# Great American FOOD

# Great American FOOD

## LESLEY ALLIN

ROSENDALE PRESS

"...I still think that one of the pleasantest of all emotions is to know that I, with my brain and my hands, have nourished my beloved few, that I have concocted a stew or a story, a rarity or a plain dish to sustain them truly against the hungers of the world."

M.F.K. Fisher
*The Gastronomical Me*

To my parents,
who so lovingly sustained me
and taught me about the beauty in all things,
especially food.

OPPOSITE TITLE PAGE : *Chocolate Fudge Turtle Cake (see page 236)*
BELOW: *Mint Julep (see page 137)*

First published in Great Britain in 1994 by:
Rosendale Press Ltd • Premier House • 10 Greycoat Place • London SW1P 1SB

Design: Robert Updegraff • Editor: Maureen Green • Copy editor: Norma MacMillan • Food photography: John Lee
Production: Edward Allhusen, Old House Books • Origination by Saik Wah Press Pte. Ltd, Singapore • Printed in Singapore

British Library Cataloguing in Publication Data.
A catalogue record for this book is available
from The British Library.

ISBN 1 872803 09 1

# Contents

# General Introduction

What is American food? There seems to be some confusion. Just as it is difficult to describe the typical American, many find it difficult to codify our cuisine. For some it may simply mean a hamburger, fries and a chocolate malt. But there is much more to it than that! To those who look further, travel through the United States or eat in an American home, generalisations about American cuisine, like generalisations about the people, retreat in the face of diverse regionalism, unique and interesting new ingredients and some brand new ways of putting them together.

After fifteen years of living outside America, I gained a unique perspective on the cooking of my native country. I knew immediately what foods were American by the feeling of comfort and connection to my home they gave me. Serving my family a meal of stuffed pork chops and apple sauce, cornbread and apple pie became more than offering them lovingly prepared food – it was memories, heritage, continuity and connection to all the things I missed and wanted to pass on.

In addition to my own love for American cooking, I met many Europeans, who returned from visits to the United States with stories of surprise and enthusiasm for the food they had found, but who could not find cookbooks to help them recreate the wonderful things they had eaten. The cookbooks that did exist, called for ingredients that were not readily available and often used measurements that were not recognised internationally. It was this opportunity that led me to write a cookbook that was intended to introduce the best of American food and to explain how American cuisine has developed.

In my research, I have focused on three major influences that have made American cuisine unique and original and have even come to define it. First, a bounty of different ingredients in the New World not only shaped our cuisine here in America, but also influenced the cooking in the Old World with ingredients that were brought back by the early explorers. Secondly, as a nation of immigrants, we have the benefit of many cooking traditions. But, American food has become more than just a collection of 'borrowed cuisines'. Immigrants' recipes were adapted and changed as surely as the immigrants themselves underwent a transformation in their new country with a very different culture and life-style. Finally, we are a country of rich diversity resulting in distinct regional variations in food and cooking styles. The combination of different cultures moving to different regions of the country with a variety of climate, topography, and indigenous ingredients has created a tapestry of regional tastes. As author, Laurie Colwin has said, "...the genius of American cooking and the secret of American life (is): a little bit of everything from everywhere put together to make something original and new."

The recipes I selected for this book are ones I love to eat and serve to my family. They include some tried-and-true classics that continue to be favourites, examples of innovative dishes and cross-cultural recipes that American chefs are creating today in their restaurants, as well as, regional and home cooking. I tried to choose recipes that I judged to be the best of their kind. I left out or found substitutes for ingredients that are difficult to find outside of the United States such as buffalo, tomatillo, soft-shell crabs and chocolate chips. There are very few beef recipes in the book because, in my experience, it is very difficult to duplicate the tenderness and taste of American beef, which is usually prepared simply on the grill.

In the following collection of recipes, I have tried to show the breadth and scope of American cuisine with numerous examples of its eclectic flavours. It is a necessarily personal collection, reflecting my own taste and a palate undoubtedly affected by living more than fifteen years in Europe. Like many today, I am conscious of how eating affects my health and that of my family and I have tried to keep deep-frying and high-fat recipes to a minimum. Some of the recipes originated with my family, others are adaptations of classic recipes and still others have been created in my kitchen from an idea or in the attempt to duplicate something I have eaten in a restaurant. There are traditional, regional and contemporary recipes here, but they were carefully chosen to demonstrate the current trends in our cooking as well as the classic cuisine that has endured. I have tried to provide a broad overview that will introduce the reader to the unknown, as well as to provide the familiar recipes for which we are now famous, such as brownies, hamburgers and chocolate chip cookies.

Are the recipes authentically American? I believe they are! Admittedly, good tasting food is more important to me than authenticity. Although I have tried to outline a procedure for producing the best results and a uniquely American taste in each recipe, the reality is that every time another cook prepares the dish, it changes. Each cook provides a unique style of cooking with ingredients substituted or varied, affected by the region or country in which it is prepared. As the prominent food writer, Raymond Dokolov, put it, "Unfortunately, authenticity is as slippery a notion as happiness."

Though our country is still young by others' standards, I think our cuisine is finally coming of age. There is a new sense of pride that our cooking tradition is alive and well and growing. Not long ago, our best restaurants would have served French cuisine but today they are more likely to serve American cuisine and with it set new standards for the way we eat. Americans have never felt the need to do things in a classic way. From the start we felt free to experiment, improvise and borrow from our many cultural traditions. Today, American chefs and cooks in homes across the nation are using a firm base of classic American recipes and building on it with the recipes, techniques and ingredients of new immigrant groups using the unique ingredients of their regions.

I hope you enjoy this book and its recipes. I hope that you find some inspiration for creating your daily meals and that along the way you also enjoy unfolding the layers of a developing and still changing American cuisine.

* * *

I would like to thank my best friend, and husband, who has always encouraged me to be the best I can be. I thank my family for tasting all the recipes in this book multiple times and giving their opinions and to friends who have given encouragement and critiques, including Pat and Bill Sproul, Donna and Jeff Franklin and Deborah Werbner, Kathy Dexter, Rosa Martella and Marie-Pierre Moine. Thanks also to Fiona Dalrymple for helping me prepare the food for photography and to Norma MacMillan, my copy editor.

# CHAPTER ONE

# THE FOOD OF THE NEW WORLD

T HOUGH SCHOOL CHILDREN still memorise the year 1492 as the discovery of America, most historians agree that Christopher Columbus was not the first to "discover" America, nor the first to visit the New World. What we must credit Columbus with is the great exchange he made possible between the Old and the New Worlds. He had gone west in search of a lucrative new trade route to the east. What he found instead was a land rich in undiscovered and valuable foods. What is surprising today is that the tomato, the potato, and the capsicum pepper, so integral to the traditional cuisines of Italy, France, England, China and India, were not known to those countries before Columbus returned with them sometime after 1492.

When the first American colonists began to arrive in the 17th century, many of the foods of the New World were totally unfamiliar to them. They had to ask for help from the Indians to prepare and cook many of the foods they found and learn to grow and eat corn to replace wheat and other Old World grains. With the Indians' help, they tapped maple trees for their syrup and sugar to use as a sweetener, roasted squashes, dried blueberries and cranberries as substitutes for raisins and currants. They adapted to their new land and learned new ways of eating, while retaining some of the old. A new way of cooking evolved using ingredients that were abundantly close at hand, ingredients that would become traditional and unique to an American style of eating still in its infancy.

There are a multitude of New World ingredients to consider. I have chosen to cover in depth those that for one reason or another remain uniquely American and have had the greatest impact on forging an American cooking style. Some ingredients have been embraced with such fervour and employed with such great style by other countries, that the adoptive nation seems their rightful owner – foods such as tomatoes, potatoes, chocolate. Some New World ingredients shine in their simplicity and are eaten on their own, but are not often used in American recipes. For example, while the cuisines of Africa and Asia are rich with recipes for peanuts, America's is not. Americans eat tons of their native peanuts, but they are primarily roasted or made into peanut butter, an ambrosia to American children.

What has kept a New World ingredient uniquely American? Colonists grew to rely on some of their new ingredients out of necessity and saw that Native Americans revered them. Foods like squash and pumpkin, corn and cornmeal became an important part of their diet and have become part of the fabric of American life. Some foods are difficult to grow outside of the U.S., foods like maple syrup and wild rice, and we claim them as our specialities. Others are simply a different but unique ingredient for which other cultures have their own traditional substitutes, such as cranberries and pecans. Although they are now familiar internationally I have included turkey and capsicum peppers because new and creative ways of using these age-old ingredients are abundant in a modern American cuisine that is still evolving and growing. I have tried to offer recipes that demonstrate the versatility of these ingredients, offering a classic recipe you may come to rely on, as well as some modern innovations that I hope will inspire you to try these foods if you have not done so already.

# SOME OF THE
# NEW WORLD INGREDIENTS

Achiote
Allspice
American Persimmon
Beans: Lima, Black, Kidney, Navy and Green 'French' Beans
Blueberries
Cassava Root (Manioc)
Chilli peppers
Chocolate
Coffee
Corn
Cranberries
Jerusalem Artichoke
Maple Syrup
Nuts: Brazil Nuts, Cashews, Black Walnuts, Pecans, Peanuts
Sunflower Seeds
Olympic Oysters
Pineapple
Potatoes
Sassafras
Squash: Summer and Winter Varieties
Sweet Potato
Tomatoes
Turkey
Vanilla
Wild Rice

PREVIOUS SPREAD: *Indians grinding corn at Lake Huron in 1845*

# CORN

## *A Most Important New World Ingredient*

"...the New World's single most important contribution to the human diet."
Harold McGee, *On Food and Cooking*

The Chinese have rice, the Irish have oats, the Germans love rye, but in America, corn is our favourite grain. It is a grain of incredible versatility. Across America, delicious foods are prepared with corn, foods developed through the influences of immigrants, regional variations, and modern innovation. We enjoy it cooked simply as corn on the cob and we process it to make such things as corn flakes, corn chips, tortillas and cornbread. We refine it further and produce corn oil, corn syrup and cornstarch (cornflour); it is even fermented to make bourbon whisky.

Of course, corn also feeds our cows, pigs and poultry, and that is how the early settlers' relationship with it first started. Europeans arriving in the New World thought of corn only as fodder for their livestock. They hesitated to eat it themselves but they saw that the Native Americans valued it so highly that its planting started their calendar year and its harvest was celebrated with a great summer feast. The Indians' maize, or corn, saved the early American colonies from starvation in their first winter. Of course, they would have preferred their familiar wheat, but it was to take a long time for wheat to grow in America. The colonists learned how to use corn from the Indians, how to eat it as a fresh vegetable, how to dry and store it and how to process it into cornmeal and flour for making breads and mush, even how to pop it for a snack. They learned to mix corn into their other foods and create dishes like succotash. (See page 21) Eventually, they came to use corn and cornmeal as substitutes in their Old World recipes, using cooking techniques and additional ingredients to which they were accustomed. The colonists continued to depend on corn for two centuries and in that time they grew to like it.

The discovery of corn, or maize as the Indians called it, came quite a bit earlier. When Cortez came to Mexico, he found Montezuma enjoying tortillas and tamales made from corn, today still staples of modern Mexican cuisine. Corn was plentiful and easy to grow, with a rustic sturdiness – it could be found growing along the roadsides – so that no one in Mexico starved, as many did in Europe. The Incan Empire of Peru, the Mayans and Aztecs of Mexico, the cliff dwelling Anasazi of the American Southwest depended on corn as a staple of their diet and had developed incredibly sophisticated practices to alleviate the problems of corn's protein and niacin deficiencies, problems that can result in a disease called pellegra. These pre-Columbian civilisations used various alkaline substances such as ashes and lime in preparing their corn in a simple but quite remarkable way to improve its nutritional value. This process removed the tough hull, balanced the essential amino acids for improved protein absorption and released corn's niacin, while providing tasty results as well. They also combined corn with beans to balance the entire meal and provide protein as vegetarians do today.

Though there is only one species of maize or corn, there are numerous varieties and sub-varieties. Popcorn varieties include the Japanese Hull-less, Red Rice and Yellow Pearl. Dent varieties include White Dent, which is ground into flours for tortillas and breads, and Yellow Dent, used for corn flakes and for animal fodder. Yellow Dent Field Corn accounts for more than 96 % of the corn grown in the U.S. Its oils, starches and sugars appear in everything from aspirin to dynamite. Flint and Flour Corn varieties are some of the original Native American varieties, still grown for their own use. Of these, Blue Corn is a special sub-variety that was cultivated by the tribes of the American Southwest, where blue was considered a sacred colour. Sweet corn, which stores more sugar than starch, is especially suitable to be eaten as a vegetable when immature or "green" and is now the favourite for human consumption. This variety has been so hybridised that the mature corn is as tender and sweet as the young one, but it is a more delicate crop than field corn and accounts for less than 3 % of corn grown in the U.S. Sub-varieties of Sweet Corn include Sugar-and-Butter (bicoloured and preferred in the Northeast and West), Silver Queen (a classic white sweet corn beloved by connoisseurs of corn), and Supersweet Yellow (one of the new genetically enhanced corns, with an extra gene that increases sugar in the kernels and slows the conversion of sugar to starch).

Corn is an excellent source of Vitamin A and provides about 75 calories per medium ear. The corn season is usually June through September, but some sub-varieties are available throughout the year. When selecting corn on the cob, look for corn that has a brown tassel that is not too dry. The husks should not be clinging to the kernels, since this is a sign of dehydration. Corn kernels should emit a milky juice when punctured, but in the high-sugar sub-varieties this juice is clear, not milky. Of course, corn is best eaten the day it is picked, but if that is not possible, store it in the refrigerator, wrapped in plastic, for up to 2 days. Remove the husks and silk just before cooking.

Cornmeal is processed in two ways: stone-ground and enriched-degerminated. Stone-ground cornmeal is not heated in the manufacturing process and retains some of the hull and the germ of the corn. It has an unctuous texture and a rich and intense flavour. Enriched-degerminated cornmeal is produced in a modern process that first dries the corn in a kiln, then grinds it. The final product is drier and almost granular. Stone-ground cornmeal, because of its higher oil content, should be kept in an airtight container or plastic bag in the refrigerator for up to three months and can be frozen as well. Enriched-degerminated cornmeal has a longer shelf-life at room temperature.

ABOVE: *Grinding corn for tortillas in New Mexico*
OVERLEAF: *New World abundance: corn, wild rice and squash, pecans and chillies*

# Corn on the Cob

The early colonists must have watched in amazement as Indian women built fires beside their cornfields, heated water to boiling and then tossed the fresh sweetcorn into it. To add insult to injury the Indians ate the sweetcorn with their hands – moving the cobs across their hungry mouths! The shocked Europeans had never seen a vegetable eaten in this way, but as with so many other new foods they were discovering, they eventually joined in and grew to enjoy it.

Today's sweetcorn is so hybridised that the mature cob is as tender and sweet as the young one, but in colonial times it was necessary to eat the corn "green" or immature to enjoy corn on the cob. About 90% of the sugar in sweetcorn turns to starch within one hour of picking – so unless the sweetcorn is eaten in the field as the Indians did, it will not be possible to know the true joy of corn on the cob. But, in an imperfect world, the following guidelines will help you to cook sweetcorn in the best way possible. Try to find the freshest sweetcorn available and choose a super-sweet hybrid, in which the sugar does not convert as quickly to starch.

TO BARBECUE CORN: Carefully pull back the husks and remove the silk (if the sweetcorn is exceedingly fresh you may leave the silk). Replace the husks and tie together at the end with kitchen string. Soak the sweetcorn in cold water for one hour or more. Place on a medium-hot charcoal fire and cook, turning frequently, for 15-20 minutes. If you prefer a rustic, smoky taste, you can pull back the husks and brown the kernels for a few minutes at the end. Serve with melted butter and salt and pepper. Try adding herbs and spices of your choice to the butter. If you buy sweetcorn without the husk, butter the cleaned cobs well and wrap in 2 layers of aluminium foil, seal well, and follow the cooking instructions (do not soak in water).

TO BOIL CORN ON THE COB: Add cleaned cobs of corn to boiling, *unsalted* water (salt toughens the kernels) and return to the boil. For very fresh, tender sweetcorn, boil for 2 minutes. If in doubt, cook up to 5 minutes for 4-6 cobs. Increase cooking time when cooking numerous cobs. When the corn is done, a sharp knife should just penetrate the cob. Restaurants serving corn on the cob in greater quantities use the following trick, as you can for entertaining larger groups of people. For a dozen or more cobs of corn: bring equal proportions of milk and water to a boil with some butter (For example, 1 litre/1 ⅔ pints [1 quart] each of water and milk with about 100 grams/3 ½ oz [7 tablespoons] of butter). Cook the sweetcorn for 8-10 minutes and hold in the milk and water mixture, over very low heat, for as long as an hour, covered.

# Popping Corn

Native American Indians have been popping corn for almost 5,000 years. Some theorise that popcorn was the first way corn was put to use by the Indians. Today, Americans eat over 900 million pounds of popcorn a year.

Popcorn pops because it contains a high ratio of protein to starch, holding moisture inside a tough husk. When heat vaporises this moisture, which must be 11 - 17 %, it explodes its skin and turns the flesh inside out. Good quality popcorn has its moisture content adjusted before it is packed in air-tight containers. And, a good quality popcorn will pop continuously once it starts, so that you can remove it from the heat quickly once it has finished popping. An inferior quality will need prolonged heat and the corn that has already popped may burn.

HOW TO POP POPCORN: Special popcorn pans are available, but any large pot with a lid will do (one used for making soup for instance). The lid should not be air-tight, but should allow steam to escape, otherwise the humidity inside may toughen the popcorn. Put about 1 table-spoon of vegetable oil in the bottom of the pan over high heat. Put 2 kernels of popcorn in immediately and cover the pan. When the 2 kernels pop, uncover the pan and add enough pop-corn to cover the bottom in one layer, or about 60-115 grams / 2-4 oz [¼ cup to ½ cup], depending on the size of your pan. (Once popped the corn will increase by about eight times the original volume.) Turn down the heat to moderately hot and shake the pan back and forth to keep the kernels moving. When popping stops remove the pan from the heat immediately and pour the popped corn into a large bowl. Sprinkle with salt and if you like, melted butter and/or freshly grated parmesan cheese.

# Skillet Corn Bread

Imagine the trouble the early colonial women had trying to bake bread in their new country without flour and yeast, but with only crudely-milled cornmeal. Through trial and error they would have discovered that the cornmeal, lacking the gluten that helps bread to rise, would not make the same kind of bread they were used to making with wheat flour. From the Indians they learned to make corn pone, a sort of porridge and when they needed to travel, they learned to make pancakes from it or "journey cakes" (later, "Johnnycakes"). The next step came when they added eggs and baked the cornmeal as a bread in spiders, or three-legged iron skillets. Much the same kind of bread is relished today for the crunchy crust that is produced by baking it in a cast iron frying pan or skillet. This bread is excellent served warm with butter and honey. With the addition of herbs and onions it is a fine accompaniment to stews, fried chicken or a bowl of *chili con carne*. The best cornmeal is stone-ground, but it may be yellow, white or blue, each distinctly different in taste, but interchangeable in this recipe. Polenta may be substituted for cornmeal.

YIELD: 6-8 SERVINGS
Equipment: a large cast iron frying pan or skillet with ovenproof handle or an enamelled gratin pan
Oven: 220°C/425°F/Gas 7

INGREDIENTS:
1 tablespoon vegetable oil to grease the frying pan or skillet
220 g/8 oz [1 ½ cups] cornmeal
105 g/3 ½ oz [¾ cup] self-raising flour [US all-purpose flour]
1 teaspoon bicarbonate of soda [US baking soda]
½ teaspoon baking powder
1 ½ teaspoons salt
1-2 tablespoons sugar or honey
55 g/2 oz [4 tablespoons] unsalted butter
50 g/1 ¾ oz [4 tablespoons] white vegetable fat [US vegetable shortening]

2 size-1 eggs [US jumbo eggs]
375 ml/12 fl oz [1 ½ cups] buttermilk (Or use the same amount of milk with 2 tablespoons of lemon juice or vinegar added. Leave this soured milk to stand for 5 minutes before using.)
2 tablespoons finely chopped fresh coriander [US cilantro] (optional)
3 spring onions [US scallions], including the green tops, chopped (optional)

METHOD:
★ Preheat the oven. Put the oil into the frying pan or skillet or gratin pan and heat in the oven for 10–15 minutes.
★ Meanwhile, combine the dry ingredients in a large bowl. Melt the butter and vegetable fat in a small pan. Cool slightly, then whisk in the eggs and buttermilk to warm them slightly. Whisk the liquid ingredients into the dry ingredients just to moisten them. Fold in the chopped coriander and spring onions, if using.
★ Remove the pan from the oven and swirl the oil around to coat the pan evenly. Pour the batter into the very hot pan or skillet and bake for 20 minutes or until nicely browned. Serve warm, cut into wedges.

# Spoon Bread with Mushrooms

Spoon bread is a classic Southern dish, probably derived from "suppawn", the cornmeal porridge of the New Netherland Dutch. Spoon bread undoubtedly developed out of a mistake, in this case the cook leaving the porridge on the fire too long.

Today, spoon bread recipes are actually a cornmeal soufflé, and this recipe also includes a surprise centre of wild and domestic mushrooms. Spoon bread is wonderful with ham or any kind of stew, especially beef. It is a dish that has withstood the test of time and become new again – you will see it on some of America's trendiest restaurant menus.

YIELD: 8-10 SERVINGS
Equipment: a low-sided baking dish, gratin dish or soufflé dish
Oven: 180°C/350°F/Gas 4

INGREDIENTS:
135 g/4 ½ oz [1 cup] stone-ground yellow cornmeal
750 ml/1 ¼ pints [3 cups] milk
3 size-1 eggs [US jumbo eggs], at room temperature, separated
30 g/1 oz [2 tablespoons] butter
1 tablespoon baking powder
Pinch of cayenne pepper
1 ¼ teaspoons salt
4 tablespoons freshly grated Parmesan cheese

FOR THE MUSHROOM FILLING:
3 tablespoons finely chopped shallot (1 large shallot)
45 g/1 ½ oz [3 tablespoons] butter
225 g/8 oz  mushrooms, finely chopped (A combination of cultivated and wild is best. If you cannot get fresh wild mushrooms, use cultivated mushrooms plus 15g/ ½ oz dried wild mushrooms. Reconstitute them by soaking in boiling water for ½ hour.)
1 teaspoon finely chopped fresh thyme, or ½  teaspoon dried thyme

METHOD:
★  Preheat the oven.
★  To prepare the mushroom filling, in a frying pan, sauté the shallots in the butter until softened and then add the mushrooms. Cook until the mixture is very soft and beginning to brown. Remove from the heat and stir in the thyme. Cool.
★  In a heavy saucepan combine the cornmeal with 500 ml/16 fl oz [2 cups] of the milk. Cook over moderate heat, stirring frequently, until the mixture is thick, like porridge.
★  Beat the egg yolks with the remaining milk and add this mixture to the cornmeal porridge. Return it to the heat and cook for an additional 2-3 minutes or until it thickens again slightly. Remove from the heat and beat in the butter, baking powder, cayenne and 1 teaspoon of the salt.
★  Beat the egg whites with the remaining ¼ teaspoon salt until they form firm peaks, but are not too dry. Gently fold the egg whites into the cornmeal mixture together with 3 tablespoons of the Parmesan cheese.
★  Butter the large baking dish, gratin dish or soufflé dish and coat the sides and bottom with the remaining tablespoon of grated Parmesan. Put half the cornmeal mixture into the dish. Sprinkle with the mushrooms and top with the rest of the cornmeal mixture. Bake in the preheated oven for 45-60 minutes depending on the shape of the baking dish. A soufflé dish will take the longer time and a gratin, the shorter. The spoon bread should be browned, puffed and feel firm to the touch in the centre. Serve immediately.

# Succotash Chowder

Succotash is the Indian word for "hodgepodge", or a mixture of whatever is at hand. An early American vegetable dish, succotash combined corn and lima beans. This delicious chowder reflects the spirit of this early dish and is easy and quick to prepare.

YIELD: 4-6 SERVINGS
Equipment: a food processor

INGREDIENTS:

4 smoked streaky bacon rashers [US 4 thick smoked bacon slices]
1–2 tablespoons vegetable oil
2 large shallots, sliced
1 leek, including green top, chopped
500 g/1 lb 1 ½ oz [3 cups] fresh sweetcorn kernels, cut from the cob (4-5 cobs in total)
275 g/scant 10 oz [1 cup] drained canned flageolet beans or lima beans (Note: flageolet beans are young haricot beans harvested before they are fully ripe. They are the closest to lima beans in sweet buttery taste. Young broad beans [US fava beans] and butter beans are also possible substitutes. A 410 g/14 ½ oz can yields the quantity needed for this recipe.)
¼ teaspoon finely chopped fresh jalapeño pepper or any fresh hot green chilli, or use a pinch of cayenne pepper
750 ml/1 ¼ pints [3 cups] chicken stock, preferably home-made
Salt and freshly ground pepper to taste
250 ml/8 fl oz [1 cup] single cream [US light cream]
250 ml/8 fl oz [1 cup] milk
40 g/1 ⅓ oz [¼ cup] diced red sweet pepper
1 teaspoon finely chopped fresh herbs such as thyme and rosemary (optional)

METHOD:

★ Cut the bacon into 1.5 cm/½ inch pieces and fry in a large saucepan until crisp. Remove and reserve for the garnish.

★ Add the oil to the pan. [American cooks will not need to add any oil.] Sauté the shallots and leek until soft. Add two-thirds of the sweetcorn, half the beans, the jalapeño or cayenne, stock and some salt and pepper. Simmer, partially covered, for 25 minutes. Strain the solids from the stock and purée them with a little of the stock in a food processor fitted with a steel blade. Return the purée to the stock in the pan.

★ Add the cream, milk, the remaining sweetcorn and beans, the red sweet pepper and the herbs, if you have them, and simmer for 10 minutes. Taste and adjust the seasonings. Serve the chowder with the bacon sprinkled over the top.

# WILD RICE

" Unmolested worked the women,
Made their sugar from the maple,
Gathered wild rice in the meadows."

*The Song of Hiawatha,* Longfellow

A romantic picture, but Longfellow was obviously writing from imagination, not fact. In reality, wild rice grows in water, mainly the lakes and rivers of Minnesota, upper Michigan, Wisconsin and adjoining parts of Canada. Longfellow may have got it wrong, but he was not the only one.

After all, wild rice is not a rice at all but an aquatic grass, *Zizania aquatic.* It is actually closer in nature to wheat and the only native North American grain, because corn originated further south. The early explorers who saw it growing from the water, about three to four feet above its surface, thought it looked very much like a rice paddy. The French explorers called it *folle avoine* or crazy oats, the Indians called it *manomin* or good berry.

Growing in the wild without human interference, wild rice is not an easy crop for man to cultivate. Since the heads of wild rice ripen from the top downward, each plant must be harvested several times. Native American Indians harvest it two to a canoe. One pushes the canoe along like a gondolier in Venice, the other bends the wild rice stalks into the canoe with a stick and threshes out the ripened grain into the boat. Once harvested, the rice must be processed immediately. Indians traditionally heated it over a fire, placed it in a hole, covered it with deer skin and jumped on it or "jigged" it, to remove the hulls.

Since the development of a cultivated 'wild' rice seed in the 1960s (the Uncle Ben company supported this development), the majority of wild rice sold is raised in man-made paddies and harvested and processed mechanically. Wild rice cultivation has been transplanted to the Old World too and it is now being grown in Hungary to adequate standards. (Hungary has the same latitude and climate as Minnesota.) But, even with all of this modern innovation, the cost of harvesting and processing still keep the price of wild rice high.

Alongside modern cultivation, wild rice is still grown and harvested in wild, natural settings, where its production is monopolised by the Native American Indians, to whom it rightfully belongs. Ninety per cent of all wild rice is produced in the northern state of Minnesota, where legislation upholds the ban on mechanical harvesting of the rice in its original habitat and on public waters, regulates the wild rice season, and gives the Native Americans rights over waters on their reservations.

There is some controversy regarding the difference in taste and quality between commercially harvested and processed rice versus the wild rice that is harvested in the traditional ways of the Indians. Undoubtedly there is a difference, but it is perhaps more subtle than most can detect. The best wild rice I have ever eaten was indeed Indian harvested with the added advantage of being free of pesticides, herbicides and chemical fertilisation. This wild rice is allowed to mature slowly and can be certified as organic.

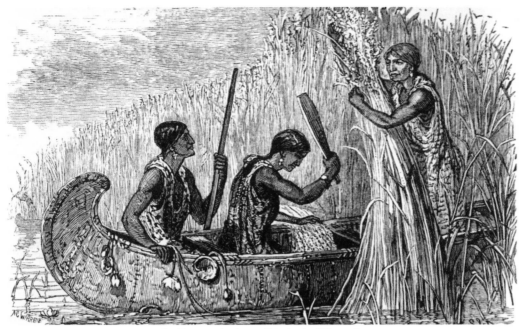

*Indians gathering wild rice in Wisconsin*

# Wild Rice

The slightly smoky, nutty taste of wild rice is an ideal complement to wild meat and fowl. Wild rice is rich in carbohydrates (72.2 mg per cup) and rich in phosphorus, magnesium, potassium, zinc, thiamine, riboflavin, and niacin, all elements of B vitamins. A cup of cooked wild rice is 130 calories (about 45 grams/1 ½ oz uncooked). Wild rice is sold in different grades from 'Giant' (uniform, long grains, never less than an inch in length), to 'Fancy' (uniform and unbroken, long grains) and finally, to 'Select' (not uniform, sometimes broken, but a good choice for making soups and puddings). Since wild rice has a high moisture content of 7.9-11.2 %, it can develop mould and mildew when stored for a long time in a warm place. To be safe, it is best to refrigerate wild rice in warm weather.

TO COOK WILD RICE: For 1 part wild rice use 3 parts water or stock and a little salt (omit if using stock). First, wash the wild rice in a strainer under running water. Put it in a heavy saucepan with the water and salt and bring to the boil. Lower the heat to moderately low and cover. Simmer the rice until most of the grains open, revealing the white interior. The rice should be just tender (taste it!), with some resistance to the bite. The cooking time will depend on the quality of the rice. Most quality rice will take 45 minutes, but it may vary from 45-60 minutes. Another method is to soak the rice overnight, drain, and cook as above, which will shorten the cooking time by about 10-15 minutes. If there is some liquid remaining in the bottom of the pan when the rice is done, cover and leave off the heat and most of it will be absorbed before serving. Or, cook over low heat, uncovered and stirring, until the liquid evaporates. Uncooked wild rice will increase in volume three to four times once cooked, depending on the quality.

# Double Rich Mushroom Soup with Wild Rice

This is a marvellously rich and earthy soup that is deceptively creamy, but without the calories, since there is very little cream. The marriage of wild and cultivated mushrooms, a mushroom stock and wild rice is one made in heaven and can be prepared in just a few hours.

YIELD: 4-6 SERVINGS
Equipment: muslin or cheesecloth and a food processor

INGREDIENTS:
55 g/2 oz [⅓ cup] wild rice
250 ml/8 fl oz [1 cup] or more water
Salt and pepper
Chicken or beef stock as required
55 g/2 oz [4 tablespoons] butter
300 g/10 oz mushrooms, sliced (Note: About 450 g/
    1 lb total fresh mushrooms are needed for this recipe.)
2 large shallots, sliced
1 garlic clove, finely chopped
3-4 tablespoons crème fraîche
Crème fraîche or whipped cream, to garnish

FOR THE MUSHROOM STOCK:
2 tablespoons olive oil
1 large onion, coarsely chopped
2 garlic cloves, coarsely chopped
15–30 g/½–1 oz dried wild mushrooms (ceps/porcini,
    morels or a mixture of whatever you have), cleaned
    and tied up in a piece of muslin or cheesecloth
115 g/4 oz fresh mushrooms, including stalks, sliced
1 carrot, chopped
1 celery stalk, chopped
6 parsley sprigs
2 bay leaves
½ teaspoon salt
1.5 litres/2 ⅛ pints [1 ½ quarts] water

METHOD:
★ Prepare the stock at least 2 hours before you intend to serve the soup. Heat the olive oil in a stockpot or large saucepan, add the onion and cook for about 15 minutes or until it is soft and well browned. Add the garlic, dried mushrooms, fresh mushrooms, carrot, celery, parsley, bay leaves, salt and water and bring to the boil. Cover and simmer for 1 hour. Remove the muslin or cheesecloth bag with the dried mushrooms and reserve. Strain the stock into a bowl and press the vegetables to get out as much liquid as possible.
★ While the stock is simmering, cook the wild rice. Rinse the rice under running water. Put it in a small saucepan with the water and ½ teaspoon salt. Bring to the boil, cover and cook for about 45 minutes. (See the general guidelines for cooking wild rice.) When it is cooked, drain and reserve.
★ Measure the stock and add enough chicken or beef stock to it so that you have 1.5 litres/2 ⅛ pints [1 ½ quarts]. Clean the stock pot and begin again. Melt the butter and add the mushrooms, shallots, garlic and the dried wild mushrooms (take them out of the muslin or cheesecloth and discard it). Sauté until softened. Add the stock and simmer for 30 minutes, partially covered.
★ Remove the solids from the stock and purée them in a food processor until quite fine. Add the purée to the stock with the wild rice and the crème fraîche. Taste and adjust the seasonings, adding freshly ground black pepper to taste. Reheat for serving. To serve, garnish each bowl with a spoonful of crème fraîche or a small mound of whipped cream. The soup can be made in advance and refrigerated or frozen.

# Wild Rice Pilaff

This pilaff is the perfect accompaniment to game, fish, and poultry and a traditional way of serving wild rice. The addition of white rice makes the pilaff lighter and more economical.

### YIELD: 3–4 SERVINGS

INGREDIENTS:

55 g/2 oz [4 tablespoons] butter
1 large shallot, sliced, or substitute the white part of a small leek
85 g/3 oz [½ cup] wild rice, well rinsed
375 ml/12 fl oz [1 ½ cups] water
100 g/3 ½ oz [½ cup] long-grain white rice, or basmati if you prefer
1 bay leaf
2 parsley sprigs

250 ml/8 fl oz [1 cup] chicken stock, preferably home-made
Salt and pepper to taste
115 g/4 oz button mushrooms, sliced
15 g/½ oz dried wild mushrooms, soaked in boiling water for ½ hour, drained and finely chopped (optional)
2 tablespoons Madeira
30 g/1 oz [¼ cup] pecans, toasted and coarsely chopped
1-2 tablespoons finely chopped fresh herbs, such as thyme and parsley

METHOD:

★ Melt half of the butter in a flameproof casserole and sauté the shallot until softened. Add the wild rice and stir to coat the grains in butter. Add the water and bring to the boil over moderate heat. When it reaches the boil, lower the temperature slightly so that the liquid is simmering. Cover the casserole and cook for 30 minutes or until all the water is absorbed.

★ Add the white rice, bay leaf, parsley, chicken stock and some salt and pepper. Bring to the boil again. Cover and simmer for a further 20-25 minutes or until all the stock is absorbed. Taste the rice to see that it is done. If necessary add more water or stock and cook for an additional 5-10 minutes. Leave the rice to rest off the heat, covered, for 10–30 minutes. Meanwhile prepare the rest of the ingredients. Toast the pecans lightly in a 180°C/350°F oven and chop.

★ Sauté all the mushrooms in the remaining butter until just beginning to brown. Add the Madeira and cook until all excess liquid evaporates completely from the pan.

★ Just before serving, toss the rice with the pecans, mushrooms and herbs.

# Smoked Salmon and Salmon Caviar with Wild Rice Pancakes

After a memorable dinner at Gustaf Ander's famous Swedish-American restaurant in Santa Ana, California, this elegant appetiser begged to be recreated. The crispy texture of the wild rice gives the pancakes great appeal. If the rice is cooked ahead of time, this is a surprisingly straightforward but impressive dish. This recipe is delicious and as close to the original as I can get.

YIELD: 10-12 pancakes (10 cm/4 inch diameter) or many more bite-size hors d'oeuvres

INGREDIENTS:

55 g/2 oz [⅓ cup] wild rice or 90 g/just over 3 oz [1 ½ cups] cooked wild rice

60 g/just over 2 oz [½ cup] buckwheat flour (available in healthfood shops)

70 g/scant 2 1/2 oz [½ cup] self-raising flour [US all-purpose flour]

1 teaspoon caster sugar [US granulated sugar]

1 teaspoon baking powder

½ teaspoon bicarbonate of soda [US baking soda]

¾ teaspoon salt

250 ml/8 fl oz [1 cup] buttermilk

Yolk from a size-1 egg [US jumbo egg]

30 g/1 oz [2 tablespoons] butter, melted, plus more for cooking pancakes

1 spring onion [US scallion], including the green top, finely chopped

Whites from 2 size-1 eggs [US jumbo eggs]

FOR THE GARNISH:

About 125 g/4 ½ oz finest quality smoked salmon, thinly sliced

1 small jar salmon caviar

60–125 ml/2–4 fl oz [¼–½ cup] sour cream

Fresh dill sprigs

METHOD:

★ If using raw wild rice, cook it in about 250 ml/8 fl oz [1 cup] or more salted water for 40–45 minutes. (See the general guidelines for cooking wild rice.) Drain and cool.

★ Sift the dry ingredients into a medium-size bowl. In a small bowl, whisk together the buttermilk and the egg yolk and add to the dry ingredients. Whisk in the melted and cooled butter, the wild rice and finely chopped spring onion. Finally, whisk the 2 egg whites until stiff peaks form, but not until they are dry. Fold carefully into the batter.

★ Lightly butter a griddle or large frying pan and heat it. Drop spoonfuls of the batter on to the griddle, to make 10 cm/4 inch discs (or smaller bite-size discs). Cook for 1–2 minutes or until bubbles form on the top, then turn and cook until golden brown on the other side. Be sure that the pancakes are cooked throughout and not still liquid on the inside. If you are frying them in advance, put them on a baking sheet in one layer and cover with cling film [US plastic wrap]. Reheat, uncovered, in a 200°C/400°F/Gas 6 oven for about 5 minutes before serving.

★ To serve, place one or two pancakes on each plate and arrange a slice of smoked salmon attractively on top. Put a dollop of sour cream on top of that and 'nest' the caviar eggs into it. Add a sprig of fresh dill and serve while the pancakes are still warm. Small bite-size pancakes make fine hors d'oeuvres and should be prepared in the same way.

Note: These pancakes would be delicious for breakfast too. Simply omit the onion and the garnish, and serve with maple syrup.

# Wild Rice Salad with Pecans and Cranberries

A sophisticated New World mix, this gutsy salad will suit any grilled meat or fowl, especially game.

YIELD: 6-12 SERVINGS
Oven: 180°C/350°F/Gas 4

INGREDIENTS:
170 g/6 oz [1 cup] wild rice
1 bay leaf
1 garlic clove, split
½ teaspoon salt
750 ml/1 ¼ pints [3 cups] water
1 small fennel bulb, chopped, or 1 celery stalk, diced
3 spring onions [US scallions] including most of the green tops, finely chopped
3 smoked streaky bacon rashers [US thick smoked bacon slices]
1–2 tablespoons vegetable oil
55 g/2 oz [½ cup] pecans or pine nuts

100 g/3 ½ oz [1 cup] fresh or frozen cranberries, or 4 tablespoons currants
1 ½ tablespoons soft brown sugar (this won't be needed if you use currants)
1 crisp apple, chopped

FOR THE DRESSING:
2 tablespoons rice vinegar
2 teaspoons soy sauce
2 tablespoons freshly squeezed orange juice
½ teaspoon grated fresh ginger
1 tablespoon finely chopped fresh coriander [US cilantro]
4 tablespoons mild fruity olive oil

METHOD:
★ Cook the wild rice with the bay leaf, garlic, salt and water, according to the guidelines at the beginning of this section. Be sure that all the rice kernels open and are well done. Leave the rice, covered, to rest and dry out for at least 10 minutes after it has finished cooking. Then discard the bay leaf and garlic.
★ In the meantime, whisk the dressing ingredients together in a medium-size bowl, adding the olive oil in a slow stream and whisking well to incorporate it. While the rice is still warm, add it to the dressing. Fold in the fennel or celery and spring onions. If you are preparing the salad in advance, refrigerate at this stage.
★ Preheat the oven if using cranberries.
★ Cut the bacon into small strips and fry until crisp. With a slotted spoon, take the bacon out of the pan and drain it on paper towels. Add the oil to the pan [American cooks will not need to add any oil]. Add the nuts and stir-fry them until they are browned and nicely toasted. Remove and drain on paper towels. Reserve these two garnishes.
★ Wash the cranberries and dry well. Put them into a small cake pan or other baking dish in one layer and sprinkle the brown sugar over them. Cover tightly with aluminium foil and bake for 20 minutes. Remove from the oven, take off the foil and allow to cool. If you are using the currants instead, cover them with water in a small saucepan, bring to the boil and remove from the heat. Cover the pan and leave to soak for about 15 minutes. Drain the currants and reserve.
★ A few hours or less before you plan to serve the salad, toss the chilled wild rice with the cranberries or currants, the pecans or pine nuts, the bacon and the chopped apple. Serve chilled or at room temperature.

OPPOSITE: *Settlers harvesting maple sap around 1856*

# MAPLE SUGAR AND SYRUP

Maple sugar and syrup are unique in being the only New World ingredients that have not been successfully produced outside North America. Numerous attempts have been made to transplant the American sugar maple, *A. platanoides* and the plane-tree maple, *A. pseudoplatanus* in Europe. Unfortunately, it is not the tree that matters so much as the climate. Only in the Northeastern United States and adjacent areas of Canada, are there sufficient long, cold periods when the temperature drops below freezing during the evening and rises above freezing the following day. This alternating temperature acts as a kind of thermal pump forcing the sap to circulate in the tree.

Maple sugar season begins anytime from mid-February to mid-April, depending on the locality and the climate and, like the wine industry, varies from year to year. The sap that maple sugar and syrup are made from is not the normal liquid found in the tree, but a special seasonal secretion whose function remains something of a mystery. One theory is that it's a kind of natural anti-freeze which protects the tree during the winter and can be dispensed with, to our benefit, once the cold winter is over. Maple sap is colourless and nearly tasteless until it is boiled down and filtered to make maple syrup or sugar. Grade 'A' maple syrup is made from the first run of sap and is light amber in colour and delicately flavoured. It is also considerably higher in price. Consumers should use some caution when buying maple syrup to be sure they are getting what they pay for. Some syrup, even under the label "pure maple syrup" may be 80-90% corn or sugar syrup and very little, if any, real maple syrup. Maple syrup is tested and graded by each producing state from Fancy Grade 'A' and 'B' to Grade 'C' – the colour gets progressively darker and the taste more intense. Ironically, maple syrup and sugar, now considered gourmet luxuries with prices that reflect that opinion, were the cheapest and most common form of sweetener to the early American settlers. In the early days, especially in the Northeast, nearly everyone had access to a maple tree or two and could draw its sap for their own private stock of sweetener.

Although a number of other foods are produced from the maple's sap, such as maple sugar, butter and honey, maple vinegar and even maple beer; maple syrup remains the most popular and versatile product. Its use should not be limited to pouring over pancakes and waffles. Its subtle sweetness and unique taste enhances many other flavours, especially fruits such as apples, pears and blueberries. It is better than honey for glazing hams or other cuts of pork and brings out the natural sweetness of root vegetables such as carrots and squash. Try substituting maple syrup for honey in your favourite recipes. Its subtle flavour can be easily overwhelmed by stronger flavours, but it can dominate harshly if you have mistakenly purchased an artificial maple product. As with all new foods, buy the best quality you can find first and then use that as a bench-mark for others you may encounter later.

# Maple Pecan Cream Cheese Spread

Bagels, originally brought to the United States by Jewish immigrants along with other breads, are ring-shaped rolls that are boiled and then baked. They have become so popular that speciality shops have sprung up all over America, selling a variety of bagels and spreads to go on top of them. This is typical of the toppings offered and you can use your imagination to create others. For example, try adding grated Cheddar cheese, chopped spring onions (scallions), and bacon, fried crisp and crumbled, for a hearty spread. For a special breakfast, offer a variety of bagels, toasted, and this spread.

### YIELD: ABOUT 170 G/6 OZ [1 CUP]

INGREDIENTS:

4 tablespoons pure maple syrup

115 g/4 oz cream cheese, at room temperature

30 g/1 oz [¼ cup] pecans, toasted and finely chopped

METHOD:

★ Bring the syrup to the boil in a small saucepan and boil it for 2 minutes. It should be slightly thickened. Cool slightly, then beat into the softened cream cheese.

★ Fold in the nuts. Refrigerate until serving. The spread will keep, covered, in the refrigerator for about 1 week.

# Grilled Goat Cheese Salad with Maple Vinaigrette

Grilled goat cheese salads have been popular around the world of late. Here is an American variation that adds the unique flavour of maple syrup to this wonderfully appetizing dish.

## YIELD: 4 SALAD SERVINGS

### INGREDIENTS:

8 large handfuls assorted greens, such as frisé or curly endive, rocket [US arugula], lamb's lettuce, Cos or romaine lettuce

4 slices bread (Choose something interesting, heavy and crusty and preferably not white.)

Olive oil to drizzle over bread

4 small goat's cheese, sliced (Ideally use Crottin de Chavignol, which is made especially for grilling.)

12-16 walnut halves

### FOR THE VINAIGRETTE:

3 tablespoons balsamic vinegar

1 tablespoon pure maple syrup

1 tablespoon finely chopped red onion or shallot

¼ teaspoon salt

Freshly ground pepper to taste

6 tablespoons extra-virgin olive oil

### METHOD:

★ Preheat the grill [US broiler].

★ Clean and dry the salad greens. Drizzle a little olive oil over both sides of the bread slices, then toast them under the grill until browned on both sides. Lay the goat's cheese slices on top of the bread to cover it completely; set aside. Toast the walnuts lightly in a 180°C/350°F oven.

★ Whisk together the vinegar, maple syrup, onion, salt and pepper in a small bowl. Add the olive oil in a stream, whisking continuously. Taste and correct the seasonings.

★ When ready to serve, cook the goat's cheese toasts under the preheated grill until nicely browned. (If you have been unable to find Crottin and have used a softer goat's cheese, you may not get a brown surface. You will have to be content with a warm, slightly melted goat's cheese.) Toss the greens with the vinaigrette in a large bowl. Distribute the greens among 4 serving plates and put the goat's cheese toasts in the centre, or slice each piece and scatter them among the greens. Garnish with the toasted walnuts.

# THE CRANBERRY
## *A Very American Berry*

As in other examples of indigenous New World ingredients, cranberries were an important food for the Native American Indians, long before the first Europeans arrived. The newcomers learned how to use them in cooking from the Indians, who sweetened the acidic berries with maple sugar or honey to eat with their meats and even ate them raw. They made pemmican, a food which travelled well and kept indefinitely, by pounding together dried meats, melted animal fats and cranberries. The early colonists bought berries from the Indians and learned from them how to sun dry them to use as substitutes for raisins and currants. Cranberries eventually became valuable as a source of Vitamin C to prevent scurvy.

Cranberries kept well, protected by their high acidity, so they were perhaps the first native American fruit to be shipped commercially to Europe. Early in the 18th century, Cape Cod Bell Cranberries were being sold on the Strand in London. From England, the cranberry spread to the continent, where it became most popular in Germany.

There are a large number of small red acid fruits called cranberries, but not all deserve the name. The name 'cranberry' may stem from the plant's blossoms which resemble the head of a crane. The American cranberry, *Vaccinium macrocarpon* is a large berry (about 1.5cm/½ inch in diameter) and a member of the same family as rhododendron and heather, thriving in bogs and moorlands.

Cranberries should be vivid in colour and firm. Reject bags with moisture inside. Their season is from September to November and because it is hard to find them out of season, it is a good idea to freeze a number of bags. No preparation is necessary, just freeze them in the bags in which they are sold. Most of the following recipes, with the exception of the cranberry orange relish, work just as well with the frozen berry as with the fresh. Cranberries are rich in Vitamins A and C and their flavour is enhanced by orange, cinnamon and ginger.

# Cranberry Claufoutis with Custard Sauce

This recipe is typical of what you may find on U.S. restaurant menus today – dishes borrowed from other countries, in this case from France, and given an American twist. The sharpness of the cranberry enlivens what can be a one-dimensional sweet flavour.

YIELD: 4–6 SERVINGS
Equipment: a 25 x 33 cm/10 x 13 inch gratin dish or equivalent
Oven: 200°C/400°F/Gas 6

INGREDIENTS:
200 g/7 oz [2 cups] fresh or frozen cranberries
55 g/2 oz [¼ cup] granulated sugar
2 tablespoons Grand Marnier or Cointreau
3 size-1 eggs [US jumbo eggs]
110 g/4 oz [½ cup] caster sugar [US granulated sugar]
50 g/1 ¾ oz [5 tablespoons] flour
250 ml/8 fl oz [1 cup] crème fraîche
Icing sugar [US confectioners' sugar] to sprinkle over the top

FOR THE CUSTARD SAUCE:
250 ml/8 fl oz [1 cup] milk
1 vanilla pod [US vanilla bean], split, or 1 teaspoon
   pure vanilla essence [US pure vanilla extract]
Yolks from 3 size-1 eggs [US jumbo eggs]
2 tablespoons sugar

METHOD:
★ First prepare the custard sauce. Bring the milk to the boil with the vanilla pod (if you are using vanilla essence, add it at the end). Remove from the heat, cover and allow the vanilla flavour to infuse the milk for 15 minutes. Whisk the egg yolks with the sugar in a small bowl. When the milk has finished infusing, add some of it to the yolks and sugar, mixing well. Return this mixture to the milk in the saucepan and cook over moderate heat, stirring constantly with a wooden spoon. Remove from the heat as soon as the sauce thickens slightly or when it coats the spoon, leaving a clean line when you run your finger across the back of the spoon. Strain into a pitcher. (The vanilla pod can be washed and stored to be used again if you wish.)
★ Preheat the oven. Butter the gratin dish and sprinkle the cranberries over the bottom. If you are using frozen cranberries, they should still be in their frozen state. Sprinkle the berries with the granulated sugar and the orange liqueur.
★ Whisk the eggs in a medium-size bowl until lightened. Whisk in the caster sugar, flour and crème fraîche. Pour this batter carefully over the cranberries in the gratin dish.
★ Bake in the preheated oven for 35 minutes or until lightly browned and puffed. Sprinkle with sifted icing sugar and serve warm with the custard sauce.

NOTE: Other seasonal fruits can be substituted for the cranberries, such as the more traditional fresh sweet cherries or pears.

# Cranberry and Orange Relish

This refreshing and easy, uncooked relish is a delicious addition to any meal involving game or turkey. When it is leftover turkey time, I enjoy this added to my turkey sandwich.

YIELD: ABOUT 450 G/1 LB [2 CUPS]
Equipment: a food processor or mincer [US meat grinder]

INGREDIENTS:
200 g/7 oz [2 cups] firm fresh cranberries
1 large thin-skinned orange

220 g/8 oz [1 cup] caster sugar [US granulated sugar]

METHOD:
★ Wash and pick over the cranberries, discarding any soft or bruised berries. Dry them with paper towels. Cut the orange into quarters.
★ Work the cranberries and orange through the coarsest blade of a mincer into a glass or ceramic bowl and then add the sugar. Or, work the ingredients in a food processor, in 4 batches, adding one-quarter of the sugar to each batch, until finely chopped and juicy.
★ Cover the bowl with cling film [US plastic wrap] and leave it at room temperature for about 24 hours before serving. Following this, the relish can be kept refrigerated, tightly covered, for 2–3 weeks.

# Crisp Oatmeal Cranberry Cookies

In recent years, some of the dried fruits popular with early Americans have returned at high prices as gourmet goodies. Dried cranberries, cherries, even blueberries are available and make delicious additions to one of America's favourite cookies – oatmeal.
If you can find dried cranberries, by all means experiment with them or try adding the fresh berries, as in this recipe.

YIELD: ABOUT 3 DOZEN COOKIES
Equipment: a food processor and an electric mixer
Oven: 180°C/350°F/Gas 4

INGREDIENTS:
200 g/7 oz [2 cups] fresh or frozen and thawed cranberries
115 g/4 oz [1 cup] sifted strong plain flour [US all-purpose flour]
½ teaspoon bicarbonate of soda [US baking soda]
½ teaspoon salt
¼ teaspoon ground cinnamon

225 g/8 oz [1 cup] unsalted butter, at room temperature
220 g/8 oz [1 cup firmly packed] light or dark soft brown sugar
110 g/4 oz [½ cup] caster sugar [US granulated sugar]
2 size-1 eggs [US jumbo eggs]
1 teaspoon pure vanilla essence [US pure vanilla extract]
4 tablespoons water
155 g/5 ¼ oz [2 cups] whole rolled oats

METHOD:
★ Preheat the oven.
★ Rinse and dry the cranberries, discarding any soft ones. Put in a food processor fitted with a steel blade and pulse a number of times until the berries are quite finely chopped. Reserve.
★ Sift the flour, soda, salt and cinnamon into a small bowl. In a medium-size bowl, beat the butter with an electric mixer until soft and creamy. Add the brown and white sugars and continue beating for a few minutes or until the mixture is creamy. Add the vanilla, water and eggs and beat well. On a slow speed, add the dry ingredients and beat again until the mixture is smooth. Stir the oats into the mixture with a wooden spoon. Finally, gently fold in the cranberries.
★ Drop the cookie mixture by tablespoons on to non-stick or foil-lined baking sheets, spacing the cookies about 7.5 cm/3 inches apart. Flatten each cookie with the back of a moistened spoon. Bake in the preheated oven for 15-17 minutes or until they are lightly browned.
★ Transfer the cookies to a wire rack or greaseproof or parchment paper. (If you have used foil, simply lift it on to the rack with the cookies in place; put fresh foil on the baking sheets to make another batch. When the cookies are cool, peel the foil away from them and let them cool upside down.) The cookies are quite fragile. Store them in an airtight container.

NOTE: You can substitute dried fruit, such as sultanas [US golden raisins], currants or dried cherries, for the cranberries.

# Cranberry Orange Bread

Americans love fruit breads and serve them for breakfast or tea. This is an especially colourful one that is delicious toasted and buttered or topped with cheese.

YIELD: 3 small loaves or 1 large and 1 small
Equipment: 3 small loaf pans, each 15 x 10 cm/6 x 4 inches, or a 15 x 10 cm/6 x 4 inch loaf pan and a larger one, perhaps 25 x 11 cm/10 x 4 ½ inches or equivalent
Oven: 180°C/350°F/Gas 4

INGREDIENTS:

2 large navel oranges
220 g/8 oz [1 cup] granulated sugar
1 tablespoon water
220 g/8 oz [1 cup] caster sugar [US granulated sugar]
2 size-1 eggs [US jumbo eggs]
250 ml/8 fl oz [1 cup] milk
30 g/1 oz [2 tablespoons] butter, melted and cooled

295 g/10 ½ oz sponge or plain flour [US cooks see note below]
125 g/4 ½ oz strong plain flour [see note]
1 tablespoon baking powder
½ teaspoon salt
200 g/7 oz [2 cups] fresh or frozen cranberries, rinsed and dried, or thawed and drained, and coarsely chopped

METHOD:

★ Remove the rind from the oranges, including some of the white pith, and slice into very thin strips. Put into a pan of salted boiling water and cook until soft and tender. Drain and refresh under cold running water. Return the strips of rind to a medium-size saucepan and add the granulated sugar and 1 tablespoon of water. Cook over very low heat until the orange rind is translucent, being careful that the sugar syrup doesn't caramelise and harden. Cool and reserve.

★ Preheat the oven. Butter the loaf pans.

★ In a large bowl, whisk together the caster sugar, eggs, milk and melted butter. Mix the flours, baking powder and salt together and sift them over the mixture in the bowl. Stir gently together with a wooden spoon until thoroughly mixed. Finally, gently fold in the orange rind with any sugar syrup and the coarsely chopped cranberries.

★ Divide the mixture into the prepared pans. The mixture should not fill the pans more than three-quarters full. Bake the bread in the preheated oven for 45-55 minutes or until a wooden skewer inserted into the centre comes out clean. Cool on a rack before removing the bread from the pans. When the bread is cold, wrap it well. Serve sliced and toasted, with cream cheese or butter, or with thinly sliced ham for tea sandwiches. This bread freezes very well.

NOTE: US cooks should use 3 ½ cups all-purpose flour in place of the sponge flour and strong plain flour.

# WINTER SQUASH AND SWEET POTATOES

Squash was perhaps the first food to be grown by Native American Indians; an important part of what is called the Indian triad – that is corn, beans and squash, the staple diet of Indians in both North and South America. Archaeological findings in Mexico, dated from 4,000-9,000 B.C., have produced squash seeds of cultivated varieties, while the beans found were still of wild varieties and corn was not found until much later. So, although it is almost unknown in the rest of the world, some of the more than 25 species of squash have been cultivated in the Americas for more than 9,000 years.

The first American colonists found a greater range of coloured squashes than we have today and their versatility was a boon to them. The colonists called all squashes 'pompion' or 'pumpion', a word believed to be derived from the Greek *pepon*, which means large melon.

The three species of squashes, *Cucurbita Pepo, C. Maxima* and *C. Moschata* are most commonly divided into summer and winter varieties. The summer varieties include: yellow or orange crookneck and straightneck squash, the British custard marrow, turban, pineapple or pattypan, cocozelle and zucchini or courgette. They are all called summer squash in America, not because they are only available in that season, but because they are perishable, and eaten when soft and immature. Winter varieties are the hubbard, winter crookneck, Boston marrow, butternut and buttercup, acorn, and the sugar pumpkin. The winter varieties are of course ideal for winter storage since they grow more slowly, are harvested late and have tough skins which protect the flesh. They can be stored in a cool place for 3 to 4 months before eating. Once cut, they will keep in the refrigerator for up to a week. Most of them have seeds which can be toasted to make a nutritious snack. Pumpkin seeds, for example, are 29% protein, more than almost any other seed or nut. Squash is a good source of Vitamin A and its flavour is enhanced by nutmeg, allspice, cinnamon, cloves and curry.

Choosing a good quality squash is a bit like choosing a sweet melon, that is, it is often a matter of luck. Avoid those that are bruised, soft or mouldy. A good squash will be heavy for its size. Acorn squash, named for its similarity to the acorn, is one of the few winter varieties that is best freshly harvested – so look for a shiny, dark green exterior that has not faded. Flavour and texture of the acorn deteriorate rapidly. Butternut is another versatile squash also found in Europe. It is club-shaped, with a tan skin and orange flesh. This squash can easily be substituted for pumpkin in recipes. Pumpkin is usually lumped with the winter squash, but botanically it is actually closer to summer squash (*C. Pepo*) and the light-flavoured juicy and more delicate squashes such as courgette. New England Pie Pumpkin or sugar pumpkins are best, but hard to find. Most pumpkins in the U.S. are being bred for Halloween, to be turned into Jack-o-Lanterns and are too large, with a stringy texture, for use in baking. To use in cooking, choose a pumpkin (preferably a sugar pumpkin) no larger than 1.8 or 2.25 kgs/4-5 lbs in weight. Because most pumpkins are watery, their flesh needs to be reduced down (in purée form) to remove most of the water before it can be used in recipes.

Sweet potatoes are not a squash at all, but have a remarkable similarity in taste. They were one of the first foods to be offered to Christopher Columbus upon arrival in the New World. He wrote, "As soon as the natives had cast off their fear, they all went to the houses and each one brought what he had to eat, consisting of yams (note: these were actually sweet potatoes, not yams), which are roots like large radishes, which they sow and cultivate in all their lands, and is their staple food. They make bread of it and roast it." (Yams, a very similar root, are native to Africa and belong to the Morning Glory family, *Convolvulaceae.*)

The sweet potato was transplanted in Spain very soon after the Spaniards found it in the New World and there it became even more popular than the white potato. But throughout the rest of the Old World, the sweet potato, like the winter squash, never really caught on. It was most appreciated where there was little other indigenous food that was filling or nutritious, such as in Africa, the Pacific Islands and parts of Asia. The sweet potato is still very important in Latin America and therefore makes its way back into American cuisine through increasing Hispanic immigration. It has also played an important part in the cooking of the South in such dishes as sweet potato pie, sweet potato biscuits and candied sweet potatoes, the latter being a traditional dish of Thanksgiving celebrations across the land.

Sweet potatoes (as well as yams – distinguishable because they are more uniform in shape and plumper) are available year round, but have a peak season of October through March. They should be stored at room temperature unwrapped and will keep for a week or two. For longer storage, they should be kept in a cool, dark place for up to 2 months. They are an excellent source of Vitamin A and potassium. They can be baked, boiled or steamed.

*A pumpkin farm in Vermont*

# Halloween Pumpkin Cake

This spice cake made with pumpkin or squash purée is a variation of the famous carrot cake that everyone seems to love. Offer this to the little spooks and goblins who come calling on All Hallow's Eve.

YIELD: 8-10 SERVINGS

Equipment: a round 20 cm/8 inch bundt pan, or a round 20–23 cm/8–9 inch cake pan with high sides, or a 20 cm/8 inch square cake pan. You'll also need a food processor.

Oven: 200°C/400°F/Gas 6 for the squash, 180°C/350°F/Gas 4 for the cake

INGREDIENTS:

450 g/1 lb winter squash such as acorn, kabocha, Japanese, pumpkin, butternut or hubbard (Or use 205 g/7 oz [¾ cup] canned pumpkin purée.)

205 g/7 oz [1 ½ cups] self-raising flour [US all-purpose flour]

330 g/12 oz [1 ½ cups] caster sugar [US granulated sugar]

½ teaspoon salt

1 ½ teaspoons bicarbonate of soda [US baking soda]

1 teaspoon ground cinnamon

½ teaspoon freshly ground nutmeg

185 ml/6 fl oz [¾ cup] vegetable oil

2 size-1 eggs [US jumbo eggs]

2 teaspoons pure vanilla essence [US pure vanilla extract]

60 g/2 oz [½ cup] sweetened desiccated coconut [US sweetened flaked coconut]

80 g/scant 3 oz [¼ cup] crushed pineapple (2 canned pineapple rings plus 1 tablespoon juice, chopped in a blender or food processor)

85 g/3 oz [¾ cup] pecans, toasted and coarsely chopped (or substitute walnuts)

FOR THE FROSTING:

115 g/4 oz cream cheese or other full fat soft cheese, at room temperature

45 g/1 ½ oz [3 tablespoons] unsalted butter, at room temperature

180 g/6 oz [1 ½ cups] icing sugar [US confectioners' sugar]

½ teaspoon pure vanilla essence [US pure vanilla extract]

2 teaspoons freshly squeezed lemon juice

METHOD:

★ To make the squash purée, preheat the oven and bake the chosen squash, whole or in wedges, depending on their size, for about 1 hour for a medium-size squash or until tender. If you bake the squash whole, be sure to make slits in the sides to allow steam to escape or you will have an explosion in your oven! Some squashes (especially the Japanese variety) are bitter around the seeds and are best split in half so the seeds and fibres can be removed before baking. You can bake the squashes upside down in a little water or right side up and brushed with honey. When they are very soft, remove from the oven, leave to cool and then scoop the flesh into a food processor fitted with a steel blade. Process to a smooth purée. You need 207 g/7 oz [¾ cup] purée for the cake.

★ Butter the cake pan generously. Reduce the oven temperature.

★ Sift the dry ingredients into a medium-size bowl. In a small bowl whisk together the oil, eggs, vanilla and squash purée. Add to the dry ingredients, beating well to combine. Fold in the coconut, pineapple and nuts and pour the mixture into the prepared pan. Bake in the preheated oven for 30-35 minutes or until a wooden skewer inserted into the centre comes out clean. Cool completely on a rack before removing from the pan to a serving plate.

★ To prepare the frosting, beat the cream cheese and butter in a small bowl until soft and creamy. Sift in the icing sugar and beat to combine. Add the vanilla and lemon juice.

★ Ice the cake. If you are serving it for Halloween you can tint the frosting orange using food colouring and make a jack-o-lantern face on the cake with edibles such as raisins, orange rind or small sweets.

# Honey-Roasted Squash Soup

This wonderful autumnal soup with aubergine croutons will satisfy on many levels – sweet and savoury, smooth and crispy, with a beautiful orange colour. If butternut squash is used the flavour will be more intense, with pumpkin the flavour will be milder.

YIELD: 4-6 SERVINGS
Equipment: a food processor
Oven: 180°C/350°F/Gas 4

INGREDIENTS:

1.35 kg/3 lb winter squash (Choose from any winter squash including hubbard, butternut, kabocha or pumpkin.)
4 tablespoons honey
Salt and pepper
165 g/5 ½ oz [2 cups] chopped onions or leeks, or a combination of both
45 g/1 ½ oz [3 tablespoons] butter
2 garlic cloves, finely chopped
1 tablespoon peeled and grated fresh ginger
1 Granny Smith apple, peeled, cored and grated
1 litre/1 ⅔ pints [1 quart] chicken stock, preferably home-made

1 teaspoon mild or medium hot curry powder
125 ml/4 fl oz [½ cup] crème fraîche

FOR THE AUBERGINE CROUTONS:

1 medium-size aubergine [US eggplant]
Salt
60 g/2 oz [½ cup] plain flour [US all-purpose flour]
½ teaspoon mild or medium hot curry powder
1 size-1 egg [US jumbo egg], beaten
100 g/3 ½ oz [1 cup] dried breadcrumbs
Vegetable oil for frying

METHOD:

★ Preheat the oven.

★ Quarter the squash of your choice, or cut into even smaller wedges, and remove the seeds and central fibres. Brush the flesh with the honey, season with salt and pepper and arrange on a baking sheet. Bake in the preheated oven for 1–1 ½ hours, brushing several times with the honey, until the squash is very tender throughout. Allow to cool, then scoop the squash flesh into a food processor and process until it is a very smooth purée. You need 900 g–1 kg/2–2 lb 2 oz [3 ½–3 ¾ cups] of purée for this soup. (If more convenient, you can make the purée in advance and refrigerate or freeze it until you want to make the soup.)

★ In a large saucepan, sweat the onions and/or leeks in the butter until very soft. To do this, cover the onions with buttered greaseproof or parchment paper, add about 4 tablespoons water, cover the pot and cook over moderately low heat. If you have the time, cook the onions very gently for 20-30 minutes, adding more water from time to time as it evaporates – the result will be very soft, sweet onions. When the onions are softened, add the squash purée, the garlic, ginger, apple, stock and curry powder. Stir well, then simmer, partially covered, for 20 minutes.

★ Remove the solids from the soup and purée them in the food processor. Return them to the soup with the crème fraîche and adjust the seasonings. Warm the soup through and serve hot, garnished with aubergine croutons. The soup can be served in a scooped-out pumpkin shell.

★ For the aubergine croutons: peel the aubergine and cut into 1.5 cm/½ inch slices. Salt them on both sides and lay on paper towels to drain for about 30 minutes. They will release any bitter juices they hold. Dry the aubergine slices and cut into 1.5 cm/½ inch cubes. Heat about 2.5–5 cm/1-2 inches of vegetable oil in a frying pan or deep-fryer. Mix the flour with the curry powder. Dip the aubergine cubes into the seasoned flour, then into the beaten egg and finally into the breadcrumbs. Fry the cubes in the hot oil until crisp and golden brown. Drain on paper towels and serve hot. (These can be made in advance and warmed on a baking sheet in the oven for serving.)

# Corn Crepes with Sweet Potato Soufflé

This is a delightful combination of sweet and savoury that overcomes any boredom in the vegetable department for both kids and adults.

YIELD: 10-12 large filled crêpes, to serve 6 as a first course or 12 as a vegetable accompaniment
Equipment: a crêpe pan or flat frying pan that is 18–23 cm/7–9 inches in diameter and a food processor or blender
Oven: 200°C/400°F/Gas 6 for the sweet potatoes, 210°C/415°F/Gas 6–7 for the filled crêpes

INGREDIENTS:
130 g/4 ½ oz [1 cup] sweetcorn kernels, cooked (Use fresh or frozen sweetcorn for best results.)
185 ml/6 fl oz [¾ cup] milk
3 size-1 eggs [US jumbo eggs]
65 g/2 ¼ oz [½ cup] self-raising flour [US all-purpose flour]
55 g/2 oz [⅓ cup] cornmeal (preferably stone-ground)
30 g/1 oz [2 tablespoons] butter, melted
2 dashes of Tabasco sauce
3 spring onions [US scallions], including the green tops, finely chopped

Clarified butter or vegetable oil for frying

FOR THE SWEET POTATO SOUFFLÉ:
2-3 large orange-fleshed sweet potatoes or yams
25 g/ ¾ oz [1 ½ tablespoons] butter
1 ½ tablespoons plain flour [US all-purpose flour]
125 ml/4 fl oz [½ cup] single cream [US light cream], or half cream and half milk
1 tablespoon pure maple syrup
¼ teaspoon salt
3 size-1 eggs [US jumbo eggs], separated
2 tablespoons freshly grated Parmesan cheese

METHOD:
★ Put the first 7 ingredients in a food processor fitted with a steel blade or in a blender and blend for about 30 seconds. The sweetcorn should be quite finely chopped in the batter. Remove the batter to a small bowl and fold in the spring onions. Leave the batter to rest for about 1 hour, covered.
★ When ready to make the crêpes, lightly grease the crêpe pan with clarified butter or vegetable oil and heat it over moderately high heat. Ladle in a small amount of the batter and tilt the pan in all directions to spread the batter evenly and as thinly as possible. Return any excess batter to the bowl. Cook the crêpe until lightly browned on each side, then turn on to a plate. Continue making crêpes, stacking them with greaseproof paper [US waxed paper] between them. Keep them covered until you use them. (They can be made in advance and frozen if they are well wrapped.)
★ Preheat the oven. Make the soufflé mixture. Bake the sweet potatoes for 1-1 ¼ hours or until they are quite soft. When they are cool enough to handle, remove the flesh from the skins and beat (or use the food processor) to make a smooth purée. Measure the purée: you need 350 g/ 12 oz [1 ¼ cups] for the soufflé.
★ In a medium-size saucepan, melt the butter and whisk in the flour. Cook for about 1 minute. Whisk in the cream and cook until the mixture thickens. Add the sweet potato purée, the maple syrup and salt and cook until heated through. Beat the egg yolks lightly in a small bowl and add a small amount of the hot purée mixture. Return this to the saucepan and cook the mixture over low heat, whisking or stirring continuously, until it thickens slightly, not more than 5 minutes.

Remove from the heat. (If more convenient, this mixture can be made in advance and refrigerated. Before continuing, reheat the mixture until it is warm.)

★ Preheat the oven for the crêpes.

★ Whisk the egg whites until they are very firm but not too dry. Whisk one-quarter of the whites into the sweet potato mixture to lighten it. Then fold the rest into the purée mixture gently but evenly. Spoon about 2 tablespoons of the soufflé mixture into the centre of each crêpe. You can fold the crêpe into quarters or smooth the soufflé mixture out and roll the crêpes up. Put them on a buttered ovenproof plate on which you plan to serve them and sprinkle the tops with the Parmesan cheese.

★ Bake in the preheated oven for about 10 minutes or until the soufflé is firm and the cheese slightly melted and browned.

NOTE: The soufflé mixture can also be baked in a buttered soufflé dish in a 200°C/400°F/Gas 6 oven for 30-35 minutes or until firm in the centre.

*Farmers with corn in Nebraska*

# Indian Fries

These home-made fries or chips are made in the oven, and will please the whole family. Feel free to change the proportions of the different root vegetables according to your likes and dislikes, but don't skip the sweet potatoes – you will love them like this. These are wonderful with turkey burgers (see page 51).

YIELD: 4 SIDE DISH PORTIONS
Oven: 230°C/450°F/Gas 8

INGREDIENTS:
2 medium-size potatoes, scrubbed clean (unpeeled)
2 orange-fleshed sweet potatoes
5 parsnips

55 g/2 oz [4 tablespoons] butter
Paprika or curry powder (optional)
Salt to taste

METHOD:
★ Fill a large bowl with cold, salted water. Cut the potatoes lengthways, without peeling them, into slices that are 1.5 cm/½ inch thick. Then cut the slices into 1.5 cm/ ½ inch sticks and put immediately into the water. Peel the sweet potatoes and parsnips and cut into sticks. Try to cut them so that they are the same dimensions as the white potatoes. Avoid cutting the long, thin ends of the parsnips – they should be left as they are because this part will be the first to brown. Add the sweet potatoes and parsnips to the salted water. Leave the vegetables to soak in the water for at least 30 minutes before baking.
★ When you are ready to start baking the fries, preheat the oven. Put the butter on a baking tray or shallow roasting pan and melt in the oven for a few minutes.
★ Drain and dry the vegetables. Add to the baking tray and toss them in the butter. Spread them out into a single layer, without overlapping too much. Sprinkle with paprika or curry powder if you like. Bake for 35-45 minutes, turning them every 10 minutes, or until they are nicely browned and tender. Drain them on paper towels and sprinkle with salt to taste. Serve hot.

# TURKEY

Benjamin Franklin, a great American statesman and wit, wrote to his daughter in 1784 to say, presumably tongue-in-cheek, "I wish the eagle had not been chosen as the representative of our country. He is a bird of bad moral character....the turkey is a much more respectable bird, and withal a true original native of America."

Alexandre Dumas disagreed with Franklin and argued that the turkey had been present in the Old World fifteen hundred years before it was found in the New. But there is enough evidence to the contrary, for us to agree that the turkey, probably a native of Mexico originally, is indeed a New World creature. In fact, it is the New World's only contribution in the area of domesticated animals.

The earliest mention of turkeys coming to the Old World is 1511, when it was reported that Miguel de Passamonte was instructed by the Bishop of Valencia to bring turkeys to Spain and returned from America with ten birds. By the end of the 16th century, turkey was well installed in almost all the European countries, an exception to other New World ingredients that were at first viewed with suspicion and took a while to be accepted. Turkey was accepted and eaten heartily, as soon as it arrived. Eighteenth century France was quite turkey-mad, and with the advent of the American Revolution eating this American bird was viewed as a symbol of solidarity.

Although turkey is not listed in the official menu of the first American Thanksgiving celebration in 1621, there are other written references to the fact that it was a part of that feast. When the pilgrims first landed on American soil, they found a profusion of wild turkeys. Since 1789, when George Washington issued a proclamation setting Thursday, November 26th the first Thanksgiving of the new nation, this holiday has become virtually "turkey's day".

Today, we serve turkey on many occasions, not just at Thanksgiving and Christmas. We are offered a great variety of cuts from almost any part of the turkey. This convenience, as well as our current health concerns, has led to a dramatic rise in turkey consumption in the U.S. and worldwide. Turkey offers similar protein to red meat but, with the skin removed, only a fraction of the fat. Comparing it to chicken, it is just as low in fat but actually lower in cholesterol. And, it has all that flavour that is sometimes lacking in chicken with a lower price per pound – making it one of the most economical ways of feeding a large group or family gathering. America, already predisposed to liking turkey, has rediscovered its virtues and found many new ways of preparing it.

Most American cookbooks advise the cook to allow about 450g/1 lb per person, when buying a turkey. Waverly Root writes in *Food*, that the quality and the size of the turkey is important to its flavour. In Root's opinion, the ideal turkey for juiciness and taste weighs about 13.5kgs/30 lbs, is wild and roasted to perfection. Most food experts advise that hens are preferred to cocks and that the consumer should look for a broad, compact bird, with a pearly white tint to the flesh. Turkeys should be hung for at least 3 days, otherwise flavour is sacrificed. Perhaps that is the problem with frozen turkeys – for they have most certainly not been hung. If you must rely on a frozen turkey, be sure to thaw it slowly in the refrigerator about 2 days before you need it. Let the defrosted bird stand at room temperature for a few hours before roasting. The following recipes reflect the versatile quality of turkey meat.

# Thanksgiving Roast Turkey with Sausage-Chestnut Stuffing

No Thanksgiving celebration would be complete without a roast turkey and an American-style stuffing like this one. The Pilgrims feasted on wild turkey, which was plentiful in the new colony. They were black-feathered and similar to a domesticated breed sold in the United States today as Bronze Turkeys. Whether you find a wild turkey, a Bronze or a simple domestic bird, try to buy a fresh rather than a frozen one. Traditionally, the Thanksgiving feast also includes mashed potatoes, sweet potatoes, a cranberry relish or sauce and, of course, pumpkin pie.

YIELD: Plan on 450 g/1 lb of turkey per serving when purchasing a small turkey of 2.25–4.5 kg/5-10 lb. Allow 350 g/12 oz per serving for larger turkeys of over 5.4 kg/12 lb. For a family gathering of 6-8 people, I suggest a 6.3–6.8 kg/14-15 lb turkey – enough to go around and assure some delicious leftovers.
Oven: 140°C/275°F/Gas 1 for the bread cubes; 220°C/425°F/Gas 7 and then 170°C/325°F/Gas 3 for the turkey

INGREDIENTS:
A fresh turkey weighing 5.9–6.8 kg/13-15 lb
115 g/4 oz [½ cup] butter, at room temperature
Salt and freshly ground pepper to taste
Flour or cornflour [US cornstarch], to thicken the gravy
Additional turkey or chicken stock, approximately 450ml–1 litre/¾–1 ⅔ pints [2-4 cups], preferably home-made

FOR THE STUFFING:
900 g/2 lb fresh pork sausagemeat (page 267)
450 g/1 lb good white bread
675 g/1 ½ lb peeled and skinned fresh chestnuts (For instructions on peeling and skinning, see page 266. Or use vacuum-packed or canned.)
2 large or 4 medium-size onions, chopped

8–10 celery stalks, chopped
115 g/4 oz [½ cup] butter
1 large bunch parsley, finely chopped
1 tablespoon finely chopped fresh thyme, or 1 ½ teaspoons dried thyme
1 tablespoon chopped fresh sage, or 1 ½ teaspoons dried sage
2 size-1 eggs [US jumbo eggs], lightly beaten

FOR THE TURKEY STOCK:
The neck and giblets from the turkey
About 1.5 litres/2 ⅓ pints [1 ½ quarts] water
A bouquet garni including parsley, bay leaf and thyme
1 celery stalk, sliced
1 medium-size onion, sliced
1 carrot, sliced

METHOD:
★ The day before roasting the turkey, prepare the sausagemeat. Refrigerate overnight.
★ As much as a day in advance, prepare the bread cubes and chestnuts for the stuffing. Preheat the oven. Cut the bread into 2.5 cm/1 inch cubes and toast in the oven for 30-40 minutes, turning once or twice, until they are crisp but not browned.
★ The day you plan to roast the turkey, make the stuffing: in a frying pan, fry the sausagemeat until it is no longer pink and is starting to brown. Remove the meat with a slotted spoon to a very large bowl. Sauté the onions and celery in the butter until they are softened slightly; the celery should still be crisp. Add to the sausagemeat. Stir in the herbs and eggs with salt and pepper to taste. Refrigerate the stuffing until you intend to use it.

★ To make a turkey stock cover the neck, giblets and any trimmings with the water and add the bouquet garni, celery, carrot and onion. Simmer, partially covered, for 2-3 hours. Add more water if necessary.

★ Preheat the oven for the turkey.

★ Rinse the turkey inside and out with cold water, dry with paper towels and salt the inside. Shortly before you intend to start roasting the turkey, stuff it loosely with the cooled (at least room temperature) stuffing mixture, filling both body and neck cavities. Put excess stuffing into a baking dish to be baked in the final hour of roasting the turkey. Truss the turkey using a trussing needle, or simply tie together the legs with kitchen twine and use skewers for the neck flap so that the stuffing is kept inside the bird. Be sure that all the appendages are secured tightly to the body, so that all of the turkey will cook evenly. Unfortunately, the dark meat of the turkey requires longer cooking than the white breast, so the breast will need to be protected.

★ Massage the turkey with the softened butter and sprinkle all over with salt and pepper. Set the turkey on a rack (so that air can circulate around it and cook it thoroughly and evenly) in a large, shallow roasting pan (preferably no deeper than 5 cm/2 inches). Make a tent of aluminium foil or cover the breast with butter-soaked muslin or cheesecloth. (Remove whatever covering you choose in the final hour of the roasting, so that the breast has a chance to brown nicely.)

★ Put into the middle of the preheated oven. Immediately turn down the temperature. Roast the turkey for 20 minutes per 450 g/1 lb. If it is not stuffed roast for 16 minutes per 450 g/1 lb. Baste the bird with the pan juices every 20 minutes, using a bulb baster or large spoon. To see if the turkey is done, insert a thermometer into the thigh, being careful not to hit a bone. It should read 90°C/195°F for the dark meat, about 85°C/185°F for the white. Other signs that the turkey is done are a sudden release of a quantity of juice, and the juices running clear yellow, not pink, when the thigh is pricked. Remove the turkey to a serving platter or carving board and cover very well with foil. Leave to rest for at least 20 minutes before carving (the bird can be left for as long as 1 hour if it is well covered). Pour the pan drippings into a tall, clear container and allow to settle for 5-10 minutes. Then carefully remove the fat from the top and reserve for making the gravy if desired.

★ If you want to use the giblets in the gravy, remove them from the stock and chop finely. Strain the stock. Set the roasting pan over two burners on your hob or range turned to moderate heat and add 1 tablespoon of reserved turkey fat for each 250 ml/8 fl oz [1 cup] of stock you have for making the gravy. Add 1 tablespoon of flour for each tablespoon of fat and whisk, mixing in all the browned pieces in the roasting pan. Whisk in the stock, starting with a little and making a smooth paste, and then adding more. Lower the heat and simmer, whisking occasionally, for at least 20 minutes (to be sure the gravy loses its floury taste). Stir in the reserved pan juices and the chopped giblets if you like. Taste and adjust seasonings. (Alternatively, for a lower fat version, thicken the stock and pan juices with a thin paste made from flour or cornflour and water. Whisk the paste into the warm stock and pan drippings in the roasting pan, adding it bit by bit and allowing it to thicken to the desired consistency.)

★ When you are ready to serve the turkey, remove all the stuffing from the cavities to a serving bowl. Carve the turkey. Serve with the stuffing and the warm gravy. Put leftovers, well wrapped, into the refrigerator within 2 hours of serving.

NOTE: If you prefer not to stuff the body cavity, put the stuffing into an oiled baking dish and bake with the turkey for the last ½–¾ hour.

# Turkey Steaks with Corn and Basil Sauce

Here's low-fat turkey in a gourmet disguise. This is quick and easy to prepare and a meal the whole family will enjoy.

YIELD: 4 SERVINGS
Oven: 170°C/325°F/Gas 3

INGREDIENTS:

4 turkey steaks, weighing about 145 g/5 oz each (This is a 2.5 cm/1 inch thick 'steak' cut across the grain from the turkey breast.)
Salt and freshly ground pepper to taste
Flour
Olive oil or vegetable oil

FOR THE SAUCE:

3 tablespoons finely chopped shallots or onions
3 tablespoons red wine vinegar

1 tomato, skin and seeds removed, chopped into large dice
3 tablespoons tomato essence (page 264), or use ready-made tomato paste
1 can (425 g/15 oz) creamed-style sweetcorn, or substitute 250 g/9 oz [1 ½ cups] fresh or frozen sweetcorn kernels and treble the amount of cream in the recipe
6 tablespoons chicken stock, preferably home-made
4 rounded tablespoons (75 g/2 ½ oz) crème fraîche or double cream [US heavy cream]
1 teaspoon Dijon mustard
4 tablespoons chopped fresh basil leaves

METHOD:

★ Preheat the oven.
★ Cover the turkey steaks with cling film [US plastic wrap] and pound lightly to flatten to a uniform thickness. Season both sides of the steaks with salt and pepper and dredge lightly in flour.
★ Heat the oil in a heavy frying pan or skillet and when it is hot, sear the turkey steaks on both sides, cooking them for about 2 minutes a side. Transfer them to an ovenproof serving platter, cover them with foil and put them into the oven to keep warm while you prepare the sauce.
★ Add the shallots or onions to the pan and sauté until softened. Add the vinegar and boil until all the liquid has evaporated. Add the tomatoes, tomato essence, sweetcorn and chicken stock. Cook over high heat until reduced to a rich, thick sauce.
★ Finally, add the crème fraîche and mustard and stir to blend. Add salt and pepper to taste. Heat until the sauce is hot and bubbling.
★ Add the basil and pour the sauce over the turkey steaks. Serve with Hashed Brown Potato Cake (page 168) and a green salad or stir-fried fresh spinach.

RIGHT: *The American Wild Turkey by John James Audubon*
OPPOSITE: *Shooting Wild Turkey before Thanksgiving*

# Turkey Burgers

This is a burger that is lower in fat, but with plenty of flavour. It is delicious served with Chilli Ketchup (see page 61) and Indian Fries (page 46).

### YIELD: 4 GENEROUS BURGERS
Equipment: a food processor

INGREDIENTS:

45 g/1 ½ oz [¼ cup] finely chopped red or ordinary onion
1 fresh or bottled jalapeño pepper or any fresh hot green chilli, stalk and seeds removed, quartered
15 g/½ oz [¼ cup firmly packed] parsley leaves
50 g/1 ¾ oz [¼ cup] soft goat's cheese, crumbled, or substitute another cheese of your choice
2 tablespoons bottled taco sauce or other Mexican-style tomato-based sauce

2 tablespoons cottage cheese
½ teaspoon ground cumin
½ teaspoon salt
Freshly ground pepper to taste
565 g/1 ¼ lb minced turkey [US ground turkey]
1 can (115 g/4 oz) diced mild green chillies, drained
Hamburger buns or baps and condiments of choice

METHOD:

★ Put the onion, jalapeño pepper and parsley leaves in a food processor fitted with a steel blade and process until very finely chopped. Add half of the goat's cheese, the taco sauce, cottage cheese, cumin, salt and pepper and process to combine well. Turn this mixture into a bowl and add the turkey. (Alternatively, finely chop the onion, jalapeño and parsley by hand and add to the rest of the ingredients.) Mix gently together with the tips of your fingers until just combined. Fold in the mild green chillies.

★ Form into 4 burger shapes, putting one-quarter of the remaining goat's cheese in the centre of each. Refrigerate, covered, until you intend to fry them. (The burgers can be made well in advance.)

★ Use a non-stick skillet or a regular frying pan with a bit of oil and butter. Fry the turkey burgers for 8-10 minutes per side. Covering them during the frying process will help to cook them through to the middle. Serve on a toasted bun with condiments of your choice.

# Turkey and Melon Salad

Here is a very modern approach to turkey, served at room temperature or cold, for a wonderful summer lunch or light dinner. For a quick alternative, buy sliced turkey from your delicatessen and cut down on the preparation time.

YIELD: 4-6 MAIN DISH SERVINGS
Oven: 200°C/400°F/Gas 6

INGREDIENTS:
2 large navel oranges, thinly sliced
A whole turkey breast with bone, weighing 1.1–1.4 kg/
  2 ⅓ lb
55 g/2 oz [4 tablespoons] butter
4 tablespoons freshly squeezed orange juice
1 tablespoon peeled and finely chopped fresh ginger
½ teaspoon salt
¼ teaspoon freshly ground pepper
2-3 small Charentais melons or 1 large muskmelon or
  canteloupe
8 large handfuls mixed greens, such as Cos or romaine lettuce, rocket [US arugula], lamb's lettuce, watercress,
  even radicchio

FOR THE VINAIGRETTE:
4 tablespoons freshly squeezed orange juice
2 tablespoons freshly squeezed lemon juice
2 tablespoons white wine vinegar or rice vinegar
1 teaspoon grated orange rind
2 teaspoons peeled and finely chopped fresh ginger
3-4 spring onions [US scallions], including green tops,
  thinly sliced
125 ml/4 fl oz [½ cup] extra virgin olive oil

METHOD:
★ Preheat the oven.
★ In a baking pan large enough to hold the turkey breast, make a layer of half of the orange slices. Put the turkey breast on top of the oranges with the bone side down. Melt the butter and add the orange juice, ginger, salt and pepper. Brush the turkey all over with this mixture and cover with the rest of the orange slices.
★ Roast the turkey breast in the preheated oven for 50-60 minutes or until a thermometer inserted in the thickest part of the breast reads 80-85°C/175–185°F. Baste the turkey with the butter mixture and the pan drippings frequently throughout the baking time. (If you do not have the time or inclination to baste the turkey, you can put all of the ingredients into a roasting bag and proceed with roasting it for the 50-60 minutes.) When the turkey is done, remove from the oven and leave it to cool for 15-30 minutes.
★ While the turkey is roasting, make the vinaigrette. Whisk together all the ingredients, except for the olive oil, in a medium-size bowl. Add the oil in a stream and whisk continuously until it becomes emulsified. Cover the vinaigrette and keep it at room temperature.
★ When the turkey has cooled for the 15-30 minutes, transfer it to a cutting board. Discard the orange slices. Remove the meat from the bone and cut it across the grain into 5 mm/¼ inch slices. Arrange the slices in a large shallow dish, overlapping them slightly, and pour the vinaigrette over them. Leave the turkey to marinate at room temperature for about 1 hour. (If you make the salad in advance, refrigerate this preparation, but let it come back to room temperature before serving.)
★ Shortly before you plan to serve the salad, peel and seed the melon and cut into slices. In a large bowl, toss the greens with some of the vinaigrette, poured off the turkey. Arrange the greens on serving plates and cover with a few melon slices and with slices of turkey. The turkey slices may be laid out flat or rolled up, as you prefer. Drizzle a little of the vinaigrette over each serving.

# PECANS

Almost all New World ingredients have gradually become integrated into other international cuisines, but the pecan has remained an almost 100% American nut. Although it is now produced in New South Wales, Australia and Natal, South Africa, it is not eaten very much outside the U.S. and Canada.

The pecan is a member of the same family as the hickory and the walnut. It is native to and grows east of the Mississippi River. The pecan may have started in Texas, where it is still greatly loved, even though its scientific name is *Carya Illinoensis* or Illinois hickory.

"Pecan" is an American Indian word and appears in the languages of all the tribes who shared the nut's habitat. Pre-Columbian Indians held pecans in high esteem and used them extensively in their diet. They used their oil, ground them to thicken stews, roasted them to carry on trips and mixed them into other foods to add texture, as well as protein and fat. Thomas Jefferson cultivated the pecan and sent trees to George Washington at Mount Vernon, where three are still standing.

So why has the pecan not become popular outside North America? Certainly it was not rejected for its taste, because that is undeniably delicate and buttery. One factor is that the pecan is difficult to grow and requires a great deal of space. Perhaps too, it was considered too similar to the walnut, a nut already well established in the Old World, when this newcomer came along.

Pecans provide 687 calories per 100 grams and most of those are from fat, 71.2 grams per 100. Because of their high fat content, pecans, like other nuts, can easily become rancid, as well as take on the odours of other things around them. They should be stored in a dark, cool and dry place in a non-reactive container – glass or plastic are ideal. To achieve a more intensely nutty flavour, pecans (like all nuts) should be toasted before using them in most recipes. (See page 268 for instructions.)

# Pecan & Cashew Crusted Trout with Mustard Sauce

Rainbow trout is fresh and abundant, especially in the American Midwest. This recipe using native nuts gives the fish a wonderful crunchiness and flavour.

YIELD: 4 SERVINGS
Oven: 200°C/400°F/Gas 6

INGREDIENTS:

55 g/2 oz [½ cup] pecans
85 g/3 oz [½ cup] cashews
4 whole trout, weighing about 225 g/8 oz each, boned and heads removed (If you prefer, have your fishmonger cut each trout into 2 fillets, leaving the skin on. Also any freshwater fish can be substituted.)
30 g/1 oz [2 tablespoons] butter
1 garlic clove, finely chopped

1 teaspoon Dijon mustard
Salt and freshly ground pepper to taste
Vegetable oil for frying

FOR THE SAUCE:

1 tablespoon Dijon mustard
15 g/ ½ oz [1 tablespoon] butter
150 ml/ ¼ pint [⅔ cup] sour cream

METHOD:

★ Chop the nuts finely using a food processor (be careful not to turn the mixture into nut butter!) or by hand. Open the trout, flesh side up, in a shallow dish or on a baking sheet covered with cling film [US plastic wrap]. In a small saucepan, melt the butter and add the garlic and mustard. Brush the trout flesh with this butter mixture and season well with salt and pepper. Dip each fillet into the finely chopped nuts (only on the flesh side) and return, flesh side up, to the dish. Pat the nuts to help them to adhere. Refrigerate, uncovered, for at least 30 minutes.

★ Preheat the oven. In a non-stick frying pan, heat a film of vegetable oil over moderately high heat (do not fry the fish at too high a heat or the nuts will burn). Sauté the trout, coated side down, for about 2 minutes. (Do this one or two fish at a time, according to the size of the pan.) As the fish are sautéed, transfer to a baking sheet, placing them coated side up again. When all the trout have been sautéed, bake them in the preheated oven for about 5 minutes, or until the fish flakes.

★ In a small saucepan, warm the mustard, butter and sour cream over a gentle heat until just warm, and serve with the fish.

OPPOSITE: *Pecan pie forms the centrepiece of Southern hospitality*

# Pecan Pie

This is a classic American-style pecan pie. Unlike the treacle version often passed off for it, this one has a custard filling with a melt-in-the-mouth consistency. It is served in inns and restaurants across the U.S. and given centre stage at holidays and celebrations. It is best served warm, accompanied by whipped cream, to offset its considerable sweetness.

YIELD: 8 SERVINGS

Equipment: a 25 cm/10 inch ceramic or china flan/quiche dish or tart tin that is at least 5 cm/2 inches deep

Oven: 150°C/300°F/Gas 2 and then 170°C/325°F/Gas 3

INGREDIENTS:

One pie shell made with Basic American Pie Crust dough (page 220)

5 size-1 eggs [US jumbo eggs]

250 g/9 oz [1 ⅛ cups] caster sugar [US granulated sugar]

330 g/12 oz [1 ½ cups firmly packed] soft brown sugar

225 g/8 oz [1 cup] unsalted butter, melted

¼ teaspoon salt

1 teaspoon pure vanilla essence [US pure vanilla extract]

175 g/6 oz [1 ½ cups] pecan halves

METHOD:

★ Preheat the oven. Prepare the pie shell and refrigerate while making the filling.

★ Whisk the eggs lightly but not until foamy (this would cause the filling to form a crust on the top). Add the sugars, melted butter, salt and vanilla, stirring with a wooden spoon until evenly mixed. Pour into the prepared pie shell.

★ Bake the pie in the preheated oven for 50 minutes. Remove from the oven and increase the temperature. Garnish the pie with the pecans; the whole surface should be covered. (They look lovely in concentric circles.) Bake for a further 15–20 minutes or until the pecans are toasted but not burned and the filling is firm throughout. Cool briefly, and serve warm with lots of whipped cream. This pie will keep well in the refrigerator for a few days and should be reheated for serving.

NOTE: If you cannot find nice pecan halves, you can chop them finely and sprinkle over the surface.

# Fettuccine and Shellfish in a Spicy Pecan Butter

This easy stir-fry is a mixed bag of cultural influences and can be made with any uncooked shell-fish such as shrimp, lobster or scallops. My favourite are rock shrimp from Florida, that taste like little morsels of lobster when stir-fried.

YIELD: 4 SERVINGS
Equipment: a food processor
Oven: 180°C/350°F/Gas 4

INGREDIENTS:

450–675 g/1–1 ½ lb raw shellfish, shelled (Choose from prawns or shrimp, lobster or scallops.)
1 red sweet pepper
35 g/1 ¼ oz [¾ cup] fresh coriander leaves [US cilantro]
15 g/1/2 oz ¼ cup] fresh flat-leaf parsley leaves
1 large garlic clove
1 fresh jalapeño pepper or other fresh hot green chilli, stalk and seeds removed, quartered

115 g/4 oz [½ cup] unsalted butter, cut into pieces
2 teaspoons freshly squeezed lime or lemon juice
½ teaspoon salt
Freshly ground pepper to taste
115 g/4 oz [1 cup] pecan halves, toasted
170 g/6 oz dried fettuccine
225 g/8 oz mangetout peas [US snow peas]
1 tablespoon olive oil
Freshly grated Parmesan cheese, to serve (optional)

METHOD:

★ Preheat the oven.
★ Rinse the shellfish in a colander and cut into bite-size pieces. Keep in a cool place.
★ Roast and peel the red pepper (see page 264). Cut the flesh into julienne (very fine strips) and reserve.
★ Have the fresh herbs, garlic, jalapeño pepper, butter, lime or lemon juice and salt and pepper ready. First, work the pecans in a food processor fitted with a steel blade until they are finely chopped. Remove and reserve. Process the fresh herbs until finely chopped. With the machine running add the garlic and jalapeño and then the butter. Finally, add the juice and salt. Process until everything is well combined. Remove from the machine and add freshly ground pepper.
★ Shortly before you plan to serve the dish, bring a large pot of salted water to the boil. Add the pasta and cook until it is *al dente*. Drain in a colander. Steam the mangetouts briefly and reserve.
★ In a large frying pan or wok, heat the olive oil. When the pan is quite hot, add the shellfish and stir-fry until opaque. Add the herb butter and melt. Add the fettuccine, the red pepper julienne and the pecans. Heat to warm through, tossing gently to mix. Taste and adjust the seasoning. Garnish with the mangetout peas. Serve with grated Parmesan cheese, if you like.

OPPOSITE: *Ristras of dried chilli peppers dyed blue, a sacred colour to Indians*

# CHILLI PEPPERS OR CAPSICUM HOT PEPPERS

European explorers frequently mistook the unknown in the New World for what they knew in the Old. Explorers from Europe were in search of spices, and one in particular was of more value than the others – pepper. So, when the Spanish found the Caribbean natives enjoying the heat-producing chilli in almost all their foods, they named it *pimiento*, the Spanish word for pepper. However chillies are actually members of the nightshade family, which includes tomatoes, potatoes, aubergine [U.S. eggplant] and tobacco and are totally unrelated to the pepper vine of India.

South American Indians in Brazil and Peru began using chillies sometime between 6,500 and 5,000 B.C. and they were the primary seasoning of the Incas and then the Aztecs. The Aztecs in particular had an elaborate chilli tradition, using a variety of different chillies that were smoked, roasted, dried and fresh. They mixed them with every conceivable meat and vegetable and, in addition, used them in medicine. The Aztecs believed the chilli to be a powerful sexual stimulant and because of its effects on the skin and mucous membrane, causing watering of eyes and nose, it was used for treating various ailments. Today, we use the chilli substance capsaicin, which causes the heat, in some cold and cough medicines and in applications for joint and muscle pain.

When the chilli was embraced in Europe and elsewhere, it was because of its fiery hotness. But a whole range of chillies from mild to hellishly hot were cultivated in the Americas and recipes for their use had been developed that were varied, subtle and even refined. There are 200 varieties of *Capsicum annuum* and *frutescens* from sweet fruity varieties used in Hungarian Paprika to peppers like anaheim (mild to hot), anchos (mildly hot and sweet), serranos (very hot), cayenne (very hot) and jalapeño (hot to very hot) and habañero (reputedly the hottest pepper in the world). The heating effect of chilli is objectively measurable on a scale of 1 to 120, relating directly to how much capsaicin each contain. Imagine that jalapeño peppers measure only 15 on this scale! Most of the capsaicin is concentrated in the membrane or rib and the seeds, so removing them can reduce the overall heat level of the chilli.

Today, hot capsicum peppers are consumed in larger quantities by more people in the world than any other spice. Americans spell the pepper 'chile', but the stew of meat and beans which often contains chilli peppers is always referred to as 'chili', as in 'a plate of chili'.

When cooking with chilli peppers it is wise to use some caution. Use the guidelines for handling chilli peppers on page 265. Experiment with the chilli peppers you find locally by adding a small amount to food and increasing that amount to your own taste by trial and error. Cayenne pepper, Tabasco sauce or both together can be used for added heat.

# Mexican-Style Turkey Fajitas

This casserole version of the very popular American-Mexican restaurant offering, fajitas, is easy to prepare and offers another interesting way to serve turkey, with warm corn and flour tortillas. This recipe has been adapted to use chillies available almost universally, in most supermarkets.

YIELD: about 16-20 filled 25 cm/10 inch tortillas, to serve 6–8
Oven: 190°C/375°F/Gas 5

INGREDIENTS:
25 cm/10 inch corn and/or flour tortillas (page 181) or use more 15 cm/6 inch tortillas
15 g/ ½ oz [1 tablespoon] butter
1 tablespoon oil
450 g/1 lb turkey breast meat, cut into julienne (very fine strips)
1 large mild onion, very thinly sliced
Salt and freshly ground pepper
2-3 fresh or bottled jalapeño peppers or any fresh hot green chillies, stalk and seeds removed, 1–2 thinly sliced and 1 finely chopped
1 green or red sweet pepper, roasted and peeled (page 264), sliced into long thin strips
250 ml/8 fl oz [1 cup] sour cream
125 g/4 oz [1 cup] Cheddar cheese, coarsely grated
125 g/4 oz [1 cup] Monterey Jack or Gruyère cheese, coarsely grated

FOR THE MEXICAN SALSA:
1 large ripe beefsteak tomato, skin and seeds removed, diced
1-2 fresh or bottled jalapeño peppers or any fresh hot green chillies, stalk and seeds removed, finely chopped
2 spring onions [US scallions], including green tops, chopped
1 tablespoon virgin olive oil
1 tablespoon red wine vinegar
½ teaspoon salt
2 tablespoons finely chopped fresh coriander leaves [US cilantro]

METHOD:
★ First make the salsa. Mix all the ingredients together in a bowl. Set aside.
★ Heat the butter and oil in a frying pan and brown the turkey quickly, stirring. Remove with a slotted spoon to a baking dish. Add the onion to the frying pan and sauté briefly. Cover the onion with a piece of buttered greaseproof or parchment paper, put a closely fitting lid on the pan and reduce the heat to low. Cook the onions like this for a good 20 minutes or until they are very soft and thoroughly caramelised. Open the pan from time to time and stir the onions; add a little water if they are starting to burn or are too dry. This may seem time consuming but the resulting taste is worth it!
★ Preheat the oven.
★ Once the onions are caramelised, remove the cover and add the salsa, sliced jalapeños (just use one if you are serving this to children, two if you like spicy food) and the sliced green or red pepper. Cook on low heat until the mixture is thick.
★ Stir the finely chopped jalapeño pepper into the sour cream, or process them together in a food processor.
★ Spread the onion mixture over the turkey in the baking dish. Spread the sour cream mixture on top and, finally, sprinkle the cheese over it all. Bake in the preheated oven for 25-30 minutes or until nicely browned on top. During the final 10 minutes of baking time, add the tortillas, wrapped well in foil, to warm through.
★ Serve the turkey mixture in the dish. Encourage guests to spoon the mixture into the tortillas, roll them up and eat them with their hands. If you like you can serve additional condiments, such as cubed avocado and tomato, shredded lettuce, and even guacamole (page 198).

# Home-made Chilli Ketchup & Barbecue Sauce

This quick, homemade ketchup surpasses its store-bought cousin by miles and enlivens any grill or burger. It is easily transformed into an authentic barbecue sauce.

YIELD: about 450 ml/ ¾ pint [2 cups] depending on thickness
Equipment: a food processor

## INGREDIENTS:

3 large ripe beefsteak tomatoes, diced
80 g/scant 3 oz [½ cup] diced onion
2 fresh jalapeño peppers, stalks and seeds removed, finely chopped (Jalapeños are about 6 cm/2 ½ inches long; 1 jalapeño finely chopped = 2 tablespoons. You can substitute any fresh hot green chillies available locally.)
2 garlic cloves, finely chopped
125 ml/4 fl oz [½ cup] red wine vinegar
140 g/scant 5 oz [½ cup] canned chopped tomatoes
3 tablespoons tomato paste
4 tablespoons golden syrup [US light corn syrup]
1 teaspoon molasses or dark treacle
½ teaspoon chilli powder [US 1–1 ½ teaspoons chilli powder] or more to taste
½ teaspoon freshly ground black pepper
¼ teaspoon salt

## EXTRA INGREDIENTS FOR BARBECUE SAUCE:

80 g/scant 3 oz [½ cup] currants
An additional 2 teaspoons molasses or dark treacle, for a total of 1 tablespoon
1 tablespoon Worcestershire sauce
2 tablespoons dark soft brown sugar or maple syrup
An additional 2 tablespoons tomato paste, for total of 5 tablespoons
Liquid smoke to taste: ¼ – 1 teaspoon

## METHOD:

★ Combine the ingredients (including the extra ones if making barbecue sauce) in a large saucepan and simmer over moderate heat for 20-25 minutes, stirring occasionally. Remove from the heat and purée in a food processor fitted with a steel blade. The texture should be slightly chunky.

★ Return to the pan and continue to simmer until the ketchup or sauce is reduced down to the desired thickness. Use warm or refrigerate. Serve the ketchup as an accompaniment to grilled meats, hamburgers (page 178) or Turkey Burgers (page 51). Use the barbecue sauce to baste grilled meat and poultry.

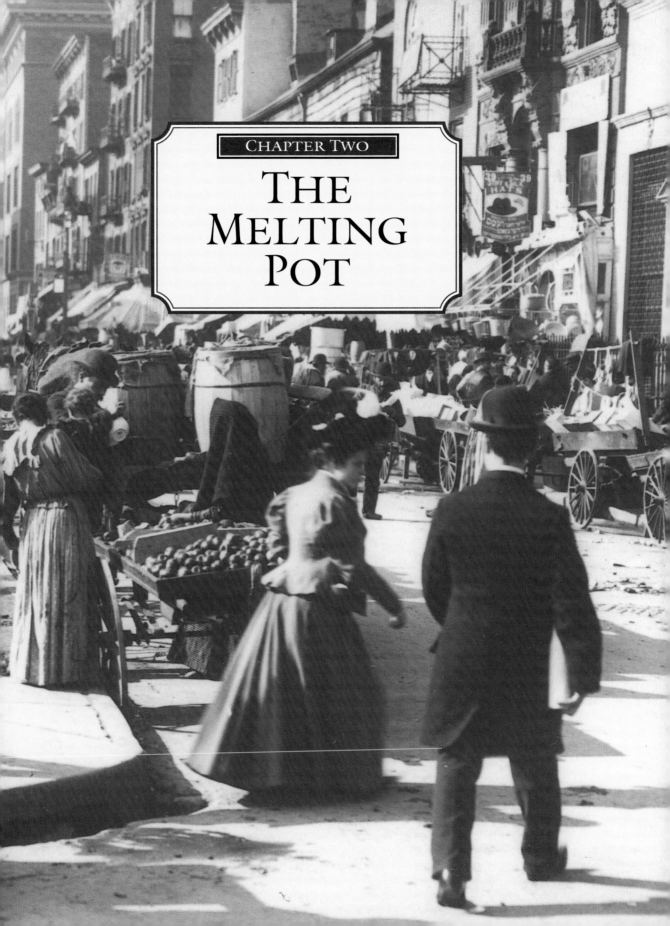

CHAPTER TWO

# THE MELTING POT

S EEKING TO DEFINE an exceptionally diverse country, America has been called a melting pot, a mosaic, a multi-cultural society, vast and variegated and "the first universal nation". What is certain is that America is a nation of immigrants, diverse yet similar, united and separate, a collection of intertwining ethnic subcultures. And many would say that in diversity lies America's strength.

Certainly this ethnic diversity makes American food more interesting. In the following chapter, we will look at a selection of immigrant groups that have had the greatest impact on American cooking. We can credit the earliest immigrant groups, the Spanish, the French, and the English with providing a base of recipes and techniques on which we built our own unique cooking. These groups struggled to tame a wild, vast, and sometimes inhospitable New World. With the help of the indigenous Native American Indians and an abundance of new foods available for the taking, the settlers began to adapt, and through an unprecedented co-operation they began to create a new cuisine. The immigrant groups that followed added more to the mix: different spices, different cooking techniques, different palates, even as they tried to assimilate and become recognised as Americans and not as foreigners. There was often resistance to the foreign foods they brought with them by the established Americans. Many immigrants opened food shops and restaurants and America was introduced to the foods of a wider world, whether they liked it or not.

American cuisine is immigrant cooking and throughout this book, the faces of our immigrants peek through the recipes. Contemporary American food reflects the new shift in our immigration. While in 1940, 70% of our immigrants came from Europe, today they make up only 15% of total immigration. Currently, 37% of our immigrants come from Asia and 44% from Latin America and the Caribbean, and our restaurants and their cooking reflect this trend.

Most immigrants coming to America today come from Mexico (22%), Vietnam (8%), the Philippines (6.3%), the Soviet Union (4.5%), Dominican Republic (4.3%), China (4%), India (3.8%), El Salvador (2.7%), Poland (2.6%) and the U.K. (2.1%). Mix this new group with our existing population and the top 10 ancestral groups (in descending order) and you will have some idea of what America is about : German (58 million), Irish (39 million), English (33 million), African (24 million), Italian (15 million), Mexican (12 million), French (10 million), Polish (9 million), Native American (9 million) and Dutch (6 million).

This chapter provides only a taste of the diversity that is America. In other parts of the book are recipes from Ireland, Scotland, Russia, Switzerland, Portugal, numerous South American and Asian countries and the many Jewish immigrants from Russia, Germany, Austria, Poland and other eastern European countries. It has been said that the Jewish people, in their many wanderings throughout the centuries, borrowed the best from every cooking culture they encountered. They brought us corned beef and pastrami, potato pancakes, bagels, rye and pumpernickel breads and cheesecake. Some American families had their first taste of wine when they were introduced to kosher Concord grape wine.

Immigrants, by nature adventurous and optimistic, came to America for freedom and opportunity and in exchange they brought their dreams and hopes and gave new energy to the so-
called 'American dream'. Throughout the history of the United States there have been those who
called for limiting or halting immigration to America, but immigration continues. America's
melting pot has become a cook pot, full of good things, enriched by new foods, new neighbours,
and a country constantly renewing itself.

The following chapter covers almost all of the largest original immigrant groups who came to
America and formed the basis for what we know as American cooking today. Some of their recipes
have remained much the same, others substitute New World ingredients, some are mixed-cultural
hybrids, others took an old idea and made it totally new. Few of these dishes would be recognis-
able in the 'old country' today – they have undergone changes, as have the immigrants themselves.

This collection is a mixed bag, just like America.

PREVIOUS PAGE: *Italian and Jewish immigrants at a New York street market in 1898*
BELOW: *An Italian family on the ferry from Ellis Island in 1905*

# SPANISH AND MEXICAN IMMIGRATION

Forty-two years before the English began to build Jamestown, the Spanish had founded settlements in Florida. Explorer, Juan Ponce de Leon, in search of the fountain of youth, founded St. Augustine, Florida, the oldest surviving community established by European colonisers. Florida remained a Spanish colony until 1763, when it came under English rule. Other Spanish colonies included settlements in present day New Mexico, California, Texas and Arizona.

The Spanish came more as adventurers in search of riches than as colonisers. But they established homes and missions in some areas, bringing with them domestic animals and planting orchards, vegetable gardens and vineyards. California was especially rich in the mission gardens that introduced olives, limes, dates, figs, pomegranates, oranges and lemons as well as the avocado to American soil.

In 1763, French King Louis XV gave New Orleans and Louisiana, west of the Mississippi, to his cousin Charles III of Spain, which the Spanish ruled from 1762 until 1803. Spain's influence on the cuisine, names of places and plants, and the architecture is still visible in this area of the country. They brought a taste for beans, such as the red kidney bean and the black bean, that took hold in Florida, where those who still remember their Spanish origins call a dish of black beans and rice, "Moors and Christians". Oranges introduced by the Spanish have become synonymous with Florida. The Spanish first encountered chilli peppers when Columbus landed at Hispaniola and incorporated them into their own cuisine, while the French rejected them. Spanish influence can be seen in American dishes of chicken and beef with the additions of raisins, olives and bacon, roasted bell peppers, tomatoes and capers.

The Spanish were the first Europeans to name the Native American's practice of grilling over a fire, *barbacoa*, or what we call barbecue today. They undoubtedly added the sauces and marinades with touches of hot pepper and garlic that we still use. The Spanish also introduced the first sheep and goats to America and their specialities included barbecued baby lamb and goat. Their love of herbs and spices has influenced the evolution of American cooking more than we realise. The Spanish started the cultivation of many ingredients important in our diets today, including garlic, bell peppers of all colours and olives and their oils. They also introduced America to wheat and sugar.

The American cowboy got his trade, his horse, his outfit and his lingo from the Spanish *vaquero*. Spanish inland exploration on horseback can be credited with bringing the horse to America, to its cowboys, to its Native American Indian population, changing forever the face of the West. The writer H.L. Mencken points out that the American language has absorbed more Spanish influences than those of any other European tongue.

The ancestors of present-day Mexico have lived along the American-Mexican border since 1598, and 75,000 Mexican citizens were scattered from the Gulf Coast to the Pacific when Mexico ceded the Southwest region to the United States. They did not immigrate to America in

*Wukoki Ruins, part of Wupatki National Monument, Arizona*

the traditional sense of leaving one country for another, but moved further into territory where their ancestors, Native Indians and Spaniards, had always lived. So, there was no thrill, no Ellis Island or Statue of Liberty to greet them when they came to America. But come they did with only 100,000 in 1900 growing to 1,500,000 known Mexican immigrants in the mid 1920s. Many Mexicans came to America to become migrant workers or to replace the original Chinese workers in building the cross-country railroad. Today, the flow of immigration continues and many Mexicans cross the border uncounted.

So many influences on what Americans eat today have come from Mexico, the Native Indians of the region and the Spaniards who settled and intermarried in states like Texas, New Mexico, California and in the Louisiana area that produced Creole and Cajun cuisine. When we eat Jambalaya, how can we not think of *paella*? The Mexicans gave us the tortilla, both corn and flour, which is a bread so versatile it is now found in supermarkets across the country. The whole world knows *chili con carne*, an Indian-Spanish inspired dish that originated among the Mexican-Americans of Texas, and other Mexican-Indian dishes such as *tacos*, *tamales*, and *enchiladas*. One of America's most interesting regional cuisines, Southwestern cooking, is an amalgam of Spanish, Mexican, Native Indian and 'Anglo' settlers' cooking and uses the corn, beans, squash and chilli peppers that are truly New World ingredients.

# Baby Chicken & Salsa Verde

This rustic, earthy dish is especially good in summer when eating out-of-doors, and demonstrates the strong influence of the Spanish on Western American cooking. It becomes an easy dish for entertaining, when you pre-bake the marinated chicken and finish it on the grill.

YIELD: 4 SERVINGS
Equipment: a barbecue or cast iron ridged grill pan
Oven: 190°C/375°F/Gas 5

INGREDIENTS:
4 poussins or baby chickens
125 ml/4 fl oz [½ cup] extra-virgin olive oil
Juice of 1 lemon
1 large bunch [½ cup] fresh mint, stalks removed, chopped
3 garlic cloves, finely chopped
Salt and freshly ground pepper

FOR THE SALSA VERDE:
1 red sweet pepper, or ½ green and ½ red
2 slices French bread, each 2.5 cm/1 inch thick

2 tablespoons red wine vinegar
1 medium-size onion, finely chopped
3 garlic cloves, finely chopped
2 tablespoons capers, rinsed in cold water, drained and chopped
25 g/ ¾ oz [½ cup] fresh flat-leaf Italian parsley, finely chopped
1 tablespoon fresh oregano, finely chopped
185 ml/6 fl oz [¾ cup] extra-virgin olive oil
3 tablespoons balsamic vinegar
Salt and freshly ground pepper

METHOD:
★ To spatchcock chickens: lay each bird breast side down on the work surface and cut up both sides of the backbone with kitchen scissors, poultry shears or a sharp knife; remove the bone. Remove interior fat and anything that shouldn't be there and press down on the whole carcass with the hand to flatten it. Turn over and flatten again. If you like, make small slits in the breast skin and insert the ends of the legs to hold them in place.
★ Whisk the olive oil into the lemon juice in a small bowl and add the mint, garlic, and salt and pepper to taste. Add the chickens to the bowl and marinate, tightly covered, overnight in the refrigerator.
★ About 1 hour before cooking, remove the chickens from the refrigerator to allow them to come to room temperature. If using an outdoor barbecue, prepare the charcoal fire; it should be medium hot (see page 212 for instructions). A grill pan needs about 10 minutes' preheating. Preheat the oven.
★ Remove the chickens from the marinade; reserve the marinade. Barbecue grill the chickens or cook on a ridged grill pan for about 5 minutes on each side or until well browned. Transfer to a baking sheet or gratin pan and spoon the reserved marinade over the birds. (The dish may be made in advance to this point.) Before serving, bake in the preheated oven for 40-50 minutes, depending on the size of the birds. Baste with the marinade frequently during baking. Serve hot or at room temperature, with salsa verde.
★ To make the salsa verde, roast the sweet pepper (do this on the barbecue if you like) and peel it (see page 264). Cut the flesh into small dice. Soak the bread in the red wine vinegar until it is totally absorbed. Flake the bread with a fork and add the diced pepper, onion, garlic, capers and herbs. Whisk the oil into the balsamic vinegar in a small bowl, add about ½ teaspoon salt and numerous grindings of pepper and pour over the other ingredients. Taste and add more seasonings if liked.

# Gazpacho with American Condiments

A gift from Spanish settlers who colonised California and areas of the Southwest United States, gazpacho has remained a favourite soup, that is especially appreciated in the warm summer months for its refreshing coolness. Be sure to serve it well chilled.

YIELD: 6 SERVINGS
Equipment: a food processor

### INGREDIENTS:
6 spring onions [US scallions]
½ medium-size cucumber [US seedless cucumber], seeds removed
1 celery stalk
½ green sweet pepper
1 large beefsteak tomato, skin removed, chopped
1 tablespoon finely chopped fresh parsley or a combination of fresh herbs such as basil, thyme and oregano
2 garlic cloves, finely chopped
500 ml/16 fl oz [2 cups] tomato-vegetable juice, such as V-8
2 tablespoons red wine vinegar
3 tablespoons extra-virgin olive oil
1 tablespoon freshly squeezed lime juice
1 teaspoon honey

1 teaspoon salt, or ½ teaspoon seasoning salt (page 264)
¼ teaspoon freshly ground pepper
½ teaspoon Worcestershire sauce
⅛–¼ teaspoon Tabasco sauce

### CONDIMENTS:
Crème fraîche, sour cream or plain yoghurt
Garlic croûtons, tortilla chips or toasted cornbread croûtons
Smoked streaky bacon, crisply fried and chopped
Avocado, diced and sprinkled with lemon juice, or guacamole (page 198)
Chopped fresh chives
Chopped black olives
Cooked peeled small prawns or shrimp

### METHOD:
★ Finely chop the spring onions, cucumber, celery and green pepper. If you like, use a food processor, but chop the green pepper by hand, otherwise it will not keep its crisp texture.
★ In a large bowl, combine all the chopped vegetables with the rest of the ingredients. Refrigerate the soup until it is very cold.
★ Serve the gazpacho in small soup bowls with a selection of condiments. The crème fraîche can be stirred into the soup to make it creamier and less acidic.

# THE ENGLISH

The English dominated the early colonisation of America. Almost all of the 14,000 colonists who came to American shores before 1624 were from London and the surrounding English counties. While most sought religious freedom, they were not wholly dissatisfied with other aspects of their lives and they tried to establish a life in their new land that was very similar to what they had experienced at home. For the many who were Puritans, they wanted to live in what they called 'the plain style' and their cooking reflected that. They had hoped to purify the church of elaborate ceremony and in the same way, they sought to purify and simplify their own lives, including the food they ate. English colonial women cooked in an honest and plain way and that meant unadorned, nourishing, economical food, in which the natural flavours of the raw ingredient would shine and no sauces or spices were needed to mask their innate goodness. 'Plain cooking' would be a recurring theme in American life in later years with the Quakers, Shakers, Amish and other religious groups. It was only in New England that cookbooks took on a moral tone, advising their readers more on frugality and manners, than on how to enjoy food. Today we still see their honest and plain way reflected in the cooking of America.

The English used simple methods of cooking, mostly spit roasting and stewing, and relied heavily on a big iron stew pot or *chaudière,* as the French called it, to cook their food. English cooks were masters of the one-pot meal. Recipes in the beginning were rustic – simple soups or stews or fish hashes that could be cooked over an open fire and suet puddings that could be steamed on the hearth. Stews that had a pastry crust or dumplings on top or fruit compotes with cake over them were popular, as the cook was able to accomplish two cooking processes in one – both stewing and baking or steaming. Most cooking had to be easy, for there were few servants in the colonies. The writers, Catherine and Harriet Beecher (Stowe) observed that: "America is the only country where there is a class of women who may be described as ladies who do their own work."

In adapting to the New World, the English colonists used the ingredients of America to produce familiar dishes they knew and loved from England. Favourites were puddings, sweet or savoury, and pies made from meat or fruit. A nation of seamen, they were familiar with fish and seafood and with an abundant supply in America, this became their most important food resource. For help with the unfamiliar, colonists visited the Indians for cooking lessons and learned how to cook with corn and maple syrup. The English started us off on our meat loving ways, for they had brought with them all the domestic animals we know today. The pig was especially popular because the animals required almost no supervision and could be raised on the leftover scraps from their meagre tables. Used to preserving, salting and smoking their food for sea voyages, the English colonists soon produced the wonderful hams and bacon for which they have become famous.

But, if puritanical New England was frugal and slightly introverted, there was more socialising going on in the hospitable homes of the Virginia colonies where the climate was easier and there were more servants. The colonial hostesses there served the kind of food fashionable in affluent homes in England and in the typical English manner of service expected there. There were soups to be ladled, roasts to be carved, home-grown vegetables and the Anglo-Saxon-style pudding to bring flaming to the table. In matters plain and fancy, the English colonists had a great influence on American food and America's table.

# Corn Pudding

Corn puddings reached a height of popularity in the early 19th century and are still being served today. This soufflé version of early American comfort food is undoubtedly more sophisticated than the early colonists prepared.

YIELD: 6-8 SERVINGS
Equipment: a food processor and a soufflé dish of 2 litre/3 ½ pint [2 quart] capacity
Oven: 180°C/350°F/Gas 4

INGREDIENTS:

330 g/11 ½ oz [2 ½ cups] fresh or frozen sweetcorn kernels
300 ml/½ pint [1 ¼ cups] single cream [US light cream] or milk
30 g/1 oz [2 tablespoons] butter
1 shallot, finely chopped, or 2–3 tablespoons finely chopped onion
¼ red or green sweet pepper, finely chopped
2 tablespoons plain flour [US all-purpose flour]
2 size-1 eggs [US jumbo eggs], separated
½ teaspoon salt
¼ teaspoon ground white pepper
Pinch of cayenne pepper
2 tablespoons freshly grated Parmesan cheese
1 tablespoon fine dried breadcrumbs

METHOD:

★ First purée 130 g/4 ½ oz [1 cup] of the sweetcorn with 125 ml/4 fl oz [½ cup] of the cream or milk: work in a food processor fitted with a steel blade until the mixture is relatively smooth. (If you are using frozen sweetcorn, gently warm it first in the cream or milk.) Reserve.

★ Preheat the oven.

★ In a frying pan, melt the butter, add the shallot and red or green pepper and sauté briefly until they soften. Add the flour and whisk for a minute, then add the remaining cream or milk and the puréed sweetcorn mixture. Whisk until the mixture is quite smooth and thick. Remove from the heat and whisk in the egg yolks, the seasonings and the remaining sweetcorn kernels.

★ Whisk the egg whites to firm but not dry peaks in a small bowl. Gently fold the egg whites into the sweetcorn mixture.

★ Butter the soufflé dish and sprinkle with 1 tablespoon of the Parmesan cheese. Gently pour the sweetcorn mixture into the dish and sprinkle with the breadcrumbs and the remaining Parmesan.

★ Bake the corn pudding in the preheated oven for 30-40 minutes or until the centre is firm. Serve as an accompaniment to meat, chicken or ham.

# Country Captain Chicken

While America only flirts with curry and East Indian cuisine, it embraced this dish as a classic from the beginning. Our introduction to what seemed quite exotic spicy food came through the English, who felt very comfortable with it. Americans adapted what must have been a spicier dish to create this recipe, which makes a nice family meal.

YIELD: 4-6 SERVINGS
Oven: 180°C/350°F/Gas 4

## INGREDIENTS:

1 chicken weighing 1.6–1.8 kg/3 ½–4 lb, cut into 6 pieces, or 6 breasts [US breast halves], with skin and bones intact
5 tablespoons plain flour [US all-purpose flour]
½ teaspoon ground turmeric
½ teaspoon seasoning salt (page 264)
30 g/1 oz [2 tablespoons] butter
2 tablespoons vegetable oil
1 medium-size onion, finely chopped
1 small green sweet pepper, finely chopped
1 garlic clove, finely chopped
1-2 tablespoons home-made curry powder (see below), or use a commercial brand
1 teaspoon salt
½ teaspoon dried thyme

2 cans (400 g/14 oz each) whole plum tomatoes, drained
4 tablespoons currants
4 tablespoons, slivered almonds, toasted
Chutney and rice, to accompany

## FOR THE CURRY POWDER:

2 teaspoons coriander seeds
2 teaspoons cumin seeds
1 teaspoon mustard seeds
1 teaspoon cardamom seeds
A 5 cm/2 inch piece of cinnamon stick
10 whole cloves
1 teaspoon ground turmeric
10 black peppercorns
2 pinches of cayenne pepper

## METHOD:

★ If you are preparing your own curry powder, put the coriander and cumin seeds in a small frying pan over moderately high heat and toast, stirring frequently, until aromatic and slightly browned. Remove from the heat and add the rest of the ingredients. Put the spices into a blender, food processor or spice grinder and process to a fine powder. Remove any large pieces by shaking the mixture through a coarse sieve into a small bowl. (This makes more curry powder than is needed for this recipe; store the excess in an airtight container.)

★ Preheat the oven.

★ Rinse the chicken pieces and dry with paper towels. Mix 4 tablespoons of the flour with the turmeric and seasoning salt in a shallow dish. Coat the chicken pieces lightly in the mixture. In a large frying pan, heat the butter and oil and fry the chicken pieces until golden brown on both sides. Remove to a baking dish.

★ Pour off all but about 2 tablespoons of the fat in the frying pan, then sauté the onion, green pepper and garlic until soft and starting to brown. Add 1 tablespoon of the curry powder, the salt, thyme and remaining 1 tablespoon flour to the vegetables and cook for 1 minute, stirring well. Then stir in the tomatoes and cook until they are hot and the sauce starts to thicken. Taste and adjust seasonings, adding more curry powder if liked.

★ Pour the sauce over the chicken pieces and cover the baking dish. Bake in the preheated oven for 1 hour. About 5 minutes before the chicken has finished cooking, stir in the currants.

★ To serve, sprinkle the chicken with the toasted almonds and offer boiled rice and chutney as accompaniments.

# New England Crab Cakes with Two Sauces

Early colonists found fish and shellfish abundant on their shores and made many simple meals by combining fish and potatoes in hash and fried cakes. Crab is perhaps the most American of all shellfish since it is available in so many regions. There is the Dungeness Crab of the West, the Atlantic Blue Crab and the huge Alaskan King Crab to choose from. Crab cakes have enjoyed a revival in recent years and are often found on restaurant menus. A hot and cold sauce are offered here – the warm sauce is more appropriate for winter, the cold for summer.

YIELD: 8-10 crab cakes (4 main course servings, 24-30 appetizer size cakes)
Equipment: a food processor

## INGREDIENTS:
2 tablespoons olive oil
½ medium-size red sweet pepper, finely chopped
½ celery stalk, finely chopped
½ medium-size red onion, diced
250 ml/8 fl oz [1 cup] double cream [US heavy cream] or crème fraîche
1 teaspoon finely chopped jalapeño pepper, fresh or canned (½ a large seeded jalapeño), or use any fresh hot green chilli pepper
1 tablespoon each chopped fresh chives, flat-leaf Italian parsley and dill
½ teaspoon chopped fresh thyme or ¼ teaspoon dried thyme
½ teaspoon salt
Pinch of cayenne pepper or 6-8 drops Tabasco sauce
1 size-1 egg [US jumbo egg], lightly beaten
100 g/3 ½ oz [½ cup] mashed potato, or 60 g/2 oz [½ cup] fresh breadcrumbs
85 g/3 oz [¾ cup] ground almonds
450 g/1 lb fresh or frozen crab meat (A proportion of ⅓ brown to ⅔ white meat is perfectly acceptable.)
30 g/1 oz [¼ cup] fresh breadcrumbs
2 tablespoons vegetable oil
30 g/1 oz [2 tablespoons] butter

## FOR THE RED PEPPER SAUCE:
45 g/1 ½ oz [3 tablespoons] unsalted butter
½ medium-size red sweet pepper, diced
½ medium-size red onion, diced
2 garlic cloves, crushed
1 teaspoon chopped fresh thyme or ½ teaspoon dried thyme
125 ml/4 fl oz [½ cup] dry white wine
185 ml/6 fl oz [¾ cup] single cream [US light cream]
Juice of ½ large lemon
Salt and freshly ground pepper to taste

## FOR THE CREOLE RÉMOULADE SAUCE:
250 ml/8 fl oz [1 cup] mayonnaise, home-made or bottled
Juice of ½ large lemon
½ teaspoon Dijon mustard
¼ teaspoon each Worcestershire sauce and Tabasco sauce
4 small pickled cornichons or gherkins
½ teaspoon capers, drained and rinsed
1 spring onion [US scallion], including the green top
1 garlic clove
¼ red sweet pepper
½ teaspoon each chopped fresh parsley and coriander [US cilantro]
Salt and freshly ground pepper to taste

## METHOD:
★ In a medium-size frying pan, heat the olive oil and sauté the red pepper, celery and onion for 5-10 minutes or until the vegetables are tender. Transfer to a large bowl and leave to cool.
★ In a small saucepan, boil the cream with the jalapeño to reduce by half. Cool and then add to the onion mixture.

*The New England coast is famous for its seafood, including lobster and crab*

★ Add the chives, parsley, dill, thyme, salt and cayenne to the mixture. Stir in the egg, the mashed potato or breadcrumbs and two-thirds of the ground almonds.

★ Carefully pick over the crab meat to remove all bits of shell and cartilage. Gently fold the crab into the mixture. Fry a small amount of the crab mixture in a frying pan and taste for seasoning; adjust if necessary. Divide the mixture into 8-10 equal portions and shape each into a small cake. Combine the breadcrumbs and remaining ground almonds and coat both sides of the crab cakes in the mixture. Refrigerate for at least 2-3 hours.

★ Shortly before you plan to serve the crab cakes, fry them in the oil and butter over moderate heat for about 4 minutes on each side or until golden brown. They should feel firm when pressed in the centre with your finger. Drain on paper towels.

★ To prepare the red pepper sauce: in a medium-size frying pan, melt the butter and add the red pepper, onion, garlic and thyme. Sauté until they are soft and the onion is translucent. Add the white wine and simmer gently until the wine is reduced to about 1 tablespoon. Add the cream and simmer for 2-3 minutes. Finish the sauce with lemon juice and seasoning to taste. This sauce may be left chunky as is or worked in a food processor to make a smoother and more refined sauce. Serve the sauce warm with the crab cakes.

★ To prepare the rémoulade sauce: combine the mayonnaise, lemon juice, mustard, and Worcestershire and Tabasco sauces in a small bowl. Put the other ingredients, except for salt and pepper, in a food processor fitted with a steel blade and process until finely chopped. Fold these ingredients into the mayonnaise mixture and season to taste with salt and freshly ground pepper. Refrigerate until serving.

# Steamed Persimmon Pudding with Brandy Sauce

America's English forefathers often made adaptations of their steamed puddings and famous Christmas pudding in the New World, and this is one of them. Persimmons grew wild in America, but now have been replaced by the larger Japanese variety grown throughout the western states. The persimmon flesh should be very ripe and like jelly. This pudding has become a traditional holiday favourite in many American homes.

YIELD: 8-10 servings

Equipment: a decorative metal or ceramic mould of 1 litre/2 pint [1 quart] capacity, a double-boiler (or a heatproof bowl that will sit over a saucepan) for the sauce and an electric mixer

INGREDIENTS:
4–6 ripe persimmons or Sharon fruit
115 g/4 oz [½ cup] unsalted butter, at room temperature
110 g/4 oz [½ cup] caster sugar [US granulated sugar]
55 g/2 oz [¼ cup firmly packed] light soft brown sugar
60 g/2 oz [½ cup] pecans, toasted and finely ground
1 size-1 egg [US jumbo egg]
85 g/3 oz [¾ cup] sifted strong plain flour [US all-purpose flour]
2 teaspoons bicarbonate of soda [US baking soda]
1 teaspoon ground cinnamon
¼ teaspoon each of ground nutmeg and ginger
¼ teaspoon salt
125 ml/4 fl oz [½ cup] milk
1 teaspoon vanilla essence [US vanilla extract]

TO SERVE FLAMING:
4 tablespoons brandy or Cognac

FOR THE SAUCE:
220 g/8 oz [1 cup] caster sugar [US granulated sugar]
115 g/4 oz [½ cup] unsalted butter, at room temperature
Yolks from 4 size-1 eggs [US jumbo eggs], beaten
125 ml/4 fl oz [½ cup] brandy, cream sherry or medium sherry
A pinch of salt
250 ml/8 fl oz [1 cup] whipping cream

METHOD:
★ Cut the persimmons or Sharon fruit in half and scoop out the flesh. Put the flesh in a food processor fitted with a steel blade and process to a purée. Measure 250 ml/8 fl oz [1 cup] purée and reserve.
★ In a medium-size bowl, beat the butter with the sugars and ground pecans until light and fluffy. Add the egg and continue to beat. Sift the flour and other dry ingredients together and add them to the butter and sugar mixture alternately with the milk, mixing well. Finally, stir in the fruit purée and the vanilla.
★ Pour the mixture into the well-buttered metal or ceramic mould. Cover the mould tightly with a lid or with a double thickness of foil. Place the mould on a rack in a large pot and fill the bottom with 2.5–5 cm/1–2 inches of warm water. Cover the pot and steam the pudding for 2 hours, keeping the water at a simmer. Check from time to time to be sure that the water has not totally evaporated, and replenish as necessary.
★ When the pudding has steamed for 2 hours, remove and allow it to cool to lukewarm (during this time, make the sauce). Turn out on to a serving plate. If you want to serve it flaming, warm the brandy or Cognac, pour over the pudding and light it. Serve with the warm brandy sauce.

★ To prepare the sauce:  beat the sugar and butter together, off the heat, in the top of a double boiler using an electric mixer. When the mixture is fluffy and light, add the yolks, brandy or sherry and salt and beat well to mix. In a small saucepan, heat the cream until it is very hot but not boiling. Slowly beat the cream into the other ingredients. Place the top pan over the bottom pan of the double boiler, containing boiling water. Continue to beat from time to time until the mixture has thickened; do not allow it to boil. It will be almost too hot to touch at this point. Serve warm. (If made in advance, refrigerate and reheat gently over warm water for serving.)

NOTE: You can steam the pudding ahead of time. Allow it to cool and wrap it well, then freeze or refrigerate it. It will keep in the refrigerator for up to 2 weeks and for a few months in the freezer. To serve it, simply wrap it in foil and steam it on a heatproof plate, keeping it above the water, until it is warm throughout.

*A Quaker farm in Pennsylvania, around the year 1800*

# THE FRENCH

The first French to set foot on American soil were not interested in colonising, but in the adventure of exploring new territory. These often colourful explorers became friendly with the Native American Indians, and ranged throughout the north and into Canada. If they stayed, they became trappers and fur traders, guides and pathfinders rather than empire builders.

It was the mere 15,000 French Huguenots of the nearly 1 million early colonists who started the French influence on American food and society, that continues to this day. The Huguenots were Protestants who left Catholic France and brought a more fun-loving spirit to the colonies and a flair for socialising and entertaining. American patriot Paul Revere was a descendant of this influential group of immigrants.

America's third President, Thomas Jefferson, had a great love of French food, which increased when he followed Benjamin Franklin to Paris as United States' envoy. During his five years in France, he reportedly spent as much time studying the food as he did on matters of state. He brought a French chef to the White House when he became President and did a great deal to promote French cuisine and elevate culinary standards in the capital and in his native South.

During his presidency, Jefferson purchased the Louisiana territory from France, trebling America's land mass. Groups of French-speaking people already living in North America came to settle in the largest French colony in the United States – in the area that is now the state of Louisiana. They became known as Cajuns and Creoles and they were to play a big part in developing American cuisine.

The Cajuns were originally from Brittany; fishermen and wetland farmers known as Acadians, who were driven out of present-day Nova Scotia and New Brunswick by the British. They settled in the isolated backwoods and bayous of Louisiana and Texas and kept their folksy ways. Today's Cajun cuisine is the unifying factor among a diverse mix of nationalities living together, including the original Acadians, African and Native Americans, Spanish, English and Irish. Through all these ethnic influences, Cajun food no longer resembles French cuisine.

Creole cuisine, on the other hand, is decidedly indebted to European cooking, with contributions from the French and the Spanish. It makes use of African, Latin American and Caribbean ingredients while retaining French cooking techniques. Creole is a term applied to people of European descent, most often French, Spanish and Portuguese, born in the New World. It also defines dishes made of tomatoes, green pepper, onion and garlic. The Creole cooking style developed in the sophistication of New Orleans, founded as a French town, and was influenced by the rich plantation culture of the area. It combines the Spanish love of highly seasoned foods, Native American Indians' wild herbs and vegetables, French know-how and the skills of African American cooks who were trained to cook it and modified it along the way. By 1850, many of the best chefs were black men, who took over the galley kitchens of the luxurious steamboats, taking French cooking up the Mississippi into settlements all along this great river, serving the public *haute cuisine* American-style. They used ingredients like crab, oysters, crawfish, hot pepper sauce and file powder. Catfish were made into *paupiettes*, stuffed with pecans and capers in a white wine sauce. The transformation of Native American ingredients using the techniques of immigrants continued in a grand style.

After the American and French revolutions, many chefs, hairdressers, fashion designers and perfumiers who had depended on the aristocracy for their livelihood, emigrated to the United States. But immigration from France has been minimal in recent years, never exceeding 4,000 in any given year.

Throughout America's history as a nation, the French have always been held in high esteem as possessing the ultimate in culinary sensibilities. In the late 1800s it became fashionable in society for young women to learn to cook and most of the teachers were French. Early American cookbooks were laced with French recipes. *The Boston Cooking-School Cook Book* by Fannie Merritt Farmer, published in 1896, defined the meaning of cookery as a demonstration of, "English thoroughness and French art". Quite a few years later, Julia Child gave America a refresher course in French *haute cuisine* and encouraged every American to try *Mastering the Art of French Cooking* at home.

Americans use many French culinary terms – bouillon, omelette, purée, fricassée, mayonnaise, pâté, hors d'oeuvres, pie à la mode, au gratin potatoes, French dressing (American French dressing is red), French fries, sauté, casserole, and fillet, to mention only a few. The French attitude towards food, their cooking techniques, their reverence for the table, wine, and service, have elevated America's culinary standards and improved the quality of American lives.

*A traditional gumbo festival*

# Cajun Gumbo

Gumbo is a speciality of Louisiana with roots in Africa and France. The word 'gumbo' comes from the Congolese *quingombo* which means okra. Cajuns claim gumbo was originally a French-Canadian *pot au feu* that was adapted in the bayou and enriched and thickened with the Africans' favourite vegetable – okra. It is a cross between a soup and a stew and served over rice.

## YIELD: 6 SERVINGS

### INGREDIENTS:

5 tablespoons olive oil

225 g/8 oz spicy sausage (kielbasa, chorizo, or gyulai from Hungary; Cajun andouille, if available, is preferable), cut into 5 mm/¼ inch slices (Remove sausage skin if it is thick and tough.)

115 g/4 oz smoked ham or pork, cut into 5 mm/¼ inch cubes

1 tablespoon finely chopped garlic (3 – 4 cloves)

1 medium-size onion, chopped (about 40 g/1 ¼ oz)

4 spring onions [US scallions], including the green tops, chopped (about 35 g/generous 1 oz)

1 small green and 1 small red sweet pepper, chopped (about 135 g/4 ½ oz)

2 celery stalks, chopped (about 115 g/4 oz)

450 g/1 lb fresh okra, sliced into 5 mm/ ¼ inch pieces

260 g/9 oz [1 cup] skinned and seeded tomatoes, chopped, or use drained, canned plum tomatoes

1 bay leaf

1 litre/1 ⅔ pints [1 quart] prawn stock (recipe follows) or fish stock

½ teaspoon Tabasco sauce, or ½ teaspoon dried hot red pepper flakes, or more to taste

1 ½ teaspoons Worcestershire sauce

Salt and freshly ground pepper to taste

900 g/2 lbs raw king prawns [US large shrimp], peeled and deveined (Keep the shells and heads to make the stock.)

1–3 teaspoons Cajun seasoning (recipe follows)

4 tablespoons plain flour [US all-purpose flour]

2 tablespoons freshly squeezed lemon juice

### METHOD:

★ Heat 1 tablespoon of the oil in a large pot, preferably cast iron. Over high heat, brown the sausage and ham or pork, stirring often. Remove with a slotted spoon and reserve. Remove all but a little of the fat from the pot.

★ Add the garlic, onion, spring onions, sweet peppers and celery to the pot and cook, stirring, until slightly wilted. Add the okra and cook until the mixture is quite dry.

★ Stir in the tomatoes, bay leaf, half of the prawn stock, the Tabasco or crushed hot red pepper, Worcestershire sauce, and the sausage and ham or pork. Season with salt and pepper. Bring to the boil and simmer for about 15 minutes.

★ Meanwhile, cut the prawns into bite-size pieces and sprinkle with 1 teaspoon Cajun seasoning (more can be added later to taste). Reserve.

★ Make the roux: heat the remaining 4 tablespoons of olive oil in a medium-size frying pan. Add the flour and cook over low heat, stirring constantly, until the roux is a deep mahogany-coloured brown. Do not allow it to go black. When the roux has reached the desired colour, add the remaining prawn stock (add carefully as it may spit!) and whisk until thickened. Stir this mixture into the vegetables and cook for an additional 10 minutes. (The gumbo can be prepared in advance to this point and refrigerated until serving time. Bring it back to the boil before finishing.)

★ Add the prawns and the lemon juice. Cook for about 3 minutes, stirring occasionally. Taste and add more Cajun seasoning if you would like the gumbo to be spicier. Serve with rice, corn-bread (page 18) and a crisp green salad.

*(See illustration overleaf)*

**PRAWN STOCK:**

Shells and heads from 900 g/2 lb raw king or tiger prawns [US large shrimp], crushed with a mallet
1.5 litres/2 ⅓ pints [1 ½ quarts] cold water, or use part fish stock if you have it

8 black peppercorns
A bouquet garni including 6 parsley sprigs, 2 thyme sprigs and 1 bay leaf
1 large onion, coarsely chopped (about 150 g/5 oz)
2 celery stalks, coarsely chopped (about 115 g/4 oz)

★ Put all the ingredients into a stock pot or large saucepan and bring to the boil. Simmer for about 20 minutes. Strain and boil to reduce to 1 litre/1 ⅔ pints [1 quart]. Once cool, the stock can be refrigerated for a few days or frozen.

**CAJUN SEASONING:**

½ teaspoon dried hot red pepper flakes
1 teaspoon freshly ground black pepper

½ teaspoon each salt, dried thyme and oregano
2 pinches of cayenne pepper

★ Grind the red pepper with the other spices in a mortar with pestle or in a blender or spice grinder.

**RICE FOR GUMBO:**

2 litres/3 ½ pints [2 quarts] water
Salt
630 g/1 lb 6 oz [3 cups] long-grain American white rice

55 g/2 oz [4 tablespoons] butter
1 teaspoon Tabasco sauce
6 tablespoons freshly squeezed lemon juice (from 2 lemons)

★ In a large pot, bring the water to the boil with the salt, then add the rice, stirring well. Bring back to the boil and simmer, uncovered, for 15-18 minutes, stirring occasionally.
★ Drain the rice in a colander. If it is not converted (parboiled), you will need to rinse out the starch with warm water. Put the rice back into the pan and add the butter, Tabasco sauce and fresh lemon juice. Stir and serve.

# Creole French Toast

While the French regard *pain perdu* as a humble and economical way to use stale brioche, Americans see it as an embellishment of the bread fit for a king's breakfast.

### YIELD: 4-6 SERVINGS

**INGREDIENTS:**

250 ml/8 fl oz [1 cup] milk
125 ml/4 fl oz [½ cup] single cream [US light cream]
2 size-1 eggs [US jumbo eggs]
Yolks from 2 size-1 eggs [US jumbo eggs]
4 tablespoons freshly squeezed orange juice
55 g/2 oz [¼ cup] caster sugar [US granulated sugar]

¼ teaspoon salt
1 tablespoon pure vanilla essence [US pure vanilla extract]
2 tablespoons Grand Marnier or 1 tablespoon Cognac
1 large baguette, or use sourdough bread or a brioche loaf
Butter and vegetable oil for frying
Icing sugar [US confectioners' sugar] and maple syrup, to serve

**METHOD:**

★ In a large shallow dish, whisk together all the ingredients, except for the bread. Cut the bread into 2.5 cm/1 inch slices, either straight across or at a diagonal. Dip the bread in the milk mixture, coating both sides, and leave it to soak for up to 1 hour. (If you are using a dense bread, soak for the full hour; a lighter bread will not be able to soak that long or it will fall apart.)
★ When you are ready to serve the French Toast, fry it in equal parts of vegetable oil and butter until golden brown on both sides. Frying slowly over moderately high heat is preferable to quick frying over high heat. Drain on paper towels, sprinkle with sifted icing sugar and serve with maple syrup or a fruit syrup of your choice.

# Classic New England Clam Chowder

One of our earliest and certainly our most famous soups is called chowder from the French *chaudière* or stew pot in which it is prepared. Americans adapted the French tradition of soups to the New World, where hearty one-pot meals made life a bit friendlier and easier. There are a number of versions of clam chowder, even a tomato based soup called Manhattan Clam Chowder, but the classic ingredients always include: clams, salt pork, onion, potato and cream or milk.

### YIELD: 6 HEARTY SERVINGS

INGREDIENTS:

115 g/4 oz salt pork, cut into strips or small cubes
15 g/ ½ oz [1 tablespoon] butter
1 medium-size onion (about 200 g/7 oz), finely chopped
3 small potatoes (about 225 g/8 oz), peeled and diced
1 teaspoon salt
500 ml/16 fl oz [2 cups] bottled clam juice or rich fish stock (If using fresh clams, replace some of the liquid with the clam broth.)
1 teaspoon freshly ground black pepper

1 teaspoon chopped fresh thyme or ½ teaspoon dried thyme
375 ml/12 fl oz [1 ½ cups] milk
500 ml/16 fl oz [2 cups] single cream [US light cream]
900 g/2 lb [2 cups] finely chopped or minced clams, fresh, frozen or canned (see page 266 for instructions on preparing fresh clams)
Chopped fresh chives or parsley to garnish
Water biscuits or soda crackers to accompany

METHOD:

★ Bring a small pan of water to the boil and add the salt pork. When the water returns to the boil, simmer for 1 minute, then drain and refresh under running cold water. Drain and dry on paper towels.

★ In a large pot, fry the salt pork until crisp; remove and set aside. Drain the fat from the pot. Add the butter and sauté the onion until softened. Add the potatoes, salt pork, salt and clam juice or stock and simmer until the potatoes are just tender.

★ Add the pepper, thyme, milk and cream and bring to the boil. Add the clams and simmer the chowder just to heat them through. Never allow the chowder to come to a full boil or it will curdle. Taste the chowder and correct the seasonings if necessary. Garnish with chives or parsley and serve with water biscuits or crackers.

OPPOSITE: *Cajun Gumbo*

# AFRICAN AMERICANS

"O, yes,
I may say it plain,
America never was America to me,
And yet I swear this oath –
America will be."
Langston Hughes, African American Poet

A group of American's who came against their will and not because of it, African Americans were first brought as slaves before America became a nation. Spanish explorers brought African slaves deep into all areas of the territories they settled and Captain John Smith brought them to Jamestown, beginning the slave trade in America. In 1790, nearly one fifth of the American population was African or had some African blood. African slaves became the foundation of the South's plantation economy, as well as their cooks. They came from many different tribes and from many different regions, but most were from modern-day Nigeria, Ghana and Cameroon. When they served as cooks they used West African foods, such as sesame seeds which they called *benne* seeds, okra and the hot spices they were used to in Africa. In the plantations of the South, where the warmth of the climate demanded that the kitchen be separate from the cool main house, the slaves who cooked became masters of their own domain and America's first group of professional (if unpaid) chefs. Slaves were often sent to Anglo-French restaurants in such cities as Charleston to train in the art of cooking and were expected to train others when they came home to the plantation.

The grandiose hospitality of the South resulted from an abundance of servants. But for every African slave who learned to cook in the European-influenced style appropriate to 'the big house' there are many more who learned to make do for their families with the wild roots and greens, beans, fish and occasional possum that was available for little or no money. This style of cooking became known as 'soul food'. Soul food was made from wild greens including collard, kale and turnip tops, the remains of the pig not choice enough for the plantation owners, and fish that could be found in the stream. This was a cooking style based on ingenuity, making something out of nothing, with little or no European influence. To African Americans 'soul' implies natural expression, openness to life and people, and sharing of common sorrows and joys – and since food was the one thing they could share, even in slavery, the name 'soul food' seems appropriate. In recent years, soul food has become popular in restaurants and cookbooks. Soul cooking is rich in recipes using peanuts, sesame seeds, okra and wild greens, for barbecue and chicken. The following recipes reflect a bit of soul and a bit of Southern plantation hospitality, both using African ingredients.

# Benne Biscuits

African slaves introduced sesame seeds, or *bennes* as they called them, to America and used them in recipes from soups to cookies, candies and cakes. Some sources say they brought the seeds to America hidden in their hair so that they had something of their own country with them. These are wonderful finger food for serving with drinks or apéritifs and are typical offerings of Southern hospitality.

YIELD: 2 DOZEN BISCUITS
Oven: 180°C/350°F/Gas 4

INGREDIENTS:

180 g/6 oz [1 ½ cups] strong plain flour [US all-purpose flour]
115 g/4 oz [½ cup] butter, at room temperature
125 ml/4 fl oz [½ cup] sour cream

35 g/1 ¼ oz [¼ cup] sesame seeds, lightly toasted
Seasoning salt (page 264) and freshly ground pepper
125 g/4 ¼ oz [1 ½ cups] Gruyère cheese, grated, or substitute another cheese of your choice

METHOD:

★ In a medium-size bowl, combine the flour, butter and sour cream and mix together very well. Be sure that all the butter has been evenly mixed into the dough. Divide the dough in half and wrap each half in cling film [US plastic wrap]. Refrigerate the dough until it is firm.

★ Put a 40 cm/16 inch long sheet of parchment or greaseproof paper on a work surface. Dust it with flour and sprinkle half the sesame seeds over the centre of the paper. Put one of the pieces of dough on the sesame seeds and top with another sheet of paper. Roll out the dough between the paper into a rectangle about 15 x 30 cm/6 x 12 inches. Peel off the top paper carefully and sprinkle the dough with seasoning salt, pepper and half of the cheese. Roll up the dough like a Swiss roll [US jelly roll], starting at a long side, and seal the edges by pinching them together. Repeat with the second piece of dough. Wrap the rolled dough in cling film and refrigerate until you plan to bake the biscuits.

★ Preheat the oven.

★ Cut each roll across into 2 cm/¾ inch slices and put them on ungreased baking sheets. (You can lay them flat to show the pinwheel effect or put them seam side down.) Bake in the preheated oven for 25–30 minutes or until golden brown. Serve warm.

NOTE: The biscuits cannot be reheated successfully, but the uncut rolls freeze well and can be kept on hand for unexpected guests.

# Okra Fritters

A fine, crunchy vegetable accompaniment to any meal, these are especially good with fried chicken.

## YIELD: 4-6 SERVINGS

### INGREDIENTS:

675 g/1 ½ lbs fresh okra
1 tablespoon extra virgin olive oil
1 tablespoon finely chopped fresh chives
60 g/2 oz [½ cup] plain flour [US all-purpose flour]
80 g/scant 3 oz [½ cup] cornmeal

1 teaspoon baking powder
1 ½ teaspoons salt
250 ml/8 fl oz [1 cup] beer
½ teaspoon Tabasco sauce
1 tablespoon vegetable oil, plus more for frying

### METHOD:

★ Wash the okra and cut across into 1.5–2.5 cm/ ½–1 inch slices. Sauté them in the olive oil until they begin to brown and are tender but still crisp. Transfer them to a small bowl and toss them with the chives. Reserve.

★ Whisk together the rest of the ingredients. Add the sautéed okra to the batter and stir to coat all the slices evenly. Heat 2.5 cm/1 inch of vegetable oil in a deep-fryer or other suitable pan. When the oil is hot, but not smoking, add the okra mixture by the tablespoon and deep fry until the fritters are golden brown. Drain on paper towels and serve hot. Unfortunately, these do not reheat well, so you must be prepared to eat them immediately.

*Slaves on a South Carolina farm around 1860*

# DUTCH, GERMAN AND EASTERN EUROPEAN IMMIGRANTS

The Dutch established colonies in America along the Hudson River from Manhattan to the Mohawk before the English and could well have been the primary colonial power, had they been able to recruit more Dutch citizens to emigrate. At the time, Holland was enjoying a time of great prosperity and despite 40 years of efforts by the Dutch West India Company to establish colonies, only 6,000 Dutch citizens came. By contrast, 100,000 English settlers arrived during the same period and by 1664, English colonists so outnumbered the Dutch that New Amsterdam was surrendered without a shot and was later renamed New York.

What is interesting is how much of a model for the future "United States" the Dutch settlement of New Amsterdam really was. The Dutch had successfully welcomed men of all nations including Flemings, Walloons, French, Danes, Poles, Norwegians, Swedes, English, Scots, Irish, Germans, Bohemians, Portuguese and Italians – all living peacefully together. But after the surrender of New Amsterdam, Dutch immigration virtually ended for nearly two centuries. In New York, which was really a Dutch town and where they had once formed more than half the population, they accounted for only one fifth of the population in 1790.

Though small in number, Dutch immigrants made large contributions. Dutch views moderated the Puritan-Calvinist austerity and rigidity. They loved to drink, eat well and dance and they loved flowers. How greatly the Dutch influenced American eating habits can be judged by the number of food names adopted directly from the Dutch language. These include some of the most popular foods: *crullers* or doughnuts, coleslaw (*kool-sla*), cookie (*koekje*) and waffle (*wafel*). Dutch contributions also included traditions of religious liberty, Santa Claus, and setting aside a day for celebration, which resulted in the American celebrations of New Year and Thanksgiving (celebrations not religiously based).

German immigration began in colonial times with the "13 families from Krefeld" who established Germantown, Pennsylvania in 1683. Between 1683 and 1783, 100,000 more Germans followed them, including the Amish, Seventh-Day Adventists and Moravians. Though they left for religious reasons and lived lives of self-denial, they were not like the Puritans, and never denied themselves good food. In fact, they prided themselves on their cooking and their reputation for bountiful, if heavy, good food spread far and wide. The first United States census in 1790, found that one out of every twelve Americans was of German descent, living primarily in Pennsylvania, and called the Pennsylvania Dutch. They were German not Dutch – a corruption of *deutsch*, meaning German. Ben Franklin was heard to complain that the Germans were threatening to Germanise the Anglo-Americans, rather than becoming American themselves. While the American Revolution brought immigration to a standstill, Germans immigrated in large numbers following a famine in 1817 and the failure of the liberal-national revolution of 1848. Today, 58 million Americans are of German ancestry, more than any other ancestral group.

In 1900, one could identify a 'German belt' where the percentage of Germans living in the area lay above the national average (10.5 % of total population and 30.7% of all immigrants and their American born children). The German belt stretched from Ohio in the east, to Nebraska in the west, from Missouri in the south and up to Wisconsin in the north. They tended to congregate in more urban settings than other immigrants. In German neighbourhoods in Chicago, Milwaukee, St. Louis and Cincinnati they produced the food and drink of their homeland, such as beer, sausages, coffee cakes and pretzels. They can be credited with contributions to many American festivals and holidays, including the importance of the Christmas tree, Easter, county and state fairs. In America's first county, state and world fairs, the public discovered German food specialities such as dill pickles, rye bread, wieners or frankfurters (today's hot dog), the hamburger, sauerkraut, noodles and schnitzels. German names such as Heinz, Gerber, Kraft and Fleischman became prominent in the food industry and beers produced by Schlitz, Miller, Blatz, and Anheuser-Busch dominate the beer industry. The sweet-sour preference in American food stems from the Germans, often called 'Sauerkraut Yankees' for their love of pickling their foods. Later, sugar was added to the sour aspect of Germanic-Slavic foods and they continued the medieval practice of mixing sweet fruits and berries with meat, fish and fowl. The Pennsylvania Dutch were so famous for their pickling and conserving, including jams and jellies, bread-and-butter pickles, relishes, spiced peaches and apple butter, that their prominence in the tinned food industry is not surprising.

Immigrants from Poland saved England's first settlement, Jamestown, after it almost collapsed when the first group of 'gentlemen adventurers' were diverted on a search for gold. Captain John Smith begged his London backers to send him craftsmen more interested in building a settlement and six Poles and their hard-working example got the colony working again. Poles escaping famine and lack of opportunity in their home have been coming to America in great numbers ever since. By 1910, nearly 2 million had arrived and in 1912 nearly 175,000 Poles immigrated in a single year.

ABOVE: *New Amsterdam around 1650*
OPPOSITE: *Waffles being cooked in Holland in the mid sixteenth century*

# Pecan Waffles

The Dutch are said to have brought waffles to American shores – little did they know what an industry would be created in the form of frozen 'toaster waffles', of which we must have at least 25 different varieties today. When I studied at the University of Minnesota, my favourite were the pecan waffles served up at the counter of Al's Breakfast.

YIELD: ABOUT 8-10 LARGE WAFFLES
Equipment: a waffle iron

INGREDIENTS:

50 g/1 ¾ oz [¼ cup] white vegetable fat [US shortening], melted
70 g/scant 2 ½ oz [⅓ cup] butter, melted
375 ml/12 fl oz [1 ½ cups] milk
2 size-1 eggs [US jumbo eggs]
2 tablespoons maple syrup, honey or sugar

180 g/6 oz [1 ½ cups] self-raising flour [US cake flour]
75 g/2 ½ oz [½ cup] buckwheat flour
1 teaspoon salt
4 teaspoons baking powder
85 g/3 oz [¾ cup] pecans, toasted and finely chopped
Maple syrup, to serve

METHOD:

★ In a small saucepan, heat the vegetable fat and butter with the milk. When the fats have melted and the mixture is warm, remove from the heat and whisk in the eggs and the maple syrup or sugar.
★ In a medium-size bowl, mix together the dry ingredients. Whisk in the milk mixture to make a smooth batter.
★ Preheat a waffle iron. Add enough batter to cover the bottom and sprinkle the waffle with 1–2 tablespoons of the chopped pecans. Close the iron and cook until the waffle is golden brown. Serve hot, with maple syrup.

NOTE: This batter should be used immediately, since the longer it sits the thicker and heavier it will become. If it should become too thick, thin it with additional milk.

# Duck Goulash with Spinach Spaetzle

A hearty, yet sophisticated dish ideal for entertaining, this goulash will evoke memories of the wonders of German hospitality and *gemutlichkeit* (cosiness)! Serve with Braised Red Cabbage (page 94) and you have the colours of Christmas and a wonderful holiday celebration dinner.

YIELD: 8-10 SERVINGS
Equipment: a spaetzle maker, or a colander with large holes, and a food processor
Oven: 220°C/425°F/Gas 7

INGREDIENTS:

2 ducks, each weighing about 2 kg/4½ lbs
30 g/1 oz dried wild mushrooms (ceps/porcini, morels etc.)
105 g/3 ½ oz [7 tablespoons] butter
450 g/1 lb fresh mushrooms, quartered
4 tablespoons plain flour [US all-purpose flour]
5 tablespoons soy sauce
3 tablespoons medium dry sherry
1 bay leaf
1 teaspoon chopped fresh tarragon or ¼ teaspoon dried tarragon
1 teaspoon chopped fresh rosemary or ¼ teaspoon dried rosemary
½ teaspoon freshly ground pepper
¼ teaspoon Tabasco sauce
3 tablespoons crème fraîche or sour cream

FOR THE DUCK STOCK:

55 g/2 oz [4 tablespoons] butter
1 large onion, chopped
4 medium-size carrots, coarsely chopped
2 celery stalks, coarsely chopped
250 ml/8 fl oz [1 cup] medium dry sherry
5-6 litres/8–9 pints [5–6 quarts] water
A bouquet garni including 8-10 parsley sprigs, a bay leaf and 3-4 thyme sprigs

FOR THE SPAETZLE:

225 g/8 oz chopped frozen spinach
1 tablespoon vegetable oil
185 ml/6 fl oz [¾ cup] milk
95 g/3 ½ oz [½ cup] semolina
180 g/6 oz [1 ½ cups] plain flour [US all-purpose flour]
1 teaspoon salt
¼ teaspoon freshly grated nutmeg
3 size-1 eggs [US jumbo eggs]
Butter

METHOD:

★ Well in advance of serving this dish, roast the duck (this can be done as much as a few days ahead). Preheat the oven. Remove the neck, liver and giblets from the ducks, as well as any extra fat. Reserve the giblets and necks for the stock. Rinse the ducks with cold running water, inside and out, and place on a rack in a roasting pan. Prick the skin all over with a sharp fork or knife, without piercing into the meat. Roast for 1 hour. Leave the ducks to cool. Remove the meat, wrap it well and refrigerate until you are ready to make the goulash. Reserve the carcasses for the stock.

★ To make the duck stock, chop up the duck carcasses into pieces. In a stock pot, melt the butter and fry the vegetables, necks and giblets until browned. Add the carcasses. Pour in the sherry and water and add the bouquet garni. The carcasses should be well covered with liquid, so add more water if necessary. Bring the liquid to the boil slowly, skimming off the froth as it rises. Leave the stock to simmer uncovered for 2-3 hours, adding more water if the carcasses become exposed. Strain the stock, then boil over high heat to reduce to 900 ml/1 ½ pints [3 ½–4 cups]. Allow to cool and then refrigerate the stock until you are ready to prepare the goulash.

★ A few hours before serving (or immediately before serving), prepare the spaetzle. Put a large pot of salted water on to boil. Put the spinach in a fine sieve and pour boiling water over it. Break up the larger pieces with a fork. Pour over more boiling water, then press down with a wooden spoon to remove most of the water from the spinach. Put the spinach, oil and milk in a food processor and process until smooth. Empty into a medium-size bowl and add the rest of the ingredients, except for the butter. Mix well to form a thick batter. Using either a spaetzle maker or a colander with large holes, press the batter through, in 125 ml/4 fl oz [½ cup] quantities, into the boiling salted water. The spaetzle are done when they float to the top. Remove with a slotted spoon and drain. Repeat with the rest of the batter. Toss the finished spaetzle with some melted butter. Just before serving, reheat the spaetzle in 30 g/1 oz [2 tablespoons] of butter in a large frying pan.

★ When you are ready to make the goulash, soak the dried mushrooms in boiling water for about 15 minutes, then drain and rinse very well (they tend to be sandy). Chop them finely and reserve.

★ In a large pot, melt 45 g/1 ½ oz [3 tablespoons] of the butter and sauté the quartered fresh mushrooms until they are dry and starting to brown. Remove them and reserve with the wild mushrooms. Add the remaining butter and the flour to the pan and cook for a few minutes, stirring, to make a roux. Whisk in the reserved duck stock, the soy sauce, sherry, herbs, pepper and Tabasco sauce. Simmer for 5-10 minutes or until the sauce thickens.

★ Remove the skin and fat from the duck meat and cut the meat into bite-sized pieces. Add to the sauce with the mushrooms and simmer for another 10 minutes. Finally, whisk in the crème fraîche or sour cream. Taste the sauce and adjust seasonings if necessary. Bring just to a simmer. Serve hot with the spaetzle.

NOTE: If you are using wild duck you may want to add more cream. The spaetzle are delicious served with any number of stews, both meat and game. They are a great last minute noodle to make any meal more festive and delicious!

*Amish farmers harvest oats in Indiana*

# Grilled Bratwurst

Wherever German immigrants settled in the United States they made beer and sausage and shared them with their friends. The frankfurter quickly became an American treat known as 'the hot dog'. Today, many of the traditional German sausages are even better when tossed on the barbecue. Here is a dramatic dish concocted from German American influences.

YIELD: 4-8 servings, depending on appetites
Equipment: a barbecue or cast iron ridged grill pan and a deep-fryer or other pan with a basket

INGREDIENTS:
8 fresh bratwurst (Pre-cooked are not as good, but will do in a pinch.)
375 ml/12 fl oz [1 ½ cups] beer
15 g/ ½ oz [1 tablespoon] butter
1 large onion, finely chopped
3 tablespoons dark soft brown sugar
3 tablespoons cider or white wine vinegar
1 tablespoon Worcestershire sauce
½ teaspoon salt
1 teaspoon Hungarian sweet paprika
1 bay leaf
1 tablespoon Dijon mustard

FOR THE MASHED POTATOES:
1.12 kg/2 ½ lb potatoes suitable for mashing, peeled and quartered
3 garlic cloves, crushed
125 ml/4 fl oz [½ cup] single cream [US light cream] or milk
45 g/1 ½ oz [3 tablespoons] butter
Salt and freshly ground pepper to taste

FOR THE TOBACCO ONIONS:
1 large Spanish or Bermuda onion, sliced paper thin
250–500 ml/8–16 fl oz [1-2 cups] buttermilk
120–240 g/4–8 oz [1-2 cups] plain flour [US all-purpose flour]
½–1 teaspoon seasoning salt (page 264)
Vegetable oil or white vegetable fat [US shortening] for frying

METHOD:
★ The day before serving, put the bratwurst in a shallow ceramic dish and pour the beer over them. Cover and refrigerate overnight.
★ To prepare the mashed potatoes, put the potatoes and garlic in a medium-size saucepan and cover with salted water. Bring to the boil and simmer until the potatoes are tender. Drain and press through a potato ricer, or mash the potatoes, so that there are no lumps (the garlic will be mashed with them). Beat in the cream or milk and the butter and season to taste. Cover and reserve until you are ready to serve. (They can be made well in advance.) Just before serving, reheat them gently in a saucepan, adding additional milk if required, or reheat in the microwave.
★ If using a barbecue, prepare and light the charcoal fire in good time; you need a medium hot fire (see page 212 for instructions). A ridged grill pan will need about 10 minutes' preheating.
★ To make the sauce, melt the butter in a medium-size saucepan, add the chopped onion and cook until lightly browned. Add the brown sugar, vinegar, Worcestershire sauce, salt, paprika and bay leaf. Remove the bratwurst from the beer and add the beer to the saucepan. Cook the sauce over moderate heat for about 5 minutes. Stir in the mustard.
★ Barbecue grill the bratwurst, or cook them on a grill pan, for about 20 minutes, turning them with tongs and not a fork (if punctured they lose their juices). When they are nicely browned, add them to the sauce in the pan and leave to simmer gently for a few minutes.
★ While the bratwurst are being grilled, prepare the tobacco onions. Put the onion slices in a bowl and add enough buttermilk to cover them. In a shallow dish, mix 120 g/4 oz [1 cup] flour with ½ teaspoon seasoning salt. Heat at least 5 cm/2 inches of vegetable oil or white vegetable fat in a deep-fryer equipped with a basket or another suitable pan for deep-frying. When the oil just begins to smoke, remove handfuls of onions from the buttermilk, toss briskly in the seasoned flour, shake off excess flour and drop into the hot oil. Fry the onions until they are "the colour of

tobacco", or a rich golden brown. If you are using a basket, lift it up and allow the oil to drain from the onions, then put them on paper towels to drain further. Alternatively, remove the onions from the oil with a large slotted spoon or wire sieve to the paper towels. Keep hot while you fry the rest of the onions, seasoning more flour as necessary.

★ To serve, make a bed of hot mashed potatoes on a large serving platter. With tongs, arrange the bratwurst decoratively on top and pour the sauce over them. Finally, pile the tobacco onions in a high stack on top of it all. Serve the dish with a spicy hot mustard, and beer of course!

NOTE: The tobacco onions can be made an hour or two in advance. Reheat them in a 150°C/300°F/Gas 2 oven for about 5 minutes.

# Braised Red Cabbage

An ideal accompaniment and foil to game, duck or meatballs; this dish epitomises the sweet-sour taste Americans love, inherited from German immigrants.

### YIELD: 6-8 SERVINGS

INGREDIENTS:

15 g/ ½ oz [1 tablespoon] bacon fat or butter
1 medium-size red cabbage weighing about 900 g/2 lbs, quartered and thinly sliced
1 medium-size red or ordinary onion, thinly sliced
2 large apples, peeled and sliced
1 teaspoon salt
55 g/2 oz [¼ cup] sugar

375 ml /12 fl oz [1 ½ cups] water
125 ml/4 fl oz [½ cup] vinegar (cider, red wine or distilled white)
1 bay leaf
4 whole allspice
2 whole cloves
6 black peppercorns
1-2 tablespoons redcurrant jelly, or any seedless red jam

METHOD:

★ In a large pot, melt the fat and add the sliced cabbage, onion and apples. Stir to coat them with the fat and cook until they begin to wilt. Add all of the other ingredients with the exception of the redcurrant jelly. Bring to the boil, then lower the heat, cover and simmer for 1-1 ½ hours or until the cabbage is tender.

★ Before serving stir in the jelly to suit your sweet-sour taste. Serve the cabbage warm with meats or stews.

NOTE: The cabbage can be made well in advance and reheated for serving. It will keep in the refrigerator for up to a week.

*Shooting duck on the marshes, 1849*

# Stuffed Cabbage Rolls

This dish is a popular family meal, as well as a potluck dinner speciality wherever immigrants of Poland, Hungary or Czechoslovakia have settled. But other nationalities know them too – they are the original Old World comfort food, especially when they are served up with mashed potatoes.

YIELD: 6–8 SERVINGS
Oven: 190°C/375°F/Gas 5

INGREDIENTS:

70 g/scant 2 ½ oz [⅓ cup] long-grain rice
250 ml/8 fl oz [1 cup] boiling salted water
1 medium-size white, green or Savoy cabbage
225 g/8 oz minced lean pork [US ground lean pork]
225 g/8 oz minced lean beef [US ground lean beef]
1 size-1 egg [US jumbo egg]
1 medium-size onion, finely chopped
2 garlic cloves, very finely chopped
¼ red sweet pepper, finely chopped
1 teaspoon Worcestershire sauce
150 ml/ ¼ pint [⅔ cup] milk or single cream [US light cream]

2 teaspoons sweet Hungarian paprika
¼ teaspoon freshly ground pepper
2 teaspoons salt
White from a size-1 egg [US jumbo egg]
30 g/1 oz [2 tablespoons] lard or white vegetable fat [US shortening]
1 tablespoon plain flour [US all-purpose flour]
2 tablespoons soft brown sugar
1 tablespoon cider or red wine vinegar
1 small can (295 g/10.4 oz) condensed beef consommé
250 ml/8 fl oz [1 cup] tomato-vegetable juice, such as V-8

METHOD:

★ Cook the rice in the boiling salted water for 18 minutes or until tender.
★ Bring a large pot of salted water to the boil. Remove the core and any bruised outer leaves from the cabbage, then plunge it into the boiling water and simmer for about 10 minutes. Remove and cool, then pull off the outer leaves carefully. Remove as many leaves as you can without breaking them. Put the rest of the cabbage back into the simmering water and cook for another 10 minutes. Remove and pull off the leaves until you have about 20-25 of them. Finely chop the inner part of the cabbage to make 45 g/1 ½ oz [½ cup] and reserve.
★ In a medium-size bowl, combine the pork, beef, whole egg, rice, onion, garlic, red pepper, Worcestershire sauce, milk or cream, paprika, pepper, salt and the finely chopped cabbage. Mix well with your hands to combine the ingredients.
★ With kitchen scissors or a sharp knife, cut the hard core from each of the large cabbage leaves. Put a few tablespoons of the meat mixture into the centre of each leaf, fold over the sides and roll up. Brush the ends with a bit of egg white and lay closed side down on a baking sheet. (The rolls can be prepared ahead of time and refrigerated.)
★ Preheat the oven.
★ In a large frying pan, heat the lard or vegetable fat and fry the cabbage rolls until lightly browned on all sides. Remove them to a casserole with a cover. When all of the rolls have been fried, add the flour to the drippings in the pan and stir well, then add the brown sugar, vinegar, beef consommé and tomato juice. Bring to the boil, stirring, and simmer until the sauce thickens slightly.
★ Pour the sauce over the cabbage rolls in the casserole. Cover and bake in the preheated oven for 1 hour. Serve with mashed potatoes.

NOTE: The cabbage rolls can be baked and then refrigerated or frozen, to be reheated for serving.

# SCANDINAVIAN IMMIGRANTS

Just one hundred Swedes came to America in 1638 with the dream of founding 'New Sweden', and settled in the area that is now Delaware. They were farmers, did not believe in slavery, treated the Native American Indians fairly and built sturdy wood houses called log cabins that would serve as a model for American pioneers. Because they were farmers used to a rugged, harsh terrain and climate, resourceful and hard-working, they became the ideal pioneers, pushing further west toward the frontier. In the 1840s three small groups of Swedes led by idealists and intellectuals spearheaded a massive immigration of their countrymen by writing 'America letters', expounding the virtues of their new-found home. Immigration grew from 4,000 in 1850 to 300,000 by 1880. In southern Sweden, some provinces lost every tenth man, woman and child to America, and before the flood of immigration stopped, 1,200,000 Swedes had come, more than a third of Sweden's entire population at the start of the exodus.

Scandinavian immigrants from Sweden, Norway and Denmark chose parts of the country where they felt most at home, like the sparsely inhabited north central states of Minnesota and Wisconsin, where there were forests and lakes and the winters were cold.

Scandinavian cooking offers a wealth of fish recipes, pastries of great delicacy, and the *smorgasbord*, that groaning board of variety, that has become a part of America's style of service and eating. Americans love the buffet, all-you-can-eat, help-yourself style first introduced by the Swedes. Scandinavians were also responsible for making us a coffee drinking country, rather than a tea drinking one. Their customary coffee break, often accompanied by a special pastry, could be at any time of the day. It has become so ingrained in our business culture that the coffee break is often written into union contracts. 'Danish' is now an American word used to describe any pastry, no matter what its origins.

# Grandma Vady's Meringue Rice Pudding

My grandmother's rice pudding was the jewel of her Swedish *smorgasbord* every Christmas Eve. This most treasured of our family's recipes actually came from a long ago neighbour. When my great-great-grandfather Magnuson died and his wife was inconsolable, her neighbour brought this pudding and she ate for the first time in days. It is irresistible, comforting, regal.

YIELD: 6-8 servings, for breakfast or dessert
Equipment: a soufflé or baking dish of at least 3 litres/4 ⅔ pints [3 quarts] capacity
Oven: 150°C/300°F/Gas 2

INGREDIENTS:
125 ml/4 fl oz [½ cup] water
125 ml/4 fl oz [½ cup] plus1 litre/1 ⅔ pints [1 quart] milk
105 g/3 ½ oz [½ cup] long-grain rice, preferably converted (which means it has been parboiled to remove starch)
1 thin strip of lemon rind, about 2.5 cm/1 inch wide and 7.5 cm/3 inches long, all white pith removed
110 g/4 oz [½ cup] caster sugar [US granulated sugar]

3 tablespoons cornflour [US cornstarch]
Yolks from 4 size-1 eggs [US jumbo eggs], beaten
1 ½ teaspoons pure vanilla essence [US pure vanilla extract]

FOR THE MERINGUE:
Whites from 6 size-1 eggs [US jumbo eggs]
¼ teaspoon cream of tartar
220 g/8 oz [1 cup] caster sugar [US superfine sugar]

METHOD:
★ Preheat the oven.
★ Bring the water and 125 ml/4 fl oz [½ cup] of milk to the boil in a heavy saucepan. Add the rice and lemon rind. Return to the boil, then lower the heat to moderately low, cover and simmer for 15-18 minutes or until all of the liquid has been absorbed. Discard the lemon rind, then add the remaining milk to the saucepan and bring back to the boil.
★ In a small bowl, combine the sugar and cornflour. When the milk and rice mixture has returned to the boil, add a little of the milk to the sugar and cornflour to make a paste, then return it all to the milk in the saucepan. Cook, stirring constantly, until the mixture just comes to the boil again. Remove from the heat and leave to cool for a few minutes.
★ Add a bit of the rice mixture to the beaten egg yolks. Stir into the rest of the rice mixture. Add the vanilla and pour into the baking dish.
★ To make the meringue, whisk the egg whites with the cream of tartar until firm peaks form. Slowly whisk in the sugar and continue to whisk until the meringue is glossy and forms stiff peaks. Gently spread the meringue over the top of the rice pudding, being sure to cover the entire top and up to the edges.
★ Bake in the preheated oven for 1 hour. Turn off the oven, open the door, leaving it ajar, and leave the rice pudding to cool. The pudding can be served warm, at room temperature or cold. Refrigerate any left-over rice pudding.

OPPOSITE: *A hearty country breakfast, painted by Edward L. Henry 1884*

# Cheese Danish Coffee Cake

Any sweet roll usually eaten for breakfast is called a "Danish" in America. Especially famous are the Cheese Danish of New York's Jewish Delicatessens that are half cheesecake, half pastry and wholly delicious! This is a large version of that speciality, inspired by Danish immigrants' finesse with pastry.

YIELD: 2 coffeecakes, 12 servings each
Oven: 180°C/350°F/Gas 4

INGREDIENTS:
One recipe of sweet bread dough for Sticky Buns
   (page 204)

FOR THE CREAM CHEESE FILLING:
2 tablespoons water
2 tablespoons sugar
250 g/9 oz [1 cup] dried apricots, chopped
2 tablespoons Kirsch

675 g/1 ½ lbs cream cheese or other full fat soft cheese, at
   room temperature
90 g/3 oz [¾ cup] icing sugar [US confectioners' sugar]
Yolks of 2 size-1 eggs [US jumbo eggs]
Grated rind of 1 lemon

FOR THE GLAZE:
6 tablespoons apricot jam
2 tablespoons Kirsch

METHOD:
★ Prepare the sweet bread dough, taking it through its second rising.
★ Meanwhile, make the filling. In a small saucepan, heat the water with the sugar until it bubbles. Add the apricots and stir until they absorb almost all of the liquid. Then add the Kirsch and stir until it is absorbed. Remove from the heat and leave to cool.
★ Beat together the cream cheese, icing sugar, egg yolks and lemon rind. Fold in the apricots.
★ Assemble the two coffeecakes as for the Chocolate Chip and Almond Coffeecake (page 208). Leave to rise until doubled in size.
★ Preheat the oven. Bake the coffee cakes for 25-30 minutes. Cool on a rack and glaze while still warm but not hot.
★ To make the glaze, melt the jam with the Kirsch in a small pan and press through a sieve. Brush all over the coffeecake and leave the glaze to set.
★ Serve warm or at room temperature. This coffeecake freezes well.

NOTE: If you would like some variety, consider halving the filling and glaze in this recipe and in the Chocolate Chip and Almond Coffeecake recipe (page 208) and making one of each coffeecake.

# Almond Coffeecake

This type of pastry has been attributed to the Danes, Swedes and Norwegians, but suffice it to say it is the invention of Scandinavian Americans. It is typical of the pastries of Scandinavia in that it is light and delicate, almond-flavoured and not too sweet. It makes a wonderful spur-of-the-moment creation to accompany coffee or tea.

YIELD: 2 LARGE COFFEECAKES
Equipment: a food processor
Oven: 200°C/400°F/Gas 6

## INGREDIENTS:

40 g/scant 1 ½ oz [¼ cup] ground almonds
80 g/scant 3 oz [¼ cup] almond paste or marzipan
95 g/3 ¼ oz [¾ cup] strong plain flour [US all-purpose flour]
85 g/3 oz [6 tablespoons] cold butter, cut into pieces
1 tablespoon cold water

### FOR THE TOPPING:

115 g/4 oz [½ cup] butter
250 ml/8 fl oz [1 cup] water
110 g/3 ¾ oz [1 cup] sponge or plain flour [US all-purpose flour]

4 size-1 eggs [US jumbo eggs]
1 teaspoon pure almond essence [US pure almond extract]

### FOR THE GLAZE:

15 g/ ½ oz [1 tablespoon] butter, at room temperature
120 g/4 oz [1 cup] icing sugar [US confectioners' sugar], sifted
1 teaspoon pure almond essence [US pure almond extract]
Single cream [US half and half]

## METHOD:

★ Preheat the oven.

★ In a food processor fitted with a steel blade, blend the almonds and almond paste or marzipan until they are combined. Add the strong flour and butter and process until well mixed. With the machine still running, add the water and process until a ball of dough is formed. Divide the dough in half and spread with your fingers on 1 or 2 ungreased baking sheets to form two rectangles, each 30 x 10 cm/12 x 4 inches.

★ To make the topping, put the butter and water in a heavy medium-size saucepan and bring to the boil. Add the flour all at once, stirring rapidly with a wooden spoon until it forms a ball. Continue to stir over the heat for about 1 minute to dry out the mixture. Remove from the heat and whisk in the eggs, one at a time, fully mixing in each egg before adding the next. Finally, whisk in the almond essence.

★ Spoon this mixture over the rectangles of dough on the baking sheet and smooth with a rubber spatula, being sure to cover all the dough. Bake in the preheated oven for 25-30 minutes. The pastry should be browned, but not too dark on the base. Remove from the oven.

★ To make the glaze, work the butter into the icing sugar in a small bowl. When well combined, add the almond essence and enough cream to make a spreading consistency. Spread the glaze over the pastries while they are still warm, but not hot. Serve the coffeecake warm or at room temperature. If well wrapped it will keep for a day, but not much longer.

# Poached Salmon in Aspic with Sweet-Sour Cucumber Fins & Mustard Sour Cream Sauce

This will be the star of any Swedish *smorgasbord* or the centrepiece of a wonderful summer picnic, and it is not that hard to prepare. The delicate flavour of poached salmon is enlivened by the addition of my favourite pickled cucumbers and a tangy mustard sauce that will titillate any taste buds.

YIELD: 10-12 or more servings
Equipment:  muslin or cheesecloth, a fish kettle or other pan large enough to hold a whole or half salmon

INGREDIENTS:
One recipe Sweet-Sour Cucumber Salad (see overleaf)
1 whole salmon or tail-end piece weighing about
    900g–1.35 kg/2–3 lbs, rinsed and cleaned
1.5 litres/2 ⅓ pints [1 ½ quarts] water
4 ½ tablespoons white distilled vinegar
1 ½ tablespoons salt
8 whole allspice
8 black peppercorns
2 bay leaves
1 small onion, chopped
1 small carrot, chopped
5 fresh dill or parsley sprigs
2 teaspoons powdered gelatine [US unflavoured gelatin]
Red sweet pepper and fresh dill, to garnish

FOR THE MUSTARD AND
SOUR CREAM SAUCE:
185 ml/6 fl oz [¾ cup] sour cream
2 tablespoons Dijon mustard
3 tablespoons white wine vinegar
1 teaspoon freshly squeezed lemon juice
1 teaspoon chopped fresh dill
2 tablespoons caster sugar [US granulated sugar]

METHOD:
★  Make the Sweet-Sour Cucumber Salad at least 2-3 hours in advance of preparing the poached salmon.
★  Rinse and clean the fish, cutting off fins, head and tail. Wrap the fish in muslin or cheesecloth, leaving ample surplus on the ends so that you can easily lift it in and out of the poaching liquid.
★  In a fish kettle or other large pan that will hold the fish comfortably, combine the water, vinegar, salt, allspice, peppercorns, bay leaves, onion, carrot and dill or parsley and bring to the boil. Cover and simmer this court bouillon for 15 minutes.
★  Lower the salmon into the court bouillon. Cover and simmer for 20-25 minutes or until the flesh is just beginning to flake when tested with the tip of a sharp knife. It should still be firm. When it is done, remove the fish from the liquid and leave to cool. Strain the court bouillon and reserve 500 ml/16 fl oz [2 cups] to make the aspic.

★   Sprinkle the gelatine over the reserved court bouillon and leave to soften for a few minutes, then heat just until the gelatine dissolves. Set this aspic mixture aside.

★   Remove the skin from the salmon and carefully scrape off any grey flesh. You can leave the fish whole or fillet it. If filleted it can be put back together or the two fillets can be finished separately. I prefer the latter because it allows you to use more of the sweet-sour cucumber and to create a very spectacular-looking dish. Lay the fish or fillets on a large serving platter.

★   Drain the sweet-sour cucumber slices and lay them in overlapping rows over the entire fish to resemble fins. You can create colour and interest by making top fins with triangles cut from red sweet pepper if you like.

★   Cool the aspic mixture over ice (or in the refrigerator) until it becomes syrupy. Remove it from the ice and spoon half of it carefully over the fish. Refrigerate the fish for 10-15 minutes to set this layer of aspic. Then spoon another layer of aspic over the fish and refrigerate until serving. If the aspic becomes too thick, it can be gently warmed and chilled again to the required consistency. Before serving, garnish the platter with dill and serve with the mustard and sour cream sauce.

★   To make the sauce, combine all the ingredients in a small bowl and whisk to mix.

# Sweet-Sour Cucumber Salad

This is a refreshing salad to serve with any meat or fish, like a quick, home-made pickle.

YIELD: 4 servings

INGREDIENTS:
2 medium-size cucumbers [US seedless cucumbers]
80 ml/2 ¾ fl oz [⅓ cup] white distilled vinegar
2 tablespoons water

55 g/2 oz [¼ cup] sugar
½ teaspoon salt
Pinch of ground white pepper
2 tablespoons chopped fresh dill or parsley

METHOD:
★   Rinse the cucumbers, but do not peel them. Slice them paper thin.
★   Mix together the rest of the ingredients in a deep bowl. Add the sliced cucumbers and rest a plate on top of them. Put a heavy can or other weight on top to keep the cucumbers submerged in the marinade. Refrigerate for 2-3 hours.
★   Drain and serve cold with meat or fish.

# ITALIAN IMMIGRANTS

Italians formed the last and largest of all the great waves of immigration to American shores with the majority coming in the late 19th and early 20th Century. A 1940 census showed Italians to be the largest foreign-born group in our population.

Italians were noticeable as restaurant owners and cooks as early as the Gold Rush of 1849, when most Californian towns had at least one Italian-style restaurant serving tomato sauce on something. At some point, Americans started a love affair with pasta, in all its varieties, and stopped calling it 'macaroni', which had been the only word for pasta previously known. On the West Coast, the growth in popularity of vegetables such as artichokes, bell peppers, aubergines [eggplants], broccoli, Savoy Cabbage, broad [fava] beans and many more can be traced to the Italians who grew them, cooked them, ate them and served them in their restaurants. They worked the vineyards of California and set up some of the large wineries famous today, such as Gallo. The Italian contribution to American cuisine is enormous. Some insist that the American habit of eating the salad as a first course was introduced by Italian immigrants who were used to eating a few raw, cold items before the heavier pasta course. Though it took a few years for Americans to explore regional variations of Italian cuisine, almost every American housewife has a favourite recipe for spaghetti sauce and whether she is Italian or not, serves it regularly to her family. Today it is hard to believe that there was a time when Americans avoided garlic and even onions and hardly knew olive oil existed. Italians have done more than almost any other ethnic group to expand America's cuisine. Today Italian food is the most popular 'ethnic food' in America and pizza now vies for popularity with the hamburger.

OPPOSITE: *Grilled Spring Vegetables on Spicy Herbed Pasta*

# Apple Pizza

Pizza - the Italian version of a quick and inexpensive flat bread with topping, that can be eaten in a wedge without the encumbrance of plate, knife and fork – has to be the international food phenomenon of all time. Americans love it so much that they take great liberties with it – like this healthy variation on apple pie, which can be popular with the whole family for brunch or breakfast.

YIELD: 6-8 SERVINGS
Equipment: a 30 cm/12 inch pizza pan
Oven: 150°C/300°F/Gas 2 and then 180°C/350°F/Gas 4

INGREDIENTS:
200 g/7 oz [1 ½ cups] wholemeal flour [US whole-wheat flour]
75 g/2 ½ oz [⅓ cup firmly packed] soft brown sugar
90 g/3 ¼ oz [1 cup] porridge oats or rolled oats
175 g/6 oz [¾ cup] butter or margarine, cut into pieces
Yolk from a size-1 egg [US jumbo egg]
1 teaspoon pure vanilla essence [US pure vanilla extract]

FOR THE TOPPING:
6 large apples, such as Cox's or Golden Delicious, that will stay firm after cooking
Juice of 1 lemon
Apple juice or water
95 g/3 ¼ oz [½ cup] raisins
55 g/2 oz [½ cup] pecans or walnuts, chopped
75 g/2 ½ oz [⅓ cup firmly packed] soft brown sugar
1 teaspoon ground cinnamon
¼ teaspoon freshly ground nutmeg
260 g/9 oz [2 ½ cups] mature (sharp) Cheddar cheese, grated

METHOD:
★ Preheat the oven to 150°C/300°F/Gas 2.
★ To make the crust, combine the wholemeal flour, brown sugar, oats and butter or margarine in a large bowl. Work the mixture with your fingertips until it is of a uniform consistency. With a fork mix in the egg yolk and vanilla. Finish mixing with your hands to form a ball of dough.
★ Set aside one-quarter of the dough (about 120 g/4 oz) in a small bowl. Press the remaining dough into a 30 cm/12 inch round pizza pan to line it evenly. Bake it in the preheated oven for 20 minutes.
★ Peel, core and slice the apples and sprinkle with the lemon juice to prevent them discolouring. Cover the bottom of a frying pan with apple juice or water and add the apples. Cook over moderate heat until they are soft. Add the raisins when the apples are almost done and cook them until soft and plump. Remove from the heat.
★ To the reserved dough add the chopped nuts, brown sugar, cinnamon and nutmeg and mix well.
★ Increase the oven temperature.
★ Scatter the grated cheese over the prebaked crust. Spread the apples and raisin mixture evenly over the whole pizza and, finally, scatter the nut topping over the apples. Bake the pizza for 40–45 minutes.
★ Allow to cool briefly and then cut into wedges as you would any pizza. Serve with yoghurt or ice-cream if you're in the mood for a dessert. This is wonderful for brunch, served with omelettes or scrambled eggs.

# American Pizza - Wholemeal Honey Crust

An Italian immigrant opened the first pizzeria in New York City in 1905, where he served a version of Neapolitan pizza. Today, the pizzeria outnumbers restaurants serving hamburgers in America. Americans are so crazy about pizza, that many new versions have been invented: 'designer pizza', a creation of Californian restauranteur and chef, Wolfgang Puck, and the Chicago 'deep dish'. For the home cook, the crisp crust of the pizzeria is difficult to achieve. I've been working on it for years and offer you my favourite crust, with directions on how to make it and suggestions for toppings.

YIELD: a 35 cm/14 inch pizza

Equipment: enough unglazed quarry tiles, less than 1.5 cm/½ inch thick, to fit your oven's dimensions with 2.5 cm/1 inch free all around (I use 8 tiles that measure 19 x 10 xm/7 ¾ x 4 inches in my oven), or a pizza baking stone. Or you can use a perforated or regular pizza pan or a baking sheet. Nice but not mandatory:  a food processor and a pizza peel

Oven: 250°C/500°F or the highest setting

INGREDIENTS:
2 ½ teaspoons dried yeast
1 tablespoon honey
150 ml/ ¼ pint [⅔ cup] warm water
2 tablespoons olive oil
35 g/1 ¼ oz [¼ cup] wholemeal flour [US whole-wheat flour]

15 g/ ½ oz [¼ cup] bran
260 g/9 oz [2 cups] strong plain flour [US bread flour]
½ teaspoon salt
Cornmeal to dust work surface and pizza pan

METHOD:
★  Mix the yeast with the honey and water in a small bowl, then leave for about 5 minutes. The mixture should bubble and become frothy. (If using easy blend yeast [US rapid-rise yeast], follow the instructions on the packet.)
★  Add the rest of the ingredients and mix to form a ball of dough. Turn the dough on to a floured surface and knead for 5-10 minutes or until it is smooth and elastic. (If you have a food processor you can add the ingredients to the yeast mixture and process until it forms a ball. Then knead it by processing for an additional 15 seconds.)
★  Put the dough in an oiled bowl and turn it to coat with oil. Cover with cling film [US plastic wrap] and put it in a warm place in your kitchen. Leave the dough to rise until it has doubled in bulk.
★  About 1 hour before you are going to bake the pizza, preheat the oven with the quarry tiles in place on the rack in the oven or on a baking sheet.
★  Punch the dough to knock out the air and turn it on to a surface sprinkled with cornmeal. Roll out into a 35 cm/14 inch round or into 4 individual pizzas about 18 cm/7 inches in diameter. Top with your choice of ingredients and place on a pizza pan, or place directly on the tiles in the preheated oven – this is where a pizza peel comes in handy. A 35 cm/14 inch pizza will take 10-15 minutes to bake, depending on toppings.

# SUGGESTED TOPPINGS FOR PIZZA

PIZZA MARGARITA (TOMATO & MOZZARELLA)
Prepare the pizza crust as directed in the master recipe. Brush the crust generously with olive oil. Cover with 450 g/1 lb grated mozzarella cheese, leaving a 1.5 cm/½ inch border clear around the edge. Cover the cheese with 450 g/1 lb skinned, chopped and drained fresh plum tomatoes (or use well-drained canned tomatoes). Sprinkle with 1 tablespoon chopped fresh oregano or basil and then with 50 g/scant 2 oz [½ cup] freshly grated Parmesan cheese. Drizzle with additional olive oil. Bake for 10–15 minutes or until golden brown and puffed.

ROASTED GARLIC & GRILLED VEGETABLE PIZZA
Preheat the oven to 150°C/300°F/Gas 2. Put 12 peeled garlic cloves in a small baking dish, add olive oil to cover and cover the dish. Roast for about 30 minutes or until tender but not browned. Drain the garlic, reserving the oil, and chop. Grill marinated vegetables of your choice as directed in the recipe for Grilled Spring Vegetables on Spicy Herbed Pasta (page 108). Prepare the pizza crust as directed in the master recipe. Brush the crust with some of the garlic-flavoured olive oil and sprinkle with the roasted garlic. Arrange the grilled vegetables on the dough and garnish with freshly grated Parmesan cheese and drained and chopped sun-dried tomatoes in olive oil. Bake for 10–15 minutes or until bubbly and browned.

DEEP-DISH CHEESE & SAUSAGE PIZZA
Roll out the dough to a 30 cm/12 inch round and fit it into a 23 cm/9 inch springform cake pan, or a deep-dish pizza pan, that has been oiled and sprinkled with cornmeal. Fry 450 g/1 lb pork sausagemeat (or use recipe for pork sausagemeat on page 267). Add 1 teaspoon fennel seeds, crushed in a mortar with a pestle, and dried hot red pepper flakes to taste. Layer on the pizza dough with 450 g/1 lb grated mozzarella cheese and 450 g/1 lb skinned, chopped and drained fresh plum tomatoes. Top with 50 g/scant 2 oz [½ cup] freshly grated Parmesan cheese and drizzle with olive oil. Bake for 30-35 minutes or until browned and bubbly.

# Grilled Spring Vegetables on Spicy Herbed Pasta

At the first sign of Spring, prepare this wonderful pasta as a celebration for family and friends. This recipe is inspired by the famous Pasta Primavera made at New York's Le Cirque restaurant.

### YIELD: 6-8 SERVINGS
Equipment: a barbecue, cast iron ridged grill pan or oven grill [US broiler]

INGREDIENTS:

1.35–1.8 kg/3–4 lbs mixed vegetables, such as:
   Small red or white onions, halved
   Leeks, cut into 7.5 cm/3 inch pieces, or use whole baby leeks
   Green asparagus, left whole if thin, or cut into 7.5 cm/3 inch pieces and skin removed if not
   Okra, left whole
   French beans [US thin green beans], left whole
   Broccoli florets
   Aubergine [US eggplant], thinly sliced (roll up for serving)
   Courgettes [US zucchini], thinly sliced, or use baby courgettes and leave whole
   Red and green sweet peppers
   Mushroom caps
   Sweet potatoes, peeled and thinly sliced
   Mangetouts [US snow peas] or sugarsnap peas
450 g/1 lb pasta of your choice, preferably fresh (Fettucine works well with the sauce.)
25–50 g/¾–1 ¾ oz [¼–½ cup] pine nuts, toasted

FOR THE MARINADE:

185 ml/6 fl oz [¾ cup] olive oil
4 tablespoons freshly squeezed lemon juice
2 tablespoons fresh oregano or 2 teaspoons dried oregano
1 garlic clove, finely chopped
2 teaspoons grated lemon rind
1 teaspoon each salt and freshly ground pepper

FOR THE PASTA SAUCE:

115 g/4 oz [½ cup] butter
1 bunch (8-10) spring onions [US scallions], finely chopped
4 garlic cloves, finely chopped
½ teaspoon dried hot red pepper flakes
4 tablespoons chicken stock, preferably home-made
250 ml/8 fl oz [1 cup] crème fraîche or double cream [US heavy cream], or a combination of both
100 g/3 ½ oz [1 cup] freshly grated Parmesan cheese
20 g/ ⅔ oz [¼ cup] fresh basil, coarsely chopped
25 g/ ¾ oz [¼ cup] fresh parsley, chopped
Salt and freshly ground pepper to taste

METHOD:

★ If using onions and leeks, they should be blanched in a cold-water method before marinating: place in a pan of cold water, bring to the boil and blanch for 1 minute, then drain and refresh under cold running water.

★ If using asparagus, okra, green beans and broccoli, they should be blanched in a hot-water method before marinating: plunge the vegetables into boiling salted water and blanch for 30 seconds, then remove and refresh under cold running water.

★ If using aubergine or courgettes, they should be salted before marinating to remove moisture and bitterness: salt the slices on both sides and set aside, either on paper towels or in a colander, for 20-30 minutes, then rinse, drain and dry well.

★ If using sweet peppers, roast and peel them (see page 264). Slice the flesh. Mushrooms, sweet potatoes and mangetouts do not need to be blanched or salted before marinating.

★ Whisk the marinade ingredients together in a glass or other non-reactive bowl. Add the vegetables, prepared as directed, and leave to marinate for at least 1 hour and up to 24 hours in the refrigerator, turning occasionally.

★  If using a barbecue, light the charcoal fire in good time; you need a medium hot fire (see page 212 for instructions). A ridged grill pan needs about 10 minutes' preheating. Bring a large pot of salted water to the boil for the pasta.

★  To make the sauce, melt the butter in a large frying pan, skillet or wok and sauté the spring onions and garlic until soft but not browned. Add the rest of the sauce ingredients with the exception of the Parmesan, basil and parsley. Bring to the boil and cook until reduced to a thick, unctuous sauce. Add the cheese, basil and parsley. Keep the sauce warm, but do not allow it to boil again.

★  Cook the pasta in the boiling salted water until it is *al dente*. At the same time, remove the vegetables from the marinade and grill them until they are nicely browned on both sides and just tender but still crisp.

★  Drain the pasta and toss in the sauce. Arrange the vegetables attractively over the pasta and garnish with the toasted pine nuts.

NOTE:  The marinade also works well with chicken breasts, pork chops and shellfish to be grilled.

# ASIAN IMMIGRANTS

Chinese and Japanese immigrant groups were among the last groups to immigrate, but their culinary influence has been dramatic and shows every sign of continuing. In 1992, 37% of those immigrating to the United States came from Asia. Food writers prophesy that with the growing interest in Asian cuisines Americans will all be eating with chopsticks some day.

Old Chinese maps indicate that Chinese navigators may have explored the California coast long before the Spanish arrived, but they didn't immigrate until the 19th century when 1,000 Chinese were brought in to help build the Transcontinental Railroad. These were not the colonising or adventurous immigrants of the past, just a temporary work force that did not invest in the New World, but sent their wages to their families back home. Some of them stayed to make their fortunes in business and mining, but many returned to China. In the first half of the 20th century when Japan invaded and occupied China, the Chinese entered the United States in great numbers, the majority from the Canton Province.

America's first Chinese restaurant was called The Canton in the rapidly growing San Francisco Chinatown of 1869. Chinese labourers found work in numerous factories as well as on the railroad, up and down the West Coast of America. But, to Americans of the time, their ways were strange and they tended to live and eat apart. Early cookbooks tried to explain the mysteries of the East to the West, but with difficulty. But Chinese cooks in Caucasian restaurants and servants cooking in private homes began to introduce cooking methods and ingredients that would become part of American cuisine. At first, there was the inevitable adaptation and compromises to suit the Western palate, that produced such dishes as chop suey and chow mein, not known in China. Today, Americans enjoy a variety of authentic regional Chinese foods from Szechwan to Hunan and most households have a wok and chopsticks as part of their *batterie de cuisine*.

The Japanese were one of the last and smallest of all immigrant groups, first arriving in 1885 and totalling 170,000 in the next forty years. They came to Hawaii first, where they were recruited by pineapple and sugar plantations. In the early 1900s, Japanese truck farms on the West Coast became legendary for their quality. During the Second World War more than 72,000 native-born Americans and their 38,000 Japanese immigrant parents were confined behind barbed wire in hastily erected internment camps. After the war, they became influential in the health-food and ecology movements, and sushi bars reached unimaginable popularity.

The contributions of both of these cuisines can be seen throughout American cooking. Techniques such as stir-frying, grilling and marinating are preferable in a health-conscious age. Americans have learned from Asian cultures how to present food in a beautiful way, and examples of their aesthetic can be found everywhere in American restaurants and cookbooks. America has acquired a taste for vegetables that are slightly crispy and not overcooked and for soy sauce, that is now used in recipes from steak to nuts.

# Sweet & Sour Chicken Stir-Fry with Pecans

A typical American adaptation of a Chinese dish – sweeter, adding indigenous pecans. This is addictive eating.

### YIELD: 6 SERVINGS

## INGREDIENTS:

6 large chicken breast fillets weighing about 900 g/2 lbs, cut into 2 cm/¾ inch pieces
2 tablespoons cornflour [US cornstarch]
¼ teaspoon salt
½ teaspoon plus 1 tablespoon caster sugar [US granulated sugar]
Vegetable oil
115 g/4 oz [1 cup] pecan halves
2 tablespoons finely chopped fresh ginger
1 tablespoon finely chopped garlic (3-4 large cloves)
4 spring onions [US scallions], including green tops, chopped
2 red sweet peppers, cut into 2.5 cm/1 inch slices and then diagonally to 2.5 cm/1 inch lengths
2 large carrots, cut into julienne (very fine strips) (If you have a mandoline use it!)
225 g/8 oz mangetouts [US snow peas]
1 bunch rocket [US arugula] (about 125 g/4 ½ oz), or use watercress or fresh spinach leaves

## FOR THE SAUCE:

125 ml/4 fl oz [½ cup] tomato ketchup
4 teaspoons soy sauce
1 teaspoon salt
4 teaspoons Worcestershire sauce
2 tablespoons honey
2 teaspoons sesame oil
Cayenne pepper to taste (2 large pinches will be a good start)
2 teaspoons cornflour [US cornstarch] mixed with 125 ml/4 fl oz [½ cup] chicken stock, preferably home-made

## METHOD:

★ Mix together the ingredients for the sauce and reserve.
★ Pat the chicken dry with paper towels and put it in a medium-size bowl. Add the cornflour, salt and ½ teaspoon sugar and toss to coat the chicken well.
★ Heat 2.5–5 cm/1–2 inches of vegetable oil in a wok or large frying pan until it is hot but not smoking. Add the chicken in batches, separating the pieces as they cook, and stir-fry until golden brown. Remove with a slotted spoon to a bowl.
★ Add the pecans to the hot oil and cook until they begin to colour, but do not burn them. Transfer to a small bowl and toss, while hot, with the remaining sugar. Discard the oil in the wok.
★ Add 2-3 tablespoons of fresh oil to the wok and heat until hot but not smoking. Add the ginger, garlic and spring onions and stir-fry for about 30 seconds. Add the red peppers and carrots and stir-fry until the peppers are tender but not soft. Add the chicken, mangetouts and rocket and stir-fry until the chicken is hot. Add the sauce and cook the mixture over high heat until the sauce comes to the boil. Stir in the pecans and serve immediately, over steamed rice.

# Chinatown Chop Suey with Crisp Noodle Pancake

In America's Chinatowns, Chinese food took western turns to gain acceptance from palates not used to spices, garlic or anything perceived as 'foreign'. How far things have come – now Americans seek out authentic Chinese regional cuisine, in search of new foods to awaken our dozing palates. Chop Suey comes from the Cantonese term *tsap sui* , meaning "miscellaneous fragments" or "odds and ends" – an economical way to use up every bit of food in the refrigerator. Feel free to improvise on the ingredients suggested here. You may create a new masterpiece.

## YIELD: 4-6 SERVINGS

### INGREDIENTS:

450 g/1 lb chicken or duck breast meat, skin and fat removed

1 tablespoon soy sauce

2 tablespoons dry sherry or Chinese Shao Shing cooking wine

3 tablespoons cornflour [US cornstarch]

1 large onion, quartered and sliced very thinly

1 tablespoon finely chopped fresh ginger

1 large garlic clove, finely chopped

100 g/3 ½ oz [½ cup] drained canned water chestnuts, sliced

50 g/ scant 2 oz [¼ cup] drained canned bamboo shoots, sliced

½ red sweet pepper, cut into julienne (very fine strips)

1 celery stalk, cut on the diagonal into 1.5 cm/½ inch slices, or 100 g/3 ½ oz [1 cup] shredded Chinese cabbage

175 g/6 oz [1 ½ cups] button mushrooms, sliced

225 g/8 oz fresh spinach, stalks removed, chopped, or 80 g/scant 3 oz [1 cup] fresh bean sprouts

5 tablespoons vegetable oil

500 ml/16 fl oz [2 cups] chicken stock, preferably home-made

Roasted cashew nuts, to garnish

### FOR THE SEASONING MIX:

1 teaspoon seasoning salt (page 264) or plain salt

1 teaspoon dry mustard

¾ teaspoon ground ginger

½ teaspoon ground black pepper

¼ teaspoon ground white pepper

¼ teaspoon garlic powder

¼ teaspoon sugar

### FOR THE NOODLE PANCAKE:

225 g/8 oz thin Chinese noodles, or substitute spaghetti-shaped pasta or thin egg noodles

3 tablespoons vegetable oil

60 g/2 oz [¼ cup] smoked ham, chopped

6 spring onions [US scallions], including the green tops, chopped

2 tablespoons chopped fresh coriander [US cilantro]

### METHOD:

★ Combine the seasoning mix ingredients in a small bowl. Reserve.

★ Cut the chicken or duck into small slivers about 5 cm/2 inches long. Combine the soy sauce, sherry or wine and cornflour in a small bowl. Add the meat and toss. Refrigerate until you are ready to cook.

★ To prepare the noodle pancake mixture, cook the noodles in boiling salted water until they are tender – most Chinese noodles take only a few minutes. Drain and turn into a medium-size bowl. Toss with 2 tablespoons of oil. Add the ham, spring onions, coriander and 1 teaspoon of the seasoning mix and toss to mix. Refrigerate until you are ready to cook.

★ Prepare all the vegetables for the chop suey so that they are ready to stir-fry.

★ About 15–20 minutes before you want to eat, cook the noodle pancake: heat the remaining 1 tablespoon of oil in a large frying pan over moderately high heat. Add the noodle mixture and press down with a palette knife [US metal spatula]. Fry for 6–8 minutes or until crisp and brown on the base, then turn the pancake over to cook the other side.

★ To stir-fry the chop suey, heat 2 tablespoons of the oil in a wok or large pan over high heat. Add the thinly sliced onion and sprinkle with 1 teaspoon of the seasoning mix. Cook until the onion is browned. Remove with a slotted spoon or strainer.

★ Add 3 more tablespoons of oil to the wok or pan followed by the chicken or duck. Stir-fry the meat until it starts to brown. Stir in the ginger and garlic and stir-fry for a few seconds. Add the rest of the vegetables, with the sliced onion, and sprinkle with another teaspoon of seasoning mix. Stir-fry for 3-5 minutes or until most of the vegetables are partially cooked and the spinach has wilted. Add the chicken stock and bring to a simmer. Cook until the sauce thickens.

★ Serve the crisp noodle pancake cut into wedges, sprinkled with additional seasoning if you like. Garnish the chop suey with cashews and serve hot.

*A 1920s advertisement for a restaurant in San Francisco's Chinatown*

# Grilled Tuna Kebabs with a Japanese Sauce & Saffron Rice

Americans have embraced all things *teriyaki*, an easy and healthy Japanese marinade for beef, fish and chicken. This sweet and sour dish served on a bed of spinach with saffron rice is a celebration of tastes and colours that will bring applause from family and guests. For such a dramatic dish, it is not difficult to prepare.

YIELD: 4 generous or 6 moderate servings
Equipment: a barbecue or cast iron ridged grill pan

## INGREDIENTS:
675 g/1 ½ lbs fresh tuna, cut into 2.5 cm/1 inch slices
1 red onion
12 mushrooms of 5 cm/2 inch diameter (about 125 g/4 ½ oz)
4 tablespoons sesame oil
4 tablespoons medium-sweet sherry
2 tablespoons soy sauce
1 tablespoon rice vinegar
1 tablespoon finely chopped fresh ginger
1 garlic clove, finely chopped

## FOR THE SAFFRON RICE:
55 g/2 oz [⅓ cup] finely chopped onion
25 g/ 3/4 oz [1 ½ tablespoons] butter
Large pinch of saffron threads, crumbled
135 g/4 ½ oz [⅔ cup] long-grain white rice
300 ml/ ½ pint [1 ¼ cups] chicken stock, preferably home-made

## FOR THE SAUCE:
1 ½ teaspoons cornflour [US cornstarch]
80 ml/2 ¾ fl oz [⅓ cup] each rice vinegar, mirin and soy sauce

## FOR THE GARNISH:
450 g/1 lb fresh spinach, stalks removed, rinsed
4 tablespoons finely chopped crystallized ginger

## METHOD:
★ Soak 4–6 long wooden skewers in water for about 15 minutes. Cut the tuna slices into 5 cm/ 2 inch pieces, discarding skin and any dark brown flesh; there should be 24 pieces of tuna. Cut the onion into 5 cm/2 inch squares and blanch in boiling water for 1 minute; drain and refresh under cold running water. Thread the tuna, mushrooms and onion on to the skewers, alternating the ingredients (for 4 large portions use 6 pieces of tuna, 2 mushrooms and 4-6 onion slices on each skewer; for 6 smaller portions use 4 pieces of tuna, 2 mushrooms and 4-6 onion slices per skewer).
★ In a shallow glass dish, whisk together the sesame oil, sherry, soy sauce, rice vinegar, ginger and garlic. Marinate the tuna kebabs in this mixture for several hours, covered, in the refrigerator. Bring the tuna out of the refrigerator about 20 minutes before grilling.
★ If using a barbecue, light the charcoal fire in good time; you need a medium hot fire (see page 212 for instructions). A ridged grill pan will need about 10 minutes' preheating.
★ To make the saffron rice, cook the onion in the butter in a heavy covered saucepan until soft-ened. Add the saffron and the rice and cook, stirring, for about 1 minute. Add the stock and bring to the boil. Lower the heat, cover and cook for about 18 minutes or until all the stock is absorbed. Remove from the heat and leave the rice to rest for 5–20 minutes, still covered, until ready to serve. (For preparation in advance, spoon the rice into buttered metal timbale or dariole moulds, cover with foil and then reheat for serving in a large shallow pan of simmering water (a bain marie). Unmould on to each plate.)

★ To make the sauce, mix the cornflour with the vinegar in a small saucepan. Add the mirin and soy sauce and simmer, stirring, until thickened and glossy. Keep warm (or make ahead of time and reheat for serving).

★ Remove the kebabs from the marinade and barbecue grill or cook on a grill pan for 10-15 minutes, turning to cook all sides. Meanwhile, stir-fry the spinach, with just the moisture retained on the leaves, in a wok or large frying pan. Remove from the heat as soon as the spinach has wilted.

★ To serve, arrange the spinach on each plate (warmed if possible). Top with a kebab, spoon over a little sauce and sprinkle with the finely chopped crystallized ginger. Serve saffron rice on the side and the remaining sauce.

# Chapter Three

# A
# Continent
# and
# its Regions

"What people of each region (in the U.S.) eat is as singular and well defined as a fingerprint.
If you don't believe it, just try to pass off spaghetti-based Cincinnati chilli to a New Mexican.
Lifetimes might go by before a Massachusetts chef would allow tomatoes in his quahog chowder,
but just over the border, in Rhode Island, tomato-clam chowder is, by law, part of the state's
official shore dinner."

*Road Food and Good Food* by Jane & Michael Stern

AMERICA IS A VAST COUNTRY, home to regions that differ radically in their history, climate, topography, the cultural backgrounds of their people, and in their very style. Food makes a marvellous focal point for bringing the history and personality of a region alive. Food changes from region to region because people cook differently depending on who and where they are and what they find locally to eat. As the writer Marshall Fishwick put it, "No one should try to separate what men eat from what they think and what they are."

The development of a regional cuisine starts with the individual cook, bringing unique beliefs, customs, and cultural experience to her cooking. Regional cooking has been influenced by the immigrant groups that settled in each region. These immigrants were often in search of a climate and terrain similar to their own homeland. We have already seen how the Puritans' religious beliefs affected the way they regarded food, which in turn had an immense impact on the cooking of the New England region.

The cooking of some regions has a long history, for others there is almost no history at all and the cooking is still evolving and changing. In regions old by American standards and colonised hundreds of years ago, the traditional food introduced by early settlers is still served with some nostalgia and even stubbornness by modern day Americans. Other parts of our country are young and brash, like the wild frontier, where immigration, experimentation and adaptation to the local ingredients have created fresh, often eclectic styles of cooking. When settlers were admonished to "go west!", a continually shifting frontier resulted in cooking styles and food habits that were purely American and adapted to each region. Examples are quick breads, first made in a skillet over an open fire, but still made today, and grilled foods, reflecting a national passion for cooking out-of-doors that stems directly from our past.

The climate, terrain, and the resulting availability of ingredients are major factors that create and influence regional cuisine. In hot climates, for instance, cooler, spicier foods are in demand and the cuisine of the Southwest and Texas certainly reflect that. The fertile terrain of the Midwest helped create a region Americans call the nation's breadbasket and dairy centre. Midwest regional cookbooks are full of recipes for cakes and cookies using the 'fruits of the land'. In California, a warm climate and a rich agricultural environment combined with the great abilities of certain immigrant groups to nurture the soil, produced an abundance of beautiful fruits and vegetables, that in turn form the basis of California cuisine.

Regional cooking is also influenced by the predominance of urban versus rural areas or vice versa. At one time, America was most truly represented by the rural farmer and the wholesome, hearty food, served in large quantities, that sustained him. Regional cooking has its roots in rural isolation and some of the best examples of this cooking is still served in home kitchens where only family and friends partake of it. Today, cookbooks and the food industry have scattered regional recipes far beyond their areas of origin and have created national appetites for regional specialities. Cosmopolitan urban centres draw regional cooking out of home kitchens and into restaurants, where it can be appreciated on a wider scale. The great cities of the East and West coasts have always set trends in American cooking. More receptive to foreign influences, cooks in cities also have greater accessibility to exotic ingredients. This was evident in early times when recipes requiring exotic, expensive ingredients often appeared on the East Coast and in the South and their inexpensive variations further west, where the ingredients were not available and rural life dictated a more frugal style. An example of this was the popularity of lemon meringue pie on the East coast and the appearance of a vinegar pie using the more common and cheaper cider vinegar in the Midwest.

In the following chapter, you will find only a small sampling of what each region has to offer. Many cookbooks available in the United States are devoted solely to one region or another, so rich is the diversity of America's regional cuisine. But I hope that this sampling will serve as an introduction to the unique character of each area of the United States.

A region's cooking style defines it in much the same way that making a new friend on a holiday can define that place forever in your memory. So travel these regions of America in your own kitchens! The folks, the atmosphere, the climate and terrain speak through regional recipes of the special places you can discover by "goin' up the road a piece."

ABOVE: *Settlers building a log cabin and cooking in the open*
PREVIOUS SPREAD: *Church of San Geronimo, New Mexico*

# THE NEW ENGLAND AND MID-ATLANTIC REGIONS

*New England* Maine, New Hampshire, Vermont, Connecticut, Rhode Island, Massachusetts
*Mid-Atlantic* New York, Pennsylvania, Maryland, Delaware, New Jersey, Washington, D.C.

These two regions are old by American standards and pervaded by history and Old World customs. In fact, New England is where traditional American cooking was born. Equating thrift with godliness, the Pilgrims, who settled the rugged, forested regions of New England, produced food that was meant to keep body and soul together. Early New England cookbooks preached economy and the wickedness of luxury and 'rich' cooking. Even Ben Franklin, one of the founding fathers of America, was heard to say, "A fat kitchen maketh a lean will."

New England's climate and seaside topography yield long winters and a short growing season. These conditions have resulted in a style of cooking with many recipes for preserving food by salting, pickling and preserving with sugar. The practical Pilgrims also made good use of the foods they found in their new land: cranberries and other wild berries, maple syrup, wild turkey, abundant supplies of fish and seafood and the Indians' crops of corn, squash and beans. New England's tradition of maritime trade accounted for an on-going supply of products from other parts of the world that also influenced the region's cooking. Molasses came from the West Indies, wines, brandy and raisins from the Mediterranean, tea and ginger from China, tapioca from South America, dates from the Middle East and spices from Indonesia.

In New England and the Mid-Atlantic Regions, quick breads such as pancakes, pone, and hasty pudding (porridge) became an important part of American cooking because of a dependence on cornmeal. Apples were plentiful and found themselves in many recipes of the two regions. Apple cider and hard cider were popular drinks and cider vinegar, an important staple, with wine vinegar not appearing until the 1970s. The emphasis by the Pennsylvania Dutch on sweet and sour accompaniments added to hearty, wholesome food started Americans off on a love affair with pickles and preserves. The American Indian's way of cooking seafood by packing it in seaweed over hot coals, laid in a pit in the ground, became a regional speciality called the clam bake that has been a New England ritual for over 350 years.

Today, these two regions are home to many of America's greatest urban centres. Cities like Boston, New York and Philadelphia are famous for having a huge number of quality restaurants. Philadelphia, christened the 'City of Brotherly Love' by founder William Penn, has an English Quaker heritage and was the national capital in 1790. As far back as that time, Philadelphia was known for its ice-cream. Other Philadelphia specialities include scrapple, pepper pot, and sticky buns. Boston became known as 'Beantown', so popular were its baked beans, a staple for the Pilgrims because they slow cooked and required no work on the Sabbath. New York today is host to more visitors than any other city in the U.S., and according to an article in *Gourmet Magazine*, "One eats in New York like nowhere else on earth. In this meeting ground and marketplace of virtually all nations, the range of culinary styles is dizzying." Just one of the highlights of this great city are its Jewish delis (delicatessens), where one can eat such delicacies as pastrami and corned beef, rye bread and bagels, chicken soup and cheesecake.

OPPOSITE: *Lobster Lasagna*

# Lobster Lasagna

A rich and dramatic start to an elegant meal, this dish is an example of East Coast restaurant cuisine that the accomplished home cook can use to wow guests. If you don't want to make your own pasta, you can substitute sheets of ready-made fresh pasta, cooked *al dente* and then cut into 15 cm/6 inch squares.

### YIELD: 6 FIRST-COURSE SERVINGS

Equipment: a pasta machine or rolling pin and a food processor or sharp chef's knife

### INGREDIENTS:
150 g/5 oz [1 ½ cups] mozzarella cheese, grated
Chopped fresh chives, to garnish

### FOR HOME-MADE PASTA:
(MAKES 450 G/1 LB)
160 g/5 ½ oz [1 cup] semolina
120 g/4 oz [1 cup] strong plain flour [US bread flour]
2 size-1 eggs [US jumbo eggs]
Yolks from 3 size-1 eggs [US jumbo eggs]
½ teaspoon salt

### FOR THE FIRST FILLING:
1 live lobster, weighing 900 g/2 lbs
1 shallot, finely chopped
3 garlic cloves, finely chopped
1 tablespoon olive oil
225 g/8 oz cream cheese or other full-fat soft cheese, at room temperature
2 tablespoons freshly grated Parmesan cheese

### FOR THE SECOND FILLING:
1 shallot
2 garlic cloves
225 g/8 oz mushrooms, stalks removed
15 g/ ½ oz [1 tablespoon] butter
1 tablespoon olive oil
2 tablespoons finely chopped roasted and peeled red sweet pepper (see page 264)
2 tablespoons finely chopped Niçoise or Kalamata olives
2 tablespoons finely chopped oil-preserved sun-dried tomatoes
1 tablespoon finely chopped fresh parsley
2 tablespoons finely chopped fresh basil

### FOR THE SAUCE:
½ shallot, finely chopped
1 garlic clove, finely chopped
Butter
375 ml/12 fl oz [1 ½ cups] whipping cream
About 125 g/4 ½ oz creamy goat's cheese, such as Montrachet
Salt and freshly ground pepper to taste

### METHOD:
★ To make the pasta dough, put the flours in a medium-size bowl or on a flat surface and make a well in the centre. Put in the eggs, yolks and salt. Mix with your fingers, gradually combining the eggs with the dry ingredients until a ball of dough is formed. (You can also make the dough in a food processor or an electric mixer fitted with a dough hook.) Knead the dough on a lightly floured surface for 5–10 minutes or until it no longer sticks to your hands and is smooth and pliant. Leave the dough to rest in a loosely closed plastic bag for an hour or two before rolling it out. The dough will also keep in the refrigerator for several days in a plastic bag.
★ Prepare the first filling: boil the lobster (see page 267); remove the meat and cut it into bite-size pieces. Set aside. Sauté the shallot and garlic cloves in the olive oil until softened, then add to the cream cheese in a small bowl. Stir in the Parmesan cheese and add salt and pepper to taste. Reserve.
★ For the second filling, chop the shallot and garlic in a food processor fitted with a steel blade, then add the mushrooms and process until finely chopped (or chop the ingredients by hand with a knife). Sauté these ingredients in the butter and oil in a large frying pan until the mixture is

fairly dry. Transfer to a bowl, add the rest of the finely chopped ingredients and stir to combine. Reserve.

★ Roll the pasta dough with a pasta machine, or by hand using a rolling pin, until it is very thin. Cut 6 squares, each 15 x 15 cm/6 x 6 inches. (Any remaining pasta dough can be saved for another use.) Bring a pot of salted water to the boil and cook the pasta squares for 3–5 minutes or until *al dente*. Add a scrap of pasta dough to the pot with the squares so that you can test the scrap from time to time to see if the pasta is done. When cooked, remove them to a bowl of warm water.

★ To assemble the lasagne: dry a pasta square on a piece of paper towel. Spread the square with about 1 tablespoon of the cream cheese filling and then with about 1 tablespoon of the mushroom filling. On one corner, place a few pieces of lobster. Fold the pasta square diagonally in half, into a triangle, and sprinkle the top with grated mozzarella cheese. Lay on a baking sheet that has been greased with olive oil. Continue with the rest of the pasta squares.

★ Preheat the grill [US broiler].

★ To make the sauce, soften the shallot and garlic in a little butter. Add one-quarter of the cream and simmer until completely reduced. Add the rest of the cream, then whisk in the goat's cheese. Taste and season with salt and freshly ground pepper. Heat until warm, but don't allow it to boil. Keep warm.

★ Grill the lasagne until it is warmed through and nicely browned on top. Put a thin layer of sauce on each serving plate, set a lasagne triangle on top and garnish with chopped chives. Serve hot.

# Monkfish Braised in Lobster Broth With Julienne Root Vegetables and Green Beans

An exquisite way of getting more for your money when you buy a fresh lobster – a rich, savoury broth is created from the crustacean's shell. It is possible to serve guests a whole meal using one lobster. Begin with the lobster lasagna (see page 122) using the lobster meat, followed by the monkfish braised in its broth.

YIELD: 6 SERVINGS
Equipment: a mandoline or sharp chef's knife
Oven: 220°C/425°F/Gas 7

INGREDIENTS:

1 live lobster, weighing 900 g/2 lbs
1 medium-size onion, chopped
2 carrots, chopped
2 celery stalks, chopped
6 garlic cloves, peeled
2 tablespoons olive oil
1.25 litres/2 pints [5 cups] water
250 ml/8 fl oz [1 cup] dry white wine
4 tablespoons tomato essence (page 264), or use ready-made tomato paste
2 large pieces of orange rind
4 sprigs each of fresh tarragon and fresh thyme

¼ teaspoon dried hot red pepper flakes
¼ teaspoon saffron
1 teaspoon black peppercorns
2 bay leaves
Salt and freshly ground pepper
700 g/1 ½ lbs monkfish, cleaned and all bone and membrane removed, or substitute another firm white fish
100 g/3 ½ oz French beans [US fine green beans]
2 leeks, white tops only, cut into julienne (very fine strips)
2 carrots and 2 parsnips, cut into julienne, preferably with a mandoline
Finely chopped fresh parsley or tarragon, to garnish

METHOD:

★ First cook the lobster (this can be done a day or two in advance): bring a large pot of salted water to the boil. Add the lobster, cover partially and cook for 10 minutes. Remove the lobster and leave it to cool, then, using a heavy knife, nut cracker and kitchen scissors, cut open the shell. Remove the large pieces of meat from the tail and claws and reserve for another dish or use in this one. Split the body open, remove the greenish head sac and discard it. Cut the shell into small pieces with kitchen scissors.

★ Preheat the oven. Put the pieces of lobster shell in a roasting pan. Add the chopped onion, carrots and celery and the garlic cloves. Drizzle over the olive oil. Roast for 30 minutes, stirring and turning the vegetables and shells a few times.

★ Transfer the shell pieces and all the vegetables to a large stock pot or saucepan. Deglaze the roasting pan with 250 ml/8 fl oz [1 cup] of the water, stirring well, and add this liquid to the stock pot with the rest of the water, the wine, tomato essence and all the herbs and spices. Bring to the boil, skimming, and then lower the heat to a simmer. Simmer the broth, partially covered, for about 1 hour. Strain and season to taste with salt and freshly ground pepper. The broth can

be made in advance up to this point and refrigerated for a few days or frozen for future use.
★ Remove any skin and central bone from the monkfish. Be extremely diligent in removing all the membrane—any left on the fish will harden and distort the fish during cooking. Cut the monkfish into 1.5 x 7.5 cm/½ x 3 inch strips or cut across the grain into medallions.
★ Steam the beans until almost tender but still crisp. Refresh under cold running water, drain and reserve. If you are using the lobster meat, cut the tail into thin medallions, but leave the claw meat in whole pieces. Prepare the julienned vegetables.
★ About 15 minutes before serving, bring the lobster broth to a simmer. Season the monkfish with salt and pepper and add to the broth. Cover and cook for about 5 minutes, then add the beans and julienned vegetables together with the lobster meat, if you are using it. Cover and cook for an additional 2-4 minutes or until the vegetables are just tender and the lobster meat is heated through. Ladle into soup bowls, garnish with finely chopped parsley or tarragon and serve with crusty bread.

# *Shrimp Cocktail*

One of America's most popular ways to begin a meal is a shrimp cocktail, served with a large helping of a tomato-based cocktail sauce. Although not the most subtle, the traditional horseradish-spiked sauce does get the old taste buds moving! My husband loves shrimp cocktail and I created this version for his birthday one year when I couldn't get fresh horseradish. Now we prefer this rather unorthodox variation.

### Yield: 4 servings

INGREDIENTS:
24 king, tiger or Mediterranean prawns or 40 large prawns [US 24 large or 40 medium shrimp], cooked, peeled and deveined
Shredded lettuce
Chopped celery

FOR THE SAUCE:
250 ml/8 fl oz [1 cup] tomato-based chilli sauce, preferably Heinz which is a chunky ketchup-type sauce
1 teaspoon freshly squeezed lime juice
3 tablespoons grated fresh ginger

METHOD:
★ To make the sauce, mix together all the ingredients and chill until serving time.
★ Arrange the prawns on a bed of shredded lettuce and chopped celery. Serve the sauce in the centre or in a separate bowl, so that guests can dip the prawns into it themselves.

# Boston Baked Beans

Boston is so famous for its beans, it is sometimes called Beantown. Colonists learned to bake beans from the Indians, who used clay pots, submerged in a hole in the ground lined with hot stones and left to cook slowly for a very long time. The result was so good that baked beans became a staple and a typical Sunday supper, especially for the Pilgrims, who did no cooking on Sunday. This recipe makes an excellent side dish or a meal-in-itself American-style cassoulet.

YIELD: 6-12 SERVINGS
Oven:180°C/350°F/Gas 4

INGREDIENTS:

450 g/1 lb [2 ½ cups] dried white haricot beans [US Great Northern or navy beans]
1 large onion, studded with 4 whole cloves
2 parsley sprigs
335 g/12 oz salt pork, or substitute unsmoked streaky bacon
450 g/1 lb smoked pork sausage (optional)
55 g/2 oz [4 tablespoons] butter

1 large onion, chopped
2 garlic cloves, finely chopped
4 tablespoons molasses or dark treacle
125 ml/4 fl oz [½ cup] tomato ketchup
55 g/2 oz [¼ cup firmly packed] dark soft brown sugar
2 teaspoons dry mustard
4 whole cloves
Tabasco sauce and freshly ground pepper to taste
1 teaspoon salt

METHOD:

★ Soak the beans overnight in cold water to cover, or use the following method: put the beans in a large pan and pour in enough cold water to cover them by at least 5 cm/2 inches. Bring to the boil and boil for 2 minutes, then cover and remove from the heat. Leave the beans to soak for 1 hour and then drain.

★ Put the prepared beans in a large pot with the clove-studded onion and the parsley and cover them well with water. Bring to the boil, then reduce the heat and simmer until the beans are just tender, but not mushy. Drain them, reserving the liquid. Discard the onion and parsley.

★ While the beans are simmering, prepare the salt pork and sausage, if using. Put the salt pork in a pan of cold water, bring to boil and simmer for 10 minutes; drain. Do the same to the sausage, but cook for 12-15 minutes. Cut the sausage into large dice.

★ In a frying pan or skillet, melt the butter and lightly brown the chopped onion. Add the garlic and cook for 1 minute without browning it. Stir in the molasses, ketchup, brown sugar, dry mustard and cloves and add a few dashes of Tabasco. Simmer until the onion is softened. Reserve.

★ Preheat the oven.

★ Make a layer of beans on the bottom of a large cast iron or enamelled casserole. Add some of the molasses mixture and some of the salt pork and sausage and season with freshly ground pepper. Continue making layers, ending with beans. Add the salt to 600 ml/1 pint [2 ½ cups] of the reserved bean cooking liquid and pour into the casserole. Cover the casserole and bake the beans in the preheated oven for about 1 ½ hours. Remove the cover and continue to bake for an additional ½-1 hour or until the liquid is almost absorbed from the top of the beans. The beans should be moist, not dry, so add more of the reserved bean cooking liquid if necessary.

NOTE: Beans should be cooked to desired tenderness during the simmering process. Once they are added to an acidic sauce (a tomato-based sauce, for example) they will not get any softer no matter how much longer they are cooked.

# Hermits

A cookie recipe almost as old as America itself, hermits apparently got their name because they kept so well. Wives of sailors off Cape Cod made them for their husbands to take to sea and they have been a favourite ever since.

YIELD: ABOUT 30-40 COOKIES OR BARS
Equipment: an electric mixer
Oven: 180°C/350°F/Gas 4

INGREDIENTS:
180 g/6 oz [1 ¾ cups] sifted plain flour [US all-purpose flour]
2 teaspoons ground cinnamon
½ teaspoon freshly grated nutmeg
¼ teaspoon each ground cardamom, cloves and ginger
¼ teaspoon salt
150 g/5 oz [⅔ cup] butter, at room temperature
220 g/8 oz [1 cup firmly packed] dark soft brown sugar
2 size-1 eggs [US jumbo eggs]
¼ teaspoon bicarbonate of soda [US baking soda]
3 tablespoons sour cream
85 g/3 oz [¾ cup] pecans or walnuts, chopped

210 g/7 oz [1 ¼ cups] chopped dried fruit and candied orange rind (I like to combine equal volumes of sultanas [US golden raisins], chopped dates, chopped dried figs, chopped dried apricots and diced candied orange peel!)

FOR THE VANILLA ICING:
15 g/ ½ oz [1 tablespoon] butter, at room temperature
90 g/3 oz [¾ cup] sifted icing sugar [US confectioners' sugar]
Pinch of salt
1 teaspoon pure vanilla essence [US pure vanilla extract]
1 tablespoon cream, or more as needed

METHOD:
★ Preheat the oven.
★ Sift the flour, spices and salt into a small bowl and reserve.
★ Beat the butter in a medium-size bowl until it is light, then add the sugar slowly, beating until the mixture is light and fluffy. Beat in the eggs, one at a time. Stir the soda into the sour cream and add to the mixture. Finally, add the flour and spice mixture and continue to beat until the mixture is smooth. Stir in the nuts and fruit.
★ Butter two baking sheets (unless they are non-stick). Drop the mixture from a tablespoon to make conventional cookies or spread the mixture out into four "logs" about 10 x 30 cm/4 x 12 inches. (I prefer the latter method because the resulting cookies or bars are softer than when they are baked individually.)
★ Bake in the preheated oven for about 10 minutes for individual cookies and 15 minutes for the logs. While they are baking, make the icing. Remove the hermits from the oven when they are lightly browned and firm and allow them to cool for a few minutes on the baking sheet.
★ To make the icing, blend the butter into the icing sugar, then add the salt, vanilla and enough cream to make a fairly thick consistency.
★ After the hermits have cooled for a few minutes on the baking sheet but while they are still warm, glaze with the icing. Remove them from the baking sheet to greaseproof paper [US waxed paper] or a cooling rack and allow them to cool completely. Then cut the logs into 2–2.5 cm/ ¾–1 inch slices. Keep in an airtight container.

# Pot Roast or Salt Beef Hash

A dish devised to use up leftovers, early seagoing New Englanders called it 'lobscouse', a name right out of a Roald Dahl story. On board ship it was made of salted meat and was not always the best loved dish, but with leftover pot roast (see Heartland Pot Roast page 140) or salt beef it achieves more interest and is wonderful for a family dinner or for breakfast with a poached egg on top.

### YIELD: 4 SERVINGS FOR A LIGHT MEAL

## INGREDIENTS:

30 g/1 oz [2 tablespoons] butter
1 medium-size onion, chopped
1 celery stalk, chopped
1 carrot, diced
3 medium-size potatoes, finely diced  (Red Russet potatoes are nice with their skins left on.)
2 tablespoons plain flour [US all-purpose flour]

500 ml/16 fl oz [2 cups] beef stock, preferably home-made, or the cooking liquid from salt beef, or a combination of leftover gravy and stock
280–300 g/about 10 oz [2 cups] cooked meat, cubed (Ideally use pot roast, roast beef or salt beef, but any meat will do.)
Salt and pepper to taste
4 eggs (optional but delicious if you are using salt beef)
Chopped fresh parsley and/or chives, to garnish

## METHOD:

★  Melt the butter in a frying pan over moderately high heat, add the vegetables and sauté until they start to brown. Add the flour to the vegetables and stir. Add the stock or cooking liquid and mix well. Simmer the mixture until the potatoes are tender.

★  Add the meat and cook for an additional 5 minutes or so or until the mixture is hot. Taste and season with salt and freshly ground pepper.

★  If you are serving poached eggs, make 4 indentations in the hash and crack an egg into each. Cover the pan, turn down the heat and cook for 3–5 minutes or until the whites are completely opaque, but the yolks are still liquid.

★  Sprinkle the hash with chopped fresh parsley and/or chives and serve from the pan.

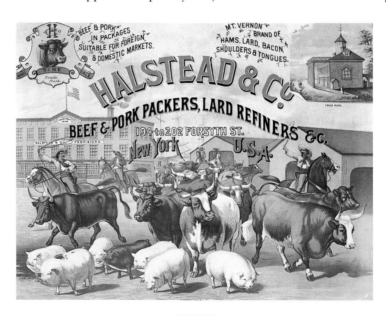

# THE SOUTH

*Virginia, West Virginia, North and South Carolina, Georgia, Florida, Alabama, Mississippi, Louisiana, Tennessee, Kentucky, Arkansas*

"People always live by the mythology of their time. The medievalists had their saints, the philosophers their reason, the British their empire. The South had its plantation. In the manor houses of the South, American cookery and hospitality reached a peak which has seldom if ever been surpassed."
Marshall Fishwick, 'Southern Cooking', *American Heritage Cookbook*

The South is a region that still remembers its elegant past and traditional lifestyle, a *Gone With the Wind* time when life centred around the plantation. From the 'big house' to the work house, rich or poor, Southerners have always prided themselves on their fine food and gracious hospitality. Food is at the centre of Southern life and the life of the family. Recipes are handed down as heirlooms. Long after most Americans left the farms for work in factories and cities, the Southern way of life remained grounded in its country ways and so did much of its food. Southerners still cherish the foods of their traditional table, whether it be earthy soul food like grits and greens, country food like biscuits with ham or fancy food like bread pudding soufflé and mint juleps.

Southern cuisine has its roots in the three distinct cultures that played a part in the region, the Native American, European and African cultures. British and French dishes were reinterpreted by African American cooks and adapted to local ingredients using the cooking techniques of Native Americans. Imported African and Caribbean ingredients such as okra, eggplant, black-eyed peas, coconut, sugar, rum, limes and lemons, chocolate and tropical fruits were added. The climate also changed what people ate in the South. There are more cakes than other desserts in the Southern repertoire because they survive better in the high humidity. Cooking out-of-doors became a natural with the heat, as did the occasional addition of spiciness or the long, tall iced drink. In fact, the South has an unquenchable thirst, consuming vast quantities of colas and ice tea, mint juleps and punches.

In the South, time-consuming cooking like barbecue and beaten biscuits were *de rigueur* when there were plenty of servants available to do the work. Greens (collards, spinach, mustard and turnip, beet tops, kale, dandelion, dock, sorrel, and chard) were more popular here than in any other region and were slow-cooked with salt pork or ham, which was always more important than beef in the region. The South combined the curing techniques of England with the Indian method of preserving with smoke and used their barbecue pits and smokehouses with wonderful results. Because their pigs ate peanuts, a cheap and abundant feed, the pork products had a taste

129

that was unique and made Southern hams and bacon famous.

The South has remained loyal to corn, while almost every other regional cooking adopted wheat as its preferred bread-making staple when it became available. Corn, whether fresh or dried and processed (hominy, grits) or distilled (bourbon, whiskey, moonshine), still plays a major role in the cuisine of this region. Not surprisingly, most of the hard alcohol consumed in the U.S. comes from the South.

Southern cities like Atlanta, Charleston and New Orleans have continued many of the original regional dishes and are famous for their restaurants and cooking styles. One of the newest of the upstart regional styles can be found in Florida, where immigration is still in full swing. The style is being called 'Floribbean' and demonstrates strong Caribbean, Latin and Cuban influences, combining the ingredients, spicing and techniques of these islands with the state's native seafood and fruit.

*Waiting at the Levee : a New Orleans scene around 1910*

# Southern Fried Chicken

This classic American dish seems to have evolved from the chicken fricassée of the late 18th century, with the first recipe for fried chicken appearing in the cookbook, *The Virginia Housewife* in 1824. Southerners take justifiable pride in their fried chicken and numerous variations exist. But for authentic Southern Fried Chicken there are a few guidelines. Southern cooks insist that you must use an old-fashioned cast-iron skillet, preferably one seasoned with long use. Their chicken is fried, not deep-fried and it must be high quality and fresh. Finally it should be turned with tongs, not a fork, and drained in a brown paper bag, which retains its crispness (paper towels can cause the chicken to go soggy).

## YIELD: 4-6 SERVINGS
Equipment: a 35–40 cm/14-16 inch cast iron or heavy enamelled frying pan or skillet

### INGREDIENTS:
A free-range chicken weighing 1.6–1.8 kg/3 ½–4 lbs
250–500 ml/8–16 fl oz [1-2 cups] buttermilk, or use milk mixed with the juice of ½ lemon
120 g/4 oz [1 cup] plain flour [US all-purpose flour]
1 teaspoon salt
½ teaspoon freshly ground pepper
Large pinch of cayenne pepper

Lard, white vegetable fat [US shortening] or vegetable oil for frying
4 smoked streaky bacon rashers [US 4 thick bacon slices], chopped into 5mm /¼ inch pieces
375 ml/12 fl oz [1 ½ cups] chicken stock, preferably home-made
125 ml/4 fl oz [½ cup] double cream [US heavy cream]
2 tablespoons freshly squeezed lemon juice
Mashed potatoes, to accompany

### METHOD:
★ Cut the chicken into 4-6 pieces and put them in a stainless steel or glass bowl. Add the buttermilk and toss to coat. Leave the chicken to marinate for at least 2 hours or overnight. Allow it to come to room temperature before cooking.
★ Combine the flour, salt, pepper and cayenne pepper in a plastic bag or brown paper bag. Reserve 2 tablespoons of this seasoned flour to thicken the gravy.
★ Heat a 1.5 cm/ ½ inch layer of lard, fat or vegetable oil in the frying pan and add the bacon. Cook until the bacon has rendered its fat and is crispy. Remove it with a slotted spoon to drain on paper towels.
★ Remove the chicken pieces from the buttermilk, one at a time, add to the seasoned flour in the bag and shake to coat evenly with flour. Then add the chicken to the hot fat in the pan, putting the serving or presentation side down first . Do not crowd the chicken in the pan – it is better to use two pans rather than to put too much chicken into one pan. When all the chicken pieces have been added, cover the pan and lower the heat to moderately hot. Cook for 15 minutes. Remove the cover, turn each piece with tongs and fry for a further 10-15 minutes uncovered. Remove the chicken to a brown paper bag to drain while you prepare the gravy.
★ Pour off all but 2 tablespoons of the cooking fat from the pan, leaving behind all the brown bits on the bottom. Stir in the reserved 2 tablespoons seasoned flour and cook until lightly browned. Add the stock, cream and lemon juice and cook, whisking, until the gravy is smooth and thickened. Taste and adjust seasoning.
★ You can add the crisp bacon bits to the gravy or sprinkle them over the gravy as a garnish, as you wish. Serve the gravy over mashed potatoes alongside the fried chicken. Never pour the gravy over the chicken – that will spoil its crispness.

# Chicken and Cornmeal Dumplings

A comforting meal in one pot that the whole family will love.

YIELD: 4-6 SERVINGS

INGREDIENTS:
A boiling fowl [US stewing chicken] weighing
    1.8–2.25 kg/4–5 lbs
2 tablespoons cornflour [US cornstarch]
250 ml/8 fl oz [1 cup] double cream [US heavy cream]
10-12 small button or pearl onions
4 carrots, sliced on the diagonal
2 celery stalks, sliced on the diagonal
140 g/scant 5 oz [1 cup] shelled fresh or frozen (not
    thawed) peas

FOR THE CHICKEN STOCK:
3–4 litres/5–7 pints [US 3–4 quarts] water
1 large onion, chopped
2 carrots, chopped

2 celery stalks, chopped
A large bouquet garni including fresh parsley, a few thyme
    sprigs and a bay leaf
8 black peppercorns
2 chicken stock cubes [US bouillon cubes]

FOR THE DUMPLINGS:
110 g/scant 4 oz [1 cup] sponge or plain flour [US cake
    flour]
2 tablespoons cornmeal
2 teaspoons baking powder
½ teaspoon each sugar and salt
15 g/ ½ oz [1 tablespoon] butter
150 ml/ ¼ pint [⅔ cup] milk
1 tablespoon chopped fresh parsley or another fresh herb

METHOD:
★  To make the stock, rinse the chicken inside and out and remove any excess fat. Cut off the tri-angular-shaped tail end, right below the body cavity (it can cause bitterness). Put the chicken in a large, heavy pot or flameproof casserole with the water, onion, carrots, celery, bouquet garni and peppercorns. The water should cover the chicken so add more if necessary. Bring to the boil, skimming well, then reduce the heat. Partially cover the pot, and simmer for 2–3 hours, depending on the age of the chicken. When the chicken is quite tender, remove it and leave it to cool.
★  Strain the stock and simmer it, uncovered, until reduced to about 2 litres/3 ½ pints [2 quarts]. Taste and add the stock cubes if necessary to make a rich broth. Mix the cornflour with the cream and add to the broth, whisking well. The texture should be thin, almost soup-like, but if you prefer a thicker sauce, add more cornflour. (You can prepare the dish in advance to this point and refrigerate it for up to 2 days.)
★  When the chicken is cool, remove all the meat, discarding the skin, and cut into bite-size pieces; reserve. Drop the button onions into a pan of boiling water, return to the boil and simmer for a few minutes. Drain and cool, then remove the skins.
★  About 2 ½ hours before you intend to serve the dish, make the dumplings:  mix the dry ingredients together in a medium-size bowl. Cut or rub in the butter until the mixture is the consistency of sand, then add the milk a little at a time, stirring until evenly moistened. Fold in the chopped herbs. Cover and chill for 2 hours.
★  About 30 minutes before service, pour the chicken sauce into a large casserole or pot with a cover that is suitable to bring to the table. Bring to a simmer. Add the button onions and carrots and cook for 5 minutes. Next, add the chicken, celery and peas. Bring back to a simmer, then drop the dumpling batter from a tablespoon in dollops on top of the chicken sauce. Cover and simmer gently for 15 minutes.
★  Serve from the pot into large soup bowls and give your guests soup spoons.

# Blackened Fish Fillets with Lemon Caper Butter

Creole and Cajun super-chef, Paul Prudhomme has made 'blackened' fish so popular that restaurants around the United States now apply the technique to more than just fish. It is perfect for the catfish or redfish of the region, that have the thickness and, shall we say, lack of delicacy necessary to stand up to such a heat and spice attack. Fish such as cod or haddock will do well. Serve with Hashed Brown Potato Cake (page 168).

### YIELD: 4 SERVINGS

INGREDIENTS:
2 teaspoons salt
1 tablespoon paprika
½ teaspoon cayenne pepper
¾ teaspoon white pepper
½ teaspoon freshly ground black pepper
½ teaspoon dried thyme

½ teaspoon dried oregano
4 fillets of white fish, each weighing 225–280 g/8–10 oz (Cod, catfish and haddock are all suitable, the thicker the better.)
115 g/4 oz [½ cup] butter
Juice of 1 lemon
1–2 tablespoons capers, drained

METHOD:
★ Mix together the spices and herbs and rub into both sides of each fish fillet. Heat a heavy cast iron frying pan or skillet until it is very hot – about 5 minutes. Dip each fillet into a little vegetable oil and cook for about 2 minutes on each side, depending on the thickness of the fillet. Remove and keep warm.
★ To make the sauce, lower the heat and add the butter to the pan. When it melts, add the lemon juice and capers and swirl to combine. Pour over the fish and serve.

# Time-Stealing Barbecue Ribs

*"Good barbecue is cooked the way a cowboy dances, slow, easy and often. It's as tender as a lady's heart, as moist as her good-night kiss, and as lean as a cowboy's wallet." - Texan Sam Higgins*

Barbecue is a slow cooking process at low temperatures, an American culinary tradition of ingredients and techniques influenced by Native American Indians and by early Spanish, French and English explorers and settlers. African Americans, Creoles and Cajuns then embraced it and made it famous. Local woods, such as hickory and mesquite, together with lusty seasonings add flavour. As early as the 1580s, John White, a member of the Roanoke Island settlement, drew Croatan Indians smoking game and fish on wooden frames, more to preserve them than for the taste it imparted. The Spanish explorers called this wooden frame a *barbacoa*. The French were fond of spit-roasting or skewering, often a whole animal from *barbe à queue* – from beard to tail. In the Southwest, the Pueblo Indians blended fiery sauces from tomatoes and chillies to use for basting their foods. In America today, there are many regional variations, but most famous of all are barbecued ribs: smoky and crusty on the out-side and juicily tender on the inside, smothered in a spicy hot sauce. For those of us with neither the time nor the technical knowledge, I offer the following recipe, which comes close to the best ribs I have tasted in my travels. Given our lack of time in general and the difficulty of keeping and regulat-ing a charcoal fire, the pre-cooking described in this recipe is, in my opinion, the only way to go.

Yield: 4 servings
Equipment: a barbecue or oven
Oven: 200°C/400°F/Gas 6

INGREDIENTS:

2 racks of pork baby back ribs (pork loin back ribs) or
    spareribs (from the centre of the ribs), weighing
    1.8–2.25 kg/4–5 lbs
¼ teaspoon each salt, freshly ground pepper and dry
    mustard
1 recipe Home-made Chilli Barbecue Sauce (page 61) or
    bottled barbecue sauce

FOR THE MARINADE:

4 tablespoons soy sauce
4 tablespoons red wine vinegar
4 tablespoons olive oil
2 garlic cloves, crushed

METHOD:

★ Prepare the ribs by loosening the white membranes on the back and removing them. Leave the racks whole for cooking. Lay them in a roasting pan large enough to hold them flat. (If they won't fit, you can cut them in half.)

★ Mix together the salt, pepper and mustard. Rub the meaty surface of the ribs with this mixture. Combine the marinade ingredients and pour over the ribs to cover evenly. Cover the pan with foil. Marinate the ribs for 6-8 hours or overnight in the refrigerator, turning over once or twice.

★ A few hours before serving, or well in advance, preheat the oven and bake the ribs, still cov-ered with foil, for at least 1 hour, turning them over once during the cooking. If the ribs you are using are extremely lean and/or thick, you may need to bake them longer—they should be ten-der when pierced with a fork or knife.

★ You can finish cooking the ribs in the oven or outdoors on the barbecue. If you are using a barbecue, prepare and light the charcoal fire in good time; you need medium hot coals (see page 212 for instructions).

★ To finish cooking in the oven: remove the ribs from the marinade and discard it. Lay the ribs meat side down in a baking dish and cover the bottom, bone side with barbecue sauce. Return to the oven and bake for 25 minutes, uncovered. Turn the ribs over and cover again with sauce. Bake for a further 25–30 minutes or until the ribs are crusty and fall-apart tender. Add additional sauce if necessary.

★ To finish cooking the ribs on a barbecue: first bake them in barbecue sauce as in the previous step, allowing 15 minutes on each side. Then transfer them to the barbecue grill and cook for 5-8 minutes on each side or until they are crispy, but not blackened. Add more sauce if necessary.

# Louisiana Bread Pudding Soufflé with Whiskey Sauce

Bread puddings have always been popular in the South, but today's version is more likely to be a lighter, soufflé-style pudding crowned with a sauce made of the region's best bourbon whiskey.

YIELD: 4-6 SERVINGS
Equipment:  an electric mixer and a soufflé dish of 2 litre/3 ½ pint [US 2 quart] capacity
Oven:  180°C/350°F/Gas 4

INGREDIENTS:
A stale French baguette, most of crust removed, cut into 2.5 cm/1 inch cubes (You need about 100 g/3 ½ oz [3 cups] of cubes.)
250 ml/8 fl oz [1 cup] single cream [US light cream]
175 ml/6 fl oz [¾ cup] milk
4 size-1 eggs [US jumbo eggs], separated
220 g/8 oz [1 cup] caster sugar [US granulated sugar]
Large pinch each freshly ground nutmeg and ground cinnamon
2 teaspoons pure vanilla essence [US pure vanilla extract]
1 teaspoon bourbon whiskey, such as Jim Beam Kentucky bourbon whiskey

3 tablespoons dried currants
4 tablespoons icing sugar [US confectioners' sugar]

FOR THE WHISKEY SAUCE:
Yolks from 2 size-1 eggs [US jumbo eggs]
75 g/2 ½ oz [1/3 cup] caster sugar [US granulated sugar]
175 ml/6 fl oz [¾ cup] milk
125 ml/4 fl oz [½ cup] whipping cream
1 teaspoon pure vanilla essence [US pure vanilla extract]
1 tablespoon + 1 teaspoon bourbon whiskey

METHOD:
★  A few hours before serving, make the whiskey sauce. Beat the egg yolks and sugar in a small saucepan until they are light. In another pan, warm the milk and cream together to just boiling point. Add to the yolks and sugar, whisking over low heat. Cook gently, stirring the mixture with a wooden spoon, until it begins to thicken enough to coat the back of the spoon. Remove from the heat and add the vanilla and bourbon whiskey. Leave to cool. Serve warm or at room temperature.

★  Put the bread cubes into a large bowl and pour over the cream and milk. In another bowl, beat the egg yolks with caster sugar until the mixture is light and lemon-coloured, then beat in the spices, vanilla and bourbon whiskey. Stir in the currants. Fold this mixture into the bread. Leave for about 10 minutes before proceeding with the recipe.

★  Preheat the oven. Prepare the soufflé dish by buttering it and coating the sides and bottom lightly with sugar.

★  Whisk the egg whites until they are foamy. Gradually add the icing sugar, whisking, then continue to whisk the egg whites until they form firm glossy peaks that are not too dry. Fold the egg whites into the bread mixture.

★  Pour into the prepared soufflé dish and set it in a large baking pan. Pour boiling water into the baking pan until it comes about one-third of the way up the side of the soufflé dish. Bake the pudding in the preheated oven for about 1 hour or until the top is puffed and brown and a knife inserted in the middle of the pudding comes out clean. Serve hot with the whiskey sauce.

# Mint Juleps

This classic cocktail is a symbol of Southern hospitality and the official drink of the Kentucky Derby. Silver goblets are traditional.

YIELD: 1 COCKTAIL
Equipment: an ice crusher or blender

INGREDIENTS:
Finely crushed ice

Fresh mint
2 teaspoons icing sugar [US confectioners' sugar]

2 teaspoons water
4 tablespoons bourbon whiskey

METHOD:
★ Fill a silver goblet or glass tumbler with finely crushed ice and refrigerate until a frost forms on the outside.
★ In a small bowl, crush 6-8 mint leaves with the back of a spoon. Add the sugar, water and bourbon whiskey and stir. Pour over the ice and garnish generously with mint. Serve with a straw.

# THE MIDWEST AND THE NORTHWEST

*Illinois, Indiana, Michigan, Ohio, Wisconsin, Minnesota, Iowa, Missouri, Kansas, Nebraska, Nevada, North and South Dakota, Wyoming, Montana, Idaho, Oregon, Washington, Alaska*

Still the frontier in many ways, these two regions include rich farmland and the "amber waves of grain" of the prairie, where rural life is still king. The cooking of this area originated with the people who settled here including German, Slavic, Irish, and Scandinavian immigrants. Here, ethnic dishes at their most traditional have tended to survive intact. The cooking is honest, unpretentious and hearty. If that sounds boring – it's not! It is family-style home cooking at its best – satisfying and comforting.

The Midwest is often called 'the bread basket', the 'dairy centre', and 'the Heartland' and it is all these things. This is meat and potatoes country, where big breakfasts and food to fuel hard work are still the norm. Competitions to judge the best home-made pies and breads are still held at the county fairs. In the cooking of the Midwest, where the winters are cold, the predominant ingredients are butter, bacon fat, lard, cream, eggs and cheese. This is also a region with abundant wild game, wild mushrooms, wild rice, orchard fruits, berries and garden vegetables. The Midwest, not surprisingly, is home to some of America's largest food manufacturers including General Foods, Pillsbury, Smucker's, Sara Lee, Quaker Oats, Armour, Kelloggs, Old El Paso and Kikkoman.

The urban centers of the Midwest benefit from the contributions and influence of the major ethnic groups that settled there. Chicago, Milwaukee, St. Louis and Cincinnati had strong German immigration, while in Detroit and Cleveland one sees a Polish influence. The Twin Cities of St. Paul and Minneapolis are strongly Scandinavian. The restaurants in these large cities can be quite sophisticated and specialise in ethnic foods as well as regional specialities.

The Northwest is still young and slightly wild in places. Settled in the 1880s, it attracted trappers and traders, prospectors and adventurers from all over the world. Seattle in Washington state, famous for its restaurants, holds a special place as the culinary capital of the Northwest. At the centre of all the excitement is the Pike Place Market, founded in 1907, which displays beautiful produce and the bounty of the sea. At Pike Market you can see some of the ingredients for which the region is famous, including salmon and shellfish, Olympia Oysters, cherries and berries, apples, Idaho potatoes, lentils, and a sweet onion known as the Walla Walla. In season, you will find fiddleheads, young unfurled fern fronds from edible varieties like ostrich, cinnamon, hay-scented and evergreen that make wonderful eating. In this last frontier of the Northwest, evocative of Jack London's Klondike, the sophistication of Seattle's cuisine is a bit surprising – a sharp contrast to the ruggedly beautiful surroundings, the snow-capped peaks of the Cascades and the turbulent waters of Puget Sound.

# Pocket Pork Chops with Corn Bread Stuffing

America loves pork and this stuffed and braised thick pork chop is a succulent and fancy way to present it. My family always like to eat these accompanied by Curried Fruit (page 169).

YIELD: 6 SERVINGS
Oven: 170°C/325°F/Gas 3

INGREDIENTS:

6 centre-cut loin pork chops, 2.5 cm/1 inch or more
 thick, well trimmed
Salt and freshly ground pepper
4 tablespoons vegetable oil
1 medium-size onion, finely chopped (about 80 g/scant
 3 oz)
2 small carrots, finely chopped (about 80 g/scant 3 oz)
¼ teaspoon fresh or dried thyme
1 tablespoon flour
375 ml/12 fl oz [1 ½ cups] chicken stock, preferably
 home-made

FOR THE STUFFING:

115 g/4 oz smoked streaky bacon, finely chopped
1 tablespoon vegetable oil
1 medium-size onion, finely chopped
2 celery stalks, chopped
3 tablespoons chopped fresh sage or 1 tablespoon dried
 sage
500 ml/16 fl oz [2 cups] chicken stock, preferably
 home-made
1 bay leaf
230 g/8 oz [2 cups] cornbread, dried and crumbled (see
 Skillet Cornbread, page 18)
225 g/8 oz pork sausages, such as chipolatas [US small
 pork link sausages], browned and diced
30 g/1 oz [¼ cup] pecans, toasted and coarsely chopped
2-3 tablespoons maple syrup
Salt and freshly ground pepper to taste

METHOD:

★ Cut a pocket horizontally in each chop, working from the opposite side to the bone and cutting a pocket about 7.5 cm/3 inches deep.

★ To make the stuffing, sauté the bacon until crisp and the fat is rendered. Add the oil [American cooks will not need this oil] and then add the onion and celery and sauté until the onion is translucent. Stir in the sage, stock and bay leaf. Boil over high heat to reduce this mixture by one-third. Add the rest of the stuffing ingredients. Remove from the heat and allow to cool.

★ Preheat the oven.

★ Divide the stuffing among the pork chops and pack it into the pockets. Seal with small skewers. Season each chop with salt and pepper. Heat the oil in a flameproof casserole or ovenproof frying pan or skillet that is large enough to hold all the chops in one layer. Brown the chops for 3-4 minutes on each side. When all the chops have been browned, remove them.

★ Drain all but a thin layer of fat from the pan. Add the onion, carrots and thyme and stir-fry until they are beginning to brown. Add the flour and mix well, then stir in the stock and bring to the boil.

★ Return the chops to the pan. Cover tightly and bake in the preheated oven for 30-45 minutes or until the chops are tender. Baste the chops occasionally during baking. You can strain the sauce or serve it chunky.

# Heartland Pot Roast

Almost all regions of America make their own version of pot roast, with each immigrant group contributing to the basic ingredients for braised beef. This Midwest version shows the influences of the dominant Scandinavian and German population with the addition of allspice, anchovies, vinegar and molasses for a rich, sweet-sour taste. This is perfect winter comfort food, and is best served with mashed potatoes or hashed brown potato cake (page 168) to absorb the generous amounts of gravy this dish produces.

YIELD: 4 SERVINGS FOR HEARTY APPETITES
Oven: 180°C/350°F/Gas 4

INGREDIENTS:
1 teaspoon ground allspice
½ teaspoon freshly ground pepper
2 teaspoons salt
1.8 kg/4 lbs braising steak to include some beef bones
    (Bottom round or blade, topside or silverside are cuts
    appropriate for pot roast in the UK; US cuts are rump,
    chuck or round steak.)
45 g/1 ½ oz [3 tablespoons] beef dripping or butter
3 tablespoons brandy, Cognac or bourbon whiskey
2 medium-size onions, sliced
1 garlic clove, finely chopped
1 celery stalk, chopped
1 small carrot, chopped

375 ml/12 fl oz [1 ½ cups] canned whole tomatoes with juice
2 whole cloves
2 bay leaves
3 canned anchovy fillets, very finely chopped, or 2 teaspoons
    anchovy paste
2 tablespoons white distilled vinegar
2 tablespoons molasses, dark treacle, golden syrup or dark soft
    brown sugar (Do not use black strap molasses full
    strength; mix it half and half with golden syrup or sugar.)
375 ml/12 fl oz [1 ½ cups] hot beef stock, preferably
    home-made
900 g – 1.35 kg/2–3 lbs mixed vegetables to braise and serve
    with the meat, to include carrots, parsnips, baby onions
    and leeks, and new potatoes

METHOD:
★ Preheat the oven.
★ Mix together the allspice, pepper and salt and rub into the meat on all sides. Heat the dripping or butter in a heavy cast iron pot or flameproof casserole and brown the meat all over. When the meat is a dark, rich brown, pour over the brandy and carefully set it alight. As the flames die down, add the rest of the ingredients, except the vegetables you intend to braise. Stir and bring to the boil. Cover the casserole and put it into the preheated oven. (Or if you prefer, you can cook over a low heat on top of the stove.) Cook for 2–3 hours. Cooking time will depend on the tenderness of the beef: you want the pot roast to be very tender, but not so well cooked that it falls apart.
★ After an hour or so, remove the casserole from the oven and turn the meat over. There should still be enough juice in the pot to almost cover the meat; if there is not add some water or tomato juice. During the last 20 minutes or so of cooking, add vegetables for braising to the pot.
★ When the pot roast is done, remove it and the braised vegetables to a heatproof platter and cover with foil. Keep warm in the oven. Spoon off as much fat as you can from the top of the sauce. (A chef's trick: lay paper towels over the sauce to "capture" the fat floating on the top and discard. Do this as many times as needed to remove all the fat from the surface.) You can leave the sauce chunky, or purée it in a food processor or press it through a sieve. Taste it and adjust the seasonings if necessary.
★ Slice the pot roast and serve with the braised vegetables, the sauce and potatoes. Leftovers, if any, can be made into hash (see page 128).

# Meatloaf with Peppers and a Sweet-Sour Glaze

Meatloaf, the common man's pâté, has become synonymous with home-cooked comfort food. It was famous American diner food in the 1800s, where its reputation became tarnished by the addition of too many cheap fillers to substitute for more expensive meat. Recently, American bistros and diners have revived meatloaf; when it is made, like this one, with care and wonderful additions it can be very special.

YIELD: 8-10 SERVINGS
Oven: 180°C/350°F/Gas 4

INGREDIENTS:
70 g/scant 2 ½ oz [¾ cup] fresh breadcrumbs
4 tablespoons cream
3 size-1 eggs [US jumbo eggs]
125 ml/4 fl oz [½ cup] tomato ketchup
½ teaspoon ground white pepper
1 teaspoon each salt and freshly ground black pepper
½ teaspoon freshly ground nutmeg
½ teaspoon ground cumin
2 pinches cayenne pepper
½ teaspoon dried hot red pepper flakes, crumbled
450 g/1 lb minced steak [US ground round]
450 g/1 lb minced pork [US ground pork]
8 fresh flat-leaf Italian parsley sprigs, finely chopped
125 g/4 ½ oz [2 cups] fresh spinach leaves, finely chopped

6 smoked streaky bacon rashers [US thick bacon slices], 2 of them chopped
1 tablespoon olive oil
½ red onion, finely chopped
1 carrot, finely chopped
1 celery stalk, finely chopped
½ red and 1 green sweet pepper, finely chopped
2 garlic cloves, finely chopped

FOR THE SAUCE:
125 ml/4 fl oz [½ cup] beef stock, preferably home-made
80 ml/2 ¾ fl oz [⅓ cup] tomato-based chilli sauce or tomato ketchup
1 tablespoon dark soft brown sugar
2 teaspoons red wine vinegar
¼ teaspoon Tabasco sauce

METHOD:
★ Preheat the oven.
★ In a large bowl, whisk together all the ingredients from the breadcrumbs to the pepper flakes. Add the meats and mix well with your hands. Add the parsley and spinach. Refrigerate while you prepare the rest of the vegetables.
★ In a large frying pan, fry the chopped bacon in the olive oil. Add all the rest of the vegetables and sauté until softened. Remove from the heat and leave to cool, then fold into the meat mixture. Form the mixture into a firm, rounded loaf in a large baking pan or gratin dish. Lay the 4 whole bacon rashers over it decoratively. Bake the meatloaf in the preheated oven for 30 minutes.
★ Combine the sauce ingredients and pour over the meatloaf. Bake for a further 30 minutes. Serve with potatoes, mashed or your preference. Cold meatloaf sandwiches are a popular use for the leftovers!

Note: All the vegetables, except the sweet peppers and garlic, can be chopped in a food processor fitted with a steel blade (the peppers lose too much liquid when they are processed, and garlic is never chopped as finely by the processor as it should be).

# Salmon Hash

This is my version of a wonderful, colourful hash that is one of the signature dishes at the Cascades restaurant in Portland, Oregon. This is the kind of dish that everyone turns to look at when it is served, wishing that they had ordered it. And it is a perfect example of how food from another era, in this case diner food, can be updated and enjoyed even more today.

### YIELD: 4–6 SERVINGS

INGREDIENTS:

4-6 medium-size Red Russet or other red-skinned potatoes (unpeeled)
125 ml/4 fl oz [½ cup] virgin olive oil
1 green, 1 yellow and 1 red sweet pepper, cut into 2.5 cm/1 inch dice
1 fennel bulb, cut into 2.5 cm/1 inch dice
1 large red onion, cut into 2.5 cm/1 inch dice
1 large shallot, finely chopped

4 garlic cloves, finely chopped
450 g/1 lb salmon fillet, skin removed, cut into 1.5 cm/ ½ inch dice
1 tablespoon each chopped fresh rosemary and thinly sliced fresh sage
¼ teaspoon dried hot red pepper flakes
¼ teaspoon salt
Freshly ground pepper to taste
3 tablespoons dry sherry

METHOD:

★ Cut the potatoes into 2.5 cm/1 inch dice and immediately cover them with cold water in a medium-size bowl. Leave to soak for about 15 minutes, changing the water a few times.

★ About 20 minutes before you plan to serve, drain the potatoes in a colander and then on paper towels. Heat the oil in a large frying pan until almost smoking. Add the potatoes and toss them in the oil until they are browned and tender. Remove them with a slotted spoon to a bowl.

★ Pour off half of the oil (save it for another use) and lower the heat a bit. Add the sweet peppers, fennel and red onion and cook for a few minutes or until they soften. Add the shallot and garlic and stir-fry for 1 minute. Add the salmon and return the potatoes to the pan. Sauté, tossing the mixture, until the salmon becomes opaque. Finally, stir in the herbs, pepper flakes, salt and a few grindings of pepper.

★ Tilt the pan to one side, add the sherry and set it alight with a match. Put the pan flat again and toss all the ingredients until the flames are extinguished. Serve immediately. Delicious with a crisp green salad and Light-as-air Buttermilk Biscuits (page 173).

OPPOSITE: *Salmon Hash accompanied by a popover (see page 211)*

# Pheasant and Mushroom Stroganoff

Game is plentiful in the Midwest and hunting is a popular sport. When wild game is available this easy method of cutting all the meat off the bones before cooking and soaking it in milk, removes some of the wild flavour and makes for wonderful eating. This rich ragout is delicious with wild rice waffles or wild rice in any form.

YIELD: 4–6 SERVINGS
Oven: 230°C/450°F/Gas 8 (if making stock)

INGREDIENTS:

2 small pheasants, weighing 675 g–1 kg/1 ½–2 ¼ lbs each, wild or farmed, cleaned
1 litre/1 ⅔ pints [1 quart] milk
30 g/1 oz dried wild mushrooms
Salt and freshly ground pepper
2 tablespoons or more olive oil
30 g/1 oz [2 tablespoons] butter
3 shallots, finely chopped
2 garlic cloves, finely chopped
225 g/8 oz fresh mushrooms, sliced
125 ml/4 fl oz [½ cup] single cream [US light cream]
175 ml/6 fl oz [¾ cup] pheasant stock (see below), or use canned beef consommé
125 ml/4 fl oz [½ cup] dry sherry
1 tablespoon sweet Hungarian paprika

A bouquet garni including 8-10 parsley sprigs, a bay leaf and 4 fresh thyme sprigs
4 juniper berries
125 ml/4 fl oz [½ cup] sour cream
125 ml/4 fl oz [½ cup] medium-sweet sherry
2 tablespoons flour mixed to a paste with 30 g/1 oz [2 tablespoons] butter (beurre manié)
1 tablespoon chopped fresh tarragon

FOR PHEASANT STOCK:

1 medium-size onion, coarsely chopped
1 carrot, coarsely chopped
1 celery stalk, coarsely chopped
A bouquet garni (as above)
6 black peppercorns
Salt

METHOD:

★ Cut all the meat off the pheasants, discarding the skin, and cut the meat into bite-size pieces. Put the meat in a bowl, pour over the milk, cover and refrigerate for 4-8 hours (or overnight). If you are using wild pheasant, the longer time would be beneficial.

★ If you have the time to make pheasant stock, cut up all the bones from the pheasants. Preheat the oven. Put the bones in a roasting pan with the carrot, onion and celery and roast for 20-30 minutes, turning often. When nicely browned, transfer these ingredients to a stock pot. Cover them amply with water and add the rest of the stock ingredients. Bring to the boil, skimming well, then partially cover the pot, reduce the heat and simmer for 1 hour. Remove the cover and simmer for 1½-2 hours or until the stock has reduced down to the quantity required for this recipe. Strain and reserve.

★ Rinse the dried wild mushrooms well, put them in a small bowl and pour boiling water over them. Leave them to soak for about 30 minutes. Drain, rinse again and finely chop. Reserve.

★ At least an hour before serving, drain the pheasant meat and discard the milk. Dry the meat on paper towels. Season the meat well with salt and pepper. In a large frying pan, heat the olive oil and brown the meat in 2 or 3 batches. As it is browned, remove the meat with a slotted spoon to a heavy casserole or pot. Add the butter to the frying pan and then add the shallots and garlic and sauté until softened. Add the sliced mushrooms and the chopped wild mushrooms and sauté until lightly browned. Add these vegetables to the pheasant in the casserole.

★ Pour the cream, pheasant stock or consommé and dry sherry into the frying pan and stir well to deglaze it. Pour into the casserole. Add the paprika, bouquet garni and juniper berries. Bring to the boil, then reduce the heat and simmer for about 1 hour or until the pheasant is tender.

★ Remove and discard the bouquet garni. Add the sour cream and the medium-sweet sherry and bring back to a simmer; don't allow the mixture to boil. Thicken the sauce with the butter and flour paste, adding it bit by bit and whisking it in; add more if you want a thicker sauce. Just before serving add the chopped tarragon.

# A Pitcher of Bloody Marys

A favourite drink, especially at brunch, with or without alcohol, the Bloody Mary mix is easy to make by the pitcher, adding alcohol as needed. The teetotal version is known as a Virgin Bloody Mary.

YIELD: 6 SERVINGS (1 PITCHER).
For individual servings, use 250 ml/8 fl oz [1 cup] of mix and 3 tablespoons vodka each.

INGREDIENTS:
4 tablespoons freshly squeezed lemon juice
4 tablespoons Worcestershire sauce
250 ml/8 fl oz [1 cup] clam juice, or substitute Clamato which is a mixture of clam juice and tomato juice
4 cans (340 ml/12 oz) V-8 juice, or substitute tomato juice
½ teaspoon Tabasco sauce

1 teaspoon Angostura bitters
1 tablespoon freshly grated horseradish
1 teaspoon sugar
Salt and freshly ground pepper to taste
275 ml/9 fl oz [1 cup + 2 tablespoons] vodka
Lemon wedges and celery stalks, to garnish
Ice

METHOD:
★ Stir together all the ingredients, except the vodka, lemon wedges, celery stalks and ice, in a large pitcher. Refrigerate.

★ To serve, add the vodka to the pitcher. Pour into glasses over ice. Alternatively, pour the mix into glasses over ice and add 3 tablespoons of vodka to each glass. Use a celery stalk to mix and garnish with a lemon wedge.

# THE SOUTHWEST & TEXAS

*Arizona, Colorado, New Mexico, Oklahoma, Texas, Utah*

One leaves the Southwest region with intense sensory memories of vibrant, vivid colours and terrain and an equally flamboyant cuisine. The colours of the Southwest are the red, yellow and orange of a setting sun reflected from the desert sand, the red sandstone of carved buttes, and the grey canyons through which fierce rivers run. One is haunted by images of ghost towns, abandoned mines, adobe buildings, cactus, sagebrush, and ristras of red chillies. Artists have flocked to the Southwest for its colour, its sun, its serenity and its primitive charm. Full of Indian legend and mysticism it is an area of the country that haunts you and brings you back.

Southwest cuisine has been called the cooking of the Sun, since its ingredients and very essence seem to be sun-drenched. Like Spain's tapas, Southwestern cuisine is strong on appetizers. Nibbling is essential in this climate and sometimes finger foods make up the whole meal. It is a colourful food, served with lots of sauces and condiments. Tortillas stand in for bread and chillies are omnipresent.

Southwestern cooking began with the simple survival techniques of the Native American Indians, including the Apaches, the Hopi, Navajo, Papago, Rio Grande, Pueblo and Zuni tribes. They lived simply on the land and depended on corn, squash, beans, wild greens, herbs, berries, game and fish. Spanish missionaries, coming north, brought with them Indians from Mexico and introduced their own ingredients to this mixture. They brought chillies, onions and garlic, tomatoes, avocados, wheat, rice, orchard fruits and grapes. After the Mexican War in 1848, Anglo-American cowboys, driving their cattle herds, added meat, stews and barbecue to the mix. The 'come and get it' chuck wagon and outdoor cooking of the cowboy fit the regional style well.

Throughout the Southwest, variations develop into local specialities. In Arizona, the flour tortilla is more common than corn tortillas and the cooking is a little milder, with specialities including the *chimichanga*, *burros* and *burritos*. In Texas, regional American cuisine is at its most flamboyant, with a style all its own. The cooking of Texas specializes in mesquite barbecue, *chili con carne* and a rough and tumble cooking called Tex-Mex. Tex-Mex started out in El Paso as a cheap, trashy kind of food from the cheapest cuts of meat, smothered in spices. Today, the tendency is to glamourize it with more expensive ingredients, but it is the kind of food best eaten from a street cart, without spending too much money.

Perhaps the best place to sample Southwestern cuisine is in the relatively sophisticated capital of New Mexico, Santa Fe, where creative chefs have succeeded in making Southwestern cooking one of the most fashionable regional cooking styles today. Look for regional specialities including: buffalo, *chili con carne*, chicken-fried steak, *chiles rellenos*, *chimichangas*, *fajitas*, Indian fry bread and *tacos*, *huevos rancheros* and mesquite-smoked barbecue.

# Black Bean Chili

This is an earthy, almost-vegetarian chili (omit the bacon if you wish) that will transport you to the Southwestern United States, where the sun is hot, the cactus high and the food is robust and anything but tame.

### YIELD: 6-8 SERVINGS

### INGREDIENTS:

340 g/12 oz [2 cups] dried black turtle or black kidney beans
4 smoked streaky bacon rashers [US thick bacon slices], chopped
1 bay leaf
1 cinnamon stick
1 tablespoon cumin seeds
1 tablespoon dried oregano
1 tablespoon paprika
¼ teaspoon cayenne pepper
1 teaspoon chilli powder [US 1 tablespoon or more chilli powder] (In the UK, Barts is a good full-strength brand – beware of those already laced with cumin.)
2 tablespoons olive oil
1 large onion, chopped

1 celery stalk, chopped
1 large green sweet pepper, chopped
3 garlic cloves, finely chopped
2 tablespoons brown sugar
2 cans (400 g/14 oz each) whole plum tomatoes and their juice
300 ml/ ½ pint [1 ¼ cups] beef or vegetable stock, prefer-ably home-made
125 ml/4 fl oz [½ cup] red wine
4 tablespoons tomato paste
½ teaspoon salt
1 tablespoon red wine vinegar
2 tablespoons cornmeal mixed with 2 tablespoons water
Sour cream and chopped fresh coriander [US cilantro], to garnish

### METHOD:

★ Sort through the beans and discard any stones or other debris. Rinse the beans well, then cover them with water and allow them to soak overnight. The next day, drain them and put into a large pan. Cover them with fresh water by about 5 cm/2 inches. Add the bacon, bay leaf and cinnamon stick and bring to the boil. Lower the heat and simmer the beans for at least 1 hour or until they are tender.

★ In the meantime, prepare the other ingredients. In a small frying pan, toast the cumin seeds, shaking the pan from time to time. When the seeds begin to brown, add the oregano. As soon as they begin to smell quite strong, remove the pan from the heat and add the paprika, cayenne and chilli powder. Stir, being careful not to get too close – the cayenne can send up vapours that could kill a horse! Grind the spices in a mortar, spice mill or blender to a coarse powder and reserve.

★ In a large frying pan, heat the olive oil and lightly brown the onion. Add the celery, green pepper and garlic and sauté until they are softened. Add the brown sugar and cook, stirring to caramelise all the vegetables. Finally, deglaze the pan with the tomatoes and their juice, stirring well. Break up the tomatoes with a spoon into small pieces. Remove from the heat and reserve this mixture to add to the cooked beans.

★ When the beans are tender, add the vegetable mixture, the stock, wine, tomato paste, salt and 2 tablespoons of the toasted spice mixture. Cook the chili uncovered for 1-3 hours or until it is rich and thick. Stir from time to time or the beans will stick to the bottom.

★ Taste and add additional spice mixture if you like a hotter chili. Discard the cinnamon and bay leaf. Add the vinegar. For a thicker chili, add the cornmeal paste: stir it in vigorously so that lumps don't form. Serve the chili topped with a dollop of sour cream and a sprinkle of chopped fresh coriander. Chili is wonderful with cornbread (page 18) or tortillas (see recipe for flour tortillas on page 181).

# Huevos Rancheros
## (RANCH-STYLE EGGS)

This is the favourite breakfast of the Southwest, and will certainly start your day with a kick! If you are bored with breakfast try poaching your eggs in salsa and you'll never be bored again.

YIELD: 2 SERVINGS
Equipment: a food processor
Oven: 200°C/400°F/Gas 6

INGREDIENTS:

4 small soft, fresh corn tortillas, or substitute flour tortillas (page 181)
100 g/3 ½ oz [1 cup] Monterey Jack cheese, grated, or substitute Cheddar or Gruyère
250 ml/8 fl oz [1 cup] Black Bean Chili (page 147 – optional)
500 ml/16 fl oz [2 cups] coriander salsa (double the recipe for salsa in Navajo Tacos, page 152), or use bottled salsa

4 size-1 eggs [US jumbo eggs]
Salt and freshly ground pepper
Sour cream and chopped fresh coriander [US cilantro], to garnish
Tabasco sauce, to add heat

METHOD:

★ Preheat the oven. Have all of your ingredients ready. Lightly grease a baking sheet and lay the tortillas on it, overlapping 2 to make each serving. Sprinkle the cheese over the tortillas and heat them in the preheated oven for about 4-5 minutes or until the cheese melts.

★ Meanwhile, warm the chili if you are using it. Put the salsa in a small frying pan with a cover and heat to a simmer. Break each egg into a small bowl and then slide it into the salsa. Adjust the heat so that the salsa simmers. Season the eggs with salt and freshly ground pepper, then cover the pan and poach the eggs for about 3–5 minutes, basting them from time to time with the salsa.

★ To assemble the *Huevos Rancheros*, put two overlapping tortillas on each plate. Cover with half of the chili if you are using it, then add two poached eggs covered in salsa. Garnish with sour cream and coriander. Put a bottle of Tabasco on the table, to add as your taste dictates.

# Texas-Style Chili con Carne

*Chili con carne* originated in the state of Texas, home of the annual World Championship Chili Cookoff. It is still the official state dish. For proof that chili is not Mexican, look in a Mexican dictionary where you will find a definition of the word roughly translated as: "A detestable food with a false Mexican name which is sold in the U.S. from coast to coast." Texans make chili a little differently from everyone else and include chopped beef marinated in beer; no onions, no bell peppers, or beans; and seasonings including chilli pepper pulp, garlic, cumin, oregano, and paprika. The fun elements of Texan chili are the condiments you can add at the table where, if you like, you can also add beans.

## YIELD: 6–8 SERVINGS

### INGREDIENTS:

16 small dried hot red chilli peppers (Those 2.5–4 cm/ 1–1 ½ inches long sold in Chinese shops are the ones to use.)

750 ml/1 ¼ pints [3 cups] boiling water

375 ml/12 fl oz [1 ½ cups] beer

1.6 kg/3 lbs braising steak, cut into 1.5 cm/½ inch cubes, or coarsely minced beef [US coarse ground beef chuck]

225 g/8 oz beef suet, preferably kidney suet, cut into 1.5 cm/½ inch cubes

2 bay leaves

750 ml/1 ¼ pints [3 cups] canned whole tomatoes, drained

1 tablespoon cumin seeds

2 large garlic cloves, finely chopped

2 teaspoons dried oregano

2 tablespoons paprika

2 teaspoons brown sugar

3 teaspoons salt

2 teaspoons mild chilli powder [In the US all chilli powder is mild.]

2 tablespoons yellow cornmeal mixed with 2 tablespoons water to make a paste

¼ teaspoon cayenne pepper

Rice, home-cooked pinto beans or black beans, sour cream, guacamole (page 198), chopped spring onions [US scallions], chopped fresh tomato, etc, to accompany

### METHOD:

★ Cut off the stalks of the dried chilli peppers, cut them in half and remove seeds. Put the chillies in a bowl and pour the boiling water over them. Leave them to soak for at least 30 minutes, then drain, reserving the liquid.

★ Pour the beer over the beef and marinate for at least 30 minutes. Drain the meat well, discarding any beer that may remain.

★ In a heavy cast iron or enamelled pot with a lid, cook the beef suet, stirring frequently, over moderate heat until it has rendered most of its fat. Remove any remaining bits of suet with a slotted spoon and discard. Pour off all but about 4 tablespoons of the fat. Heat the fat in the pot until it is very hot but not smoking. Add the meat and fry, stirring, until it is firm but not brown. Add all but about 125 ml/4 fl oz [½ cup] of the reserved chilli-soaking liquid together with the bay leaves and the tomatoes. Partially cover the pot and simmer for 1 hour.

★ Toast the cumin seeds in a small frying pan over low heat for about 5 minutes, shaking the pan frequently. Grind the seeds in a blender (or use a spice mill or a mortar and pestle) until totally fine. Add the soaked red chillies, the remaining chilli-soaking liquid, the garlic, oregano, paprika, brown sugar, salt and chilli powder to the blender and blend to a smooth purée. Add this to the meat mixture and continue to simmer, partially covered, for a further 30 minutes.

★ Finally, add the cornmeal paste, stirring briskly, to thicken the chili slightly. Taste and adjust seasonings, adding the cayenne pepper if you would like a hotter chili.

★ Serve the *chili con carne* from the pot or a soup tureen surrounded by bowls of rice, cooked pinto beans and optional condiments such as sour cream, guacamole, chopped spring onions tomatoes and grated Cheddar cheese. Skillet Cornbread (page 18) is the ideal bread to eat with this, and to drink – Mexican beer, of course!

*Texas beef on the hoof in Robert Lindneux's painting 'The Stampede'*

# Navajo Tacos

I once ate these in a small restaurant in Moab, Utah before embarking on a white-water rafting trip with my family. Call it a last supper if you will, but I still remember how good it was – and it still is, every time I make it. I like to offer bowls of toppings so that each diner can create his own taco. It's more fun and they are more satisfied for having a hand in it.

YIELD: 4 SERVINGS
Equipment: a food processor
Oven: 200°C/400°F/Gas 6 (if using beans)

## INGREDIENTS:

One recipe of dough for Navajo Fry Bread (page 170)
1 can (453 g/1 lb) refried beans (optional)
125 g/4 ½ oz [1 cup] mature (sharp) Cheddar cheese, grated
½ small iceberg lettuce, shredded
1 avocado, chopped and tossed in lemon juice, or guacamole (page 198)
Sour cream and chopped fresh coriander [US cilantro], to garnish

### FOR THE BEEF TOPPING:

450 g/1 lb minced steak [US ground beef steak]
1 shallot, finely chopped
2 garlic cloves, finely chopped
¼ teaspoon chilli powder, or more to taste
½ teaspoon each of dried oregano, paprika, ground cumin, salt and freshly ground pepper
1 teaspoon Worcestershire sauce
125 ml/4 fl oz [½ cup] tomato sauce or mild taco sauce

### FOR THE CORIANDER SALSA:

2 garlic cloves
1 fresh or canned jalapeño pepper, or other fresh hot green chilli, stalks and seeds removed
12 g/scant ½ oz [¼ cup] fresh coriander leaves [US cilantro]
2 medium-size tomatoes, skin and seeds removed
1 tablespoon extra-virgin olive oil
1 teaspoon freshly squeezed lemon or lime juice
¼ teaspoon ground cumin
Salt and freshly ground pepper to taste

## METHOD:

★ Prepare the dough for Navajo Fry Bread and leave it to rest.
★ To make the meat topping, fry the beef in a medium-size frying pan until it begins to brown, stirring to break up lumps. Pour off any fat, then add the shallot and garlic and cook until they soften. Stir in the spices and the sauces and simmer, uncovered, until the mixture is thick. Taste and adjust the seasoning. (Note: This mixture is not particularly hot with spice – let each diner adjust spiciness with the salsa.) Set aside.
★ To make the coriander salsa, put the garlic in the bowl of a food processor fitted with a steel blade and chop finely. Add the jalapeño and chop finely, then add the coriander and chop finely too. Finally, add the tomato and pulse to chop coarsely. Put these ingredients into a small bowl and add the oil, juice and cumin. Taste and adjust the seasonings.
★ If you are using refried beans, preheat the oven. Spread the beans in a shallow ovenproof serving dish, drizzle with a little olive oil and sprinkle with some of the cheese. Heat them in the preheated oven for 10–15 minutes or until bubbly. Put the remaining cheese, the lettuce and avocado or guacamole in small serving bowls. Reheat the meat topping.
★ Just before serving, fry the Navajo Fry Bread as directed in the recipe. Provide each diner with a hot fry bread and suggest they top it with the meat and/or refried beans (for vegetarians) and garnish with salsa, lettuce, cheese, sour cream, and avocado or guacamole. Serve with Mexican beer!

# Goat Cheese Chiles Rellenos

*Chiles Rellenos* is a popular Mexican dish, adopted by Southwestern cooks, who love the versatility of it. Many of the fancy Southwestern restaurants around the country claim a version of *Chiles Rellenos* as their signature dish, stuffing the chillies with everything from lobster to goat cheese. In the Southwest, poblano peppers are used, but since they are not readily available outside the United States, this recipe uses grilled red peppers to spectacular results. This makes a great start to a Southwestern-style meal.

YIELD: 6 first-course or side-dish servings
Oven: 190°C/375°F/Gas 5

## INGREDIENTS:

6 red sweet peppers
2 garlic cloves
225 g/8 oz firm goat's cheese, at room temperature, crumbled
225 g/8 oz Monterey Jack cheese, grated, or substitute another mild cheese such as Gruyère or Havarti
1 large shallot, finely chopped
1 fresh or canned jalapeño pepper or other fresh hot green chilli, finely chopped
4 oil-preserved sun-dried tomato halves, finely chopped

12 g/scant ½ oz [¼ cup] each of fresh coriander leaves [US cilantro] and fresh basil leaves, finely chopped
Salt and freshly ground pepper
1 size-1 egg [US jumbo egg]
2 tablespoons double cream [US heavy cream]
Cornmeal for dredging
Vegetable oil for deep-frying
Double quantity coriander salsa (see Navajo Tacos, page 152)
1 ripe avocado, sliced and dipped in lemon juice
Sour cream and fresh coriander sprigs [US cilantro], to garnish

## METHOD:

★ Roast and peel the peppers (see page 264). Carefully slit open on one side and remove seeds and veins. Reserve the peppers. (They can be prepared several days in advance.)

★ Preheat the oven. Blanch the garlic cloves in boiling water for 5 minutes. Drain and chop them finely.

★ In a medium-size bowl, mix the garlic with the cheeses, shallot, jalapeño, sun-dried tomatoes, coriander and basil. Taste and add salt and pepper as required. Divide this mixture into 6 equal portions and press each one into a small roll.

★ Dry the red peppers on paper towels. Put a roll of cheese mixture at the end of each pepper and roll it up in the pepper to conceal it totally. Beat the egg and cream together. Dip each stuffed pepper into this mixture and then dredge well in the cornmeal.

★ Heat about 5 cm/2 inches of vegetable oil in a deep pan until very hot but not smoking. Fry the stuffed peppers until they are golden brown. Drain on paper towels and keep warm in the oven until all are fried.

★ Serve each stuffed pepper with a portion of salsa and a few slices of avocado. Top with a dollop of sour cream and a sprig of coriander.

# Grilled Chilli-Marinated Pork Tenderloin with Corn and Black Bean Salsa

One trip to the Southwestern United States, where the influence of Indian, Spanish, Mexican and Anglo American cuisine is all at work, and you will be hooked on their earthy, sun-drenched food. In the Southwest, there are numerous varieties of chillies that deliver all levels of spicy heat. This recipe captures some of the wonderful nuances of the regional cuisine, using readily available chillies.

YIELD: 4-6 SERVINGS

Equipment: a barbecue or cast iron ridged grill pan and a food processor

INGREDIENTS:

6 pork fillets or tenderloins, weighing 225–450 g/ ½-1 lbs each

FOR THE MARINADE:

½ teaspoon coriander seeds
½ teaspoon cumin seeds
125 ml/4 fl oz [½ cup] vegetable oil
1 large onion, chopped
5 large garlic cloves, finely chopped
1 teaspoon dried hot red pepper flakes (see note), or 30 g/1 oz milder New Mexican dried chilli, in small pieces
450 g/1 lb fresh plum tomatoes, chopped
1 large bunch fresh coriander [US cilantro], about 50 g/1 ¾ oz, stalks removed, coarsely chopped
¼ teaspoon each ground cinnamon and cloves
500 ml/16 fl oz [2 cups] freshly squeezed orange juice
4 tablespoons olive oil
3 tablespoons each maple syrup and red wine vinegar

FOR THE SALSA:

80 ml/2 ¾ fl oz [⅓ cup] olive oil
1 shallot, finely chopped (2 tablespoons)
3-4 garlic cloves, finely chopped (2 tablespoons)
Kernels from 2 ears of fresh sweetcorn, or 453 g/1 lb [2 cups] frozen sweetcorn kernels
1 red and 1 yellow sweet pepper, finely diced
1 teaspoon chopped jalapeño peppers, fresh or canned, or use any other fresh hot green chilli
½ teaspoon salt
Freshly ground pepper to taste
¼ teaspoon ground coriander
1 tablespoon tequila
1 tablespoon Grand Marnier or other orange liqueur
1 ½ teaspoons freshly squeezed lime juice
1 ½ teaspoons raspberry vinegar
1 tablespoon white wine vinegar
1 tablespoon frozen orange juice concentrate
170 g/6 oz [1 cup] dried black turtle or black kidney beans, soaked overnight and cooked in salted water until tender, or substitute 1 can (425 g/15 oz) black beans, drained
12–25 g/scant ½–¾ oz [¼–½ cup] mixed fresh herbs, such as coriander [US cilantro], marjoram and parsley, or basil, thyme, marjoram and parsley, chopped

METHOD:

★ First make the marinade. Toast the coriander and cumin seeds in a small heavy frying pan until they become aromatic, stirring often. Reserve. Heat half the oil in a large frying pan over moderate heat and add the onion and garlic. Sauté until the onion is tender, then add the reserved cumin and coriander seeds, the hot pepper flakes, tomatoes, fresh coriander, cinnamon and cloves. Sauté for about 5 minutes, stirring frequently. Stir in the orange juice and bring to the boil. Simmer for about 20 minutes or until the sauce has reduced to about 500 ml/16 fl oz [2 cups], stirring frequently. Allow to cool slightly, then transfer the mixture to a food processor. Add the rest of the vegetable oil, the olive oil, maple syrup and vinegar. Process until smooth. Refrigerate if not using immediately.

★ Arrange the pork fillets in a shallow dish, in one layer, and pour over half the marinade; reserve the other half to serve as a sauce. Leave the pork to marinate in the refrigerator for at least 1 day and as much as 2 days, turning often. One hour before you are ready to grill, remove the pork from the refrigerator to allow the meat to come to room temperature.

★ If using a barbecue, prepare and light the charcoal fire in good time; you need a medium hot fire (see page 212 for instructions). A grill pan will need about 10 minutes' preheating.

★ To make the salsa, heat the olive oil in a large frying pan or skillet and sauté the shallots, garlic, sweetcorn, red and yellow peppers and jalapeños for about 5 minutes. Season with salt, pepper and coriander. Remove from the heat and add the rest of the salsa ingredients, except for the fresh herbs. Stir in the herbs just before serving. (The salsa can be prepared in advance and refrigerated. Warm slightly for serving and then add the fresh herbs. This is also good cold.)

★ Scrape the marinade off the pork fillets and reserve it for basting. Salt and pepper the pork well and barbecue grill or cook on a hot grill pan for 15–25 minutes, turning to brown all sides. Baste with the marinade from time to time. Warm the reserved marinade to serve as a sauce with the pork.

★ Cut the pork across, at an angle, into 2.5 cm/1 inch pieces and serve 2-3 slices overlapping on each plate. Garnish with sauce and fresh coriander. Serve with the salsa and warm corn tortillas.

NOTE: Small dried hot red chilli peppers are available at Chinese food shops. To substitute them for dried hot red pepper flakes (which are sold in bottles), remove the stalks and roughly chop the chillies, with the seeds.

# Fresh Fruit and Tequila Dip

This light, refreshing and easy dessert is wonderful after a spicy Mexican meal, either as a dip or poured over fresh fruit.

YIELD: about 500 ml/16 fl oz [2 cups]

INGREDIENTS:
500 ml/16 fl oz [2 cups] sour cream
4 tablespoons honey
3 tablespoons ground almonds
3 tablespoons finest-quality tequila
2 teaspoons finely grated lime rind
2 teaspoons freshly squeezed lime juice

2 teaspoons finely grated orange rind
4 teaspoons freshly squeezed orange juice
¼ teaspoon ground cinnamon
Assorted fresh fruits, such as pineapple, pears, tangerines, grapes and melon, cut into small slices or pieces for dipping

METHOD:
★ Combine all of the ingredients, except for the fruit, in a small bowl and mix well. Cover and refrigerate for at least 1 hour before serving.
★ Offer guests a variety of sliced fruits to dip into the mixture.

# Killer Margaritas

While in Mexico tequila is more often drunk straight with salt and lime on the side, Americans love the margarita cocktail, in a salt-rimmed glass or by the pitcher. These are 'killers' offering a powerful punch, the ultimate refresher on a hot summer day.

YIELD: 4-6 LARGE COCKTAILS
Equipment: an ice crusher or blender and 4-6 over-size balloon-type red wine glasses. An automatic juicer is also very handy.

INGREDIENTS:
375 ml/12 fl oz [1 ½ cups] freshly squeezed lime juice
Salt
500 ml/16 fl oz [2 cups] freshly squeezed orange juice
4 tablespoons caster sugar [US granulated sugar]

300 ml/ ½ pint [1 ¼ cups] Cointreau or Grand Marnier
300 ml/ ½ pint [1 ¼ cups] tequila, preferably Cuervo Gold
Crushed ice

METHOD:
★ First prepare the glasses: put a little lime juice in a small saucer and a good quantity of salt in another. Dip the rims of the glasses into the lime juice and then into the salt. Reserve.
★ Combine the juices, sugar and alcohol in a pitcher and refrigerate until serving time.
★ Crush enough ice to partially fill all the glasses. Pour the Margarita mixture over the ice, without disturbing the salt-crusted rim.

# CALIFORNIA

To include California among the traditional American regions speaks of the influence it has had on American cuisine and American culture in general. The state of California is America at its most brash, imaginative and free-wheeling, open and responsive to ethnic influences whether they be Thai, Japanese or Mexican. Former United States president Jimmy Carter once said, "Whatever starts in California unfortunately has an inclination to spread." Although he wasn't referring to culinary trends, he could well have been. California has given America some of its most exciting food, in a style that is light and healthy.

California was named by early explorers for a land "very near to terrestrial paradise". People have flocked there ever since: colonisation by the Spanish, Mexican, and Mexican Indians has been followed since the gold rush by the enthusiastic influx of nationalities as disparate as the French, German, English, Italian, Chinese and Japanese.

Much of California's climate is like that of the Mediterranean coast of Europe. Grilling, whether inside or outside, is the most important mode of cooking, and vinaigrettes and marinades are substituted for sauces. Oriental ingredients and techniques abound and the abundant local fruits and vegetables are always the centrepiece. The state contributes wines so good they can compete with European vintages, and restaurants here set the standards and ideas for restaurants across the United States. Like Mediterranean food, Californian cuisine is olive oil based, and resplendent with raisins, dates, pistachios, artichokes, olives, grapes and figs. The idea is to eat cool to stay cool, and the cuisine supports a health and fitness conscious population that cannot get enough salads, pasta, pizza or stir-fry.

Today, the restaurants in Los Angeles and San Francisco are often cross-cultural and non-traditional and offer some of the most trend-setting of all the regional cooking in the United States. In the 1970s French-trained, Japanese-American chefs began fusing Eastern and Western ingredients and cooking techniques to create a style that was totally new. Californian cooking is bold and fresh, full of fruits and vegetables, with Oriental spices and ingredients combined with those of Spain and Mexico. Traditional foods, in so far as there are any in California, are Cioppino, Sourdough bread, Cobb Salad and perhaps the date shakes that have fortified the muscle men on the beaches of this sunny state for years.

In California one lives a bit precariously, under the threat of earthquakes, fires and mudslides that seem to be trying to pitch the whole state into the ocean. Yet Californians seem undaunted and are proud of their beautiful state: flanked by an ocean on one side and by mountain ranges and deserts on the other; supporting lifestyles which range from the glamour of Hollywood to the easy-going casualness of the beach. How does one describe a state that gave us the McDonald's drive-in of the 1950s, the flower children in the 1960s, and the natural food movement in the 1980s? If we are to describe it we must not forget Californian cuisine. This is a cooking style light and healthy enough to propel America full-force into the 1990s and beyond.

# Grilled Teriyaki Chicken Breasts

Japanese immigrants brought teriyaki sauce to the United States – Americans fell in love with it and put it on everything from steak to chicken in the 1970s and 1980s. But it is too good to be a mere novelty, and has stayed in the American repertoire as a wonderful sauce for grilled foods and, to my mind, the best marinade for grilling chicken.

YIELD: 4 SERVINGS
Equipment: a barbecue or cast iron ridged grill pan
Oven: 180°C/350°F/Gas 4

INGREDIENTS:

2 spring onions [US scallions], including the green tops, finely chopped
1 tablespoon finely chopped fresh coriander [US cilantro]
1 garlic clove, finely chopped
1 teaspoon finely chopped fresh ginger
4 tablespoons soy sauce
4 tablespoons medium-dry or medium-sweet sherry

55 g/2 oz [¼ cup] sugar
1 teaspoon rice wine vinegar
1 tablespoon sesame oil
1 teaspoon molasses or dark treacle
Freshly ground pepper to taste
4 chicken breasts [US chicken breast halves], with skin and bones

METHOD:

★ Combine the spring onions, coriander, garlic and ginger in a small bowl and add the soy sauce, sherry, sugar, vinegar, oil, molasses and pepper. Whisk well to blend. Arrange the chicken breasts in a non-reactive container and pour over the soy sauce mixture. Cover and leave to marinate in the refrigerator for 4-8 hours or overnight.

★ Bring the chicken to room temperature before cooking. If using a barbecue, prepare and light the charcoal fire in good time; you want a medium hot fire (see page 212 for instructions). A grill pan will need about 10 minutes' preheating. Preheat the oven.

★ Remove the chicken breasts from the teriyaki sauce (reserve it!) and barbecue grill them, or cook on a hot grill pan, for 3-5 minutes on each side or until nicely browned. Remove the chicken breasts to a baking dish and pour over the reserved teriyaki sauce. Finish cooking the chicken breasts in the preheated oven, allowing 20-30 minutes depending on size. Baste the breasts with the sauce frequently. Teriyaki chicken is great served with Asian-style Spicy Cold Noodles (page 166).

NOTE: Teriyaki sauce can be used to marinate steak, fish or any other cut of chicken or other poultry.

# Green Goddess Dressing

The Palace Hotel Restaurant in San Francisco, especially during its heyday in the 1920s, invented many glamorous dishes that other restaurants copied and which then became prominent in American cookbooks. One of these was Green Goddess dressing, named for a famous play of the same name, starring the British actor, George Arliss. I include this classic because it is especially good with some of the specialities of California: artichokes, avocados and pasta salads. It holds a firm place in this region's cuisine and fits as easily into modern cooking as it did in the '20s. Use the dressing for salad greens, pasta salads, avocados or as a dipping sauce for boiled and chilled artichokes.

YIELD: about 250 ml/8 fl oz [1 cup]

INGREDIENTS:
Yolk from a size-1 egg [US jumbo egg]
2 teaspoons Dijon mustard
2–3 tablespoons tarragon white wine vinegar
185 ml/6 fl oz [¾ cup] fruity olive oil

4 canned anchovy fillets, drained and soaked in milk for 5-10 minutes
1 garlic clove, finely chopped
Salt and freshly ground pepper
2 tablespoons each chopped fresh parsley and chives
1 tablespoon chopped fresh tarragon

METHOD:
★ For successful mayonnaise, all ingredients must be at room temperature! In a small bowl whisk together the egg yolk, mustard and 1 tablespoon of the vinegar. Add the oil slowly in a stream, whisking continuously, until the sauce emulsifies and is thick and smooth.
★ With a mortar and pestle, make a paste of the anchovies and garlic with a pinch of salt. Add this to the mayonnaise with the chopped herbs and fold together. Taste and adjust the seasonings. Add the remaining tarragon vinegar to taste.

# San Francisco Cioppino

Cioppino is the most famous dish from a city well-known for its fine food. This soup, which originated in a restaurant on Fisherman's Wharf, is enough for a main course.

### YIELD: 6-8 SERVINGS

INGREDIENTS:

2 tablespoons olive oil

30 g/1 oz [2 tablespoons] butter

510 g/1 lb 2 oz [3 cups] onions, chopped

2 leeks, most of the green end trimmed off, finely chopped

2-4 garlic cloves, finely chopped

2 green sweet peppers, cut into thin strips

640 g/1 lb 7 oz [4 cups] tomatoes, skin and seeds removed, chopped

250 ml/8 fl oz [1 cup] tomato essence (page 264), or use fresh or bottled tomato-based pasta sauce [US canned tomato sauce]

1 bay leaf

1 tablespoon chopped fresh oregano or 1 teaspoon dried oregano

1 tablespoon chopped fresh thyme or 1 teaspoon dried thyme

3 tablespoons chopped fresh basil or 1 tablespoon dried basil

Dried hot red pepper flakes to taste

Salt and freshly ground pepper to taste

875 ml/scant 1 ½ pints [3 ½ cups] fish stock, preferably home-made

375 ml/12 fl oz [1 ½ cups] dry white wine

Juice of ½ lemon

450 g/1 lb boneless firm-fleshed fish, such as monkfish, turbot, bass etc.

225 g/8 oz shelled scallops [US sea scallops]

450 g/1 lb raw king or tiger prawns [US large shrimp], peeled and deveined

225 g/8 oz lobster tail in the shell (optional)

1 crab (optional)

1 dozen small clams in their shells, well washed, or substitute frozen cockles

4–6 [¼ cup] freshly shelled oysters with their liquor

METHOD:

★ Heat the oil and butter in a large flameproof casserole or saucepan and add the onions, leeks and garlic. Cook, stirring often, until lightly browned. Add the green peppers and cook just until wilted. Add the tomatoes, tomato essence, herbs and about ¼ teaspoon red pepper flakes. Season with salt and pepper. Add 500 ml/16 fl oz [2 cups] of the fish stock and bring to the boil. Leave to cook gently for about 2 hours, partially covered. Add the rest of the stock, the wine and lemon juice and continue cooking for about 10 minutes. (The soup can be made in advance up to this point.)

★ Prepare the fish and seafood well in advance and refrigerate it until use. Cut the white fish into 2.5 cm/1 inch pieces. Halve the scallops if they are large. Cut the prawns in half lengthways or butterfly them (cut open down the centre, leaving the two halves attached). The lobster and/or crab can be steamed over the soup's broth during the initial cooking process. Simply lay them on top and cook until their shells are bright red and their meat is opaque. When cooled, remove the shell and cut or flake the meat into bite-sized pieces. Clams can be steamed open in the same way as the lobster and crab, or as explained in the note opposite. Remove the empty top shells, leaving the clams in the bottom shells.

★ About 20 minutes before serving, return the soup to the boil and add the firm-fleshed fish. Cook for about 5 minutes, then add the scallops and the prawns. Simmer for another 5 minutes and then add the rest of the seafood, including the oyster liquor. Cook gently just until hot. Serve in large bowls, with sourdough bread and a green salad.

NOTE: Before cooking clams, discard any open ones. Sauté 1 finely chopped shallot in 15 g/ ½ oz [1 tablespoon] butter for a few minutes. Add 250 ml/8 fl oz [1 cup] dry white wine and bring to the boil. Add the clams and cover the pan. Cook for 3–5 minutes, shaking the pan from time to time, then check to see if the shells have opened. If most are open, remove them with a slotted spoon and continue cooking the others. If they still won't open, discard them. Strain the cooking liquid and add to the soup.

# Chinese Chicken Salad with Parmesan Pitta Toasts

This dish displays the diversity of California, where cultures mix and contribute different ingredients and flavours to the cooking. This wonderful spicy main dish salad is addictive and variations of it appear on menus everywhere. If you have children who don't like spicy foods, make extra chicken and serve it to them with french fries, so that you can have more of the salad yourself. Although this may involve some advance preparation and a trip to your local Chinese food shop, you will be very glad you made the effort.

YIELD: 6-8 SERVINGS
Oven: 200°C/400°F/Gas 6

INGREDIENTS:
55 g/2 oz transparent noodles (also known as beanthread or cellophane noodles), or use rice sticks or rice vermicelli
1 iceberg lettuce or 2 Cos or romaine lettuces, finely shredded
2 bunches spring onions [US scallions], thinly sliced
1 large bunch fresh coriander [US cilantro], stalks removed, chopped*
85–170 g/3–6 oz [½ –1 cup] roasted and salted cashews, chopped

FOR THE SESAME CHICKEN BREASTS:
6 chicken breasts [US chicken breast halves], skinned and boned
80 ml/2 ¾ fl oz [⅓ cup] plus 4 teaspoons soy sauce
2 garlic cloves, crushed
1 tablespoon sugar
2 tablespoons sherry or rice wine
3 tablespoons hoisin sauce*
Yolks from 4 size-1 eggs [US jumbo eggs]

Approximately 250 g/9 oz [2 cups] or more sesame seeds
115 g/4 oz [1 cup] rice flour*
Vegetable oil for deep frying

FOR THE DRESSING:
125 ml/4 fl oz [½ cup] sesame oil (Use the Chinese-type toasted sesame oil.)*
125 ml/4 fl oz [½ cup] white wine vinegar
4 tablespoons soy sauce
5 tablespoons honey
1 ½ teaspoons dried hot red pepper flakes
4 garlic cloves, finely chopped
2 spring onions [US scallions], including green tops, finely chopped

FOR THE PARMESAN PITTA TOASTS:
6-8 large pitta breads
Butter
100 g/3 ½ oz [1 cup] freshly grated Parmesan cheese
* These ingredients are available at Chinese food shops.

METHOD:
★ The day before, begin the preparation of the chicken. Mix together the 80 ml/2 ¾ fl oz [⅓ cup] soy sauce, the garlic, sugar, sherry and hoisin sauce in a shallow dish. Add the chicken breasts, cover well and leave to marinate overnight in the refrigerator.
★ The next day, prepare to cook the chicken (or you can do this the day before). Have ready three bowls for the coating ingredients. In one bowl, whisk the egg yolks with the remaining soy sauce (1 teaspoon sauce for each egg yolk). In another, put the sesame seeds and in the third, the rice flour. Remove the chicken breasts from the marinade and slice them in half horizontally, so that they are quite thin 'sheets' and will cook more quickly. Dip each piece of chicken into the egg, then into the sesame seeds and finally into the rice flour. You may coat all the chicken in this way before beginning to fry.

★ Heat vegetable oil in a wok or deep-fryer until it just begins to smoke and shimmer. While the oil is still clean, deep-fry the transparent noodles for the garnish: add the noodles by the handful and fry until puffed up and opaque. Do not allow the noodles to brown. With a large slotted spoon or strainer, remove the noodles quickly from the hot oil and drain on paper towels. Then deep fry the chicken, a few pieces at a time, until crisp and deep brown in colour. Drain well on paper towels. Leave to cool and then refrigerate until ready to use.

★ Whisk together the dressing ingredients and reserve.

★ To make the Parmesan pitta toasts, preheat the oven. Split the pita bread in half (cutting around the pitta with kitchen scissors works well). Butter on the rough inside part and sprinkle with freshly grated Parmesan cheese. Lay on a baking sheet and bake in the preheated oven until lightly browned. Serve warm. (If you have any left over these can be broken up and used as croûtons for salads.)

★ When you are ready to assemble the salad, put the lettuce, spring onions and chopped coriander in the salad bowl. Cut the chicken into thin strips and add to the bowl with the cashews. Toss together with enough dressing to coat but not float in the bottom (you may have a little dressing left over). Finally, garnish with the fried noodles and serve with the Parmesan pitta toasts. This salad is great with Chinese beer.

OVERLEAF: *Chinese Chicken Salad with Parmesan Pitta Toasts*
BELOW: *San Francisco's Chinatown, home to a lively cooking tradition*

# Asian-Style Spicy Cold Noodles

Some of the most fashionable new cooking in America is pan-cultural, so don't be surprised to find restaurants in California and New York offering Italian-Vietnamese or Thai-Southwestern cuisine, to name only a few of the combinations being made today. This recipe is so popular that a variation of it appears in almost every modern American cookbook. A stunning example of a mixture of cultures, this Italian pasta with a sauce concocted of Asian ingredients is great with any grilled meat, poultry or fish.

YIELD: 6-8 SERVINGS
Equipment: a food processor

INGREDIENTS:

450 g/1 lb spaghetti or other thin pasta
125 ml/4 fl oz [½ cup] sesame oil (Use the Chinese-style toasted sesame oil.)
7 spring onions [US scallions]
35 g/1 ¼ oz (4 slices) peeled fresh ginger
75 g/2 ½ oz [⅓ cup] smooth peanut butter
4 tablespoons soy sauce
4 tablespoons rice wine vinegar
4 tablespoons honey
4 tablespoons freshly squeezed lime juice

2 tablespoons mirin (sweet cooking rice wine) or sherry
Grated rind of 2 limes
2 teaspoons dried hot red pepper flakes
½ teaspoon salt
4 tablespoons vegetable oil
4 carrots
1 cucumber [US seedless cucumber]
4 tablespoons chopped fresh mint
80 g/scant 3 oz [½ cup] dry-roasted peanuts, chopped
Fresh mint sprigs, to garnish

METHOD:

★ Cook the pasta in a large pan of boiling salted water until *al dente*. Drain in a colander, then turn into a bowl and toss with 2 tablespoons of the sesame oil. Reserve while you prepare the sauce.

★ Use a food processor fitted with a steel blade. Drop in 4 of the spring onions and the ginger while the machine is running and process until finely chopped. Add the peanut butter, soy sauce, rice vinegar, honey, lime juice, mirin, lime rind, pepper flakes and salt and process until smooth. Add the vegetable oil and the remaining sesame oil through the feed tube in a stream, while the machine is running, and process until smooth. Reserve this sauce.

★ Cut the carrots into long strips, as finely as possible. Use a mandoline if you have one. Cut the cucumber in half lengthways and remove all the seeds with a teaspoon. Cut across into slices, sprinkle with salt and leave to "sweat" in a colander for about 20 minutes; rinse, drain and pat dry with paper towels. Chop the remaining spring onions finely.

★ To assemble the salad, toss the pasta with enough of the sauce to coat the strands, but not so much that it pools at the bottom of the bowl. Add the carrots and chopped spring onions and toss again. Turn into a serving bowl and sprinkle the cucumber, mint and peanuts over the top. Refrigerate until serving. Garnish with sprigs of fresh mint.

# REGIONAL SIDE DISHES

# Savoury Wild Rice Waffles

These are more wild rice than waffle and make an unusual accompaniment to stews and ragouts of game, veal or beef. Once you've tasted them, you may also crave them for breakfast doused in maple syrup.

YIELD: 8 WAFFLES
Equipment: a waffle iron and an electric mixer or whisk

INGREDIENTS:

165 g/5 ½ oz [1 cup] wild rice
750 ml/1 ¼ pints [3 cups] water
Salt
55 g/2 oz [4 tablespoons] butter
1 shallot, finely chopped
115 g/4 oz [1 cup] sponge or plain flour [US all-purpose flour]

1 teaspoon baking powder
2 size-1 eggs [US jumbo eggs], separated
180 ml/6 fl oz [¾ cup] sour cream
125 ml/4 fl oz [½ cup] milk
¼ teaspoon freshly grated nutmeg

METHOD:

★ Rinse the wild rice thoroughly and cook in the water with 1 teaspoon salt for about 30-40 minutes or until almost all of the kernels have popped open. Drain in a sieve and reserve. (The rice can be cooked well in advance and refrigerated or frozen for later use.)

★ Melt the butter in a small frying pan and add the shallot. Sauté until the shallot is softened. If you have cooked the rice in advance, add it to the pan to warm it before folding it into the batter.

★ Sift the flour, baking powder and ¼ teaspoon salt into a medium-size bowl. In another bowl, beat the egg yolks until they are lemon-coloured, then whisk in the sour cream, milk and nutmeg. Add to the dry ingredients and whisk just to combine. Fold in the wild rice and butter and shallot. Whisk the egg whites with a pinch of salt until they have formed stiff, glossy peaks. Fold into the batter.

★ Preheat a waffle iron. Add a large spoonful of batter and spread it thin with a spatula, so that there is only one layer of rice. Cook the waffle until it is brown and crispy—it should be thin. Serve hot. These are especially good with Pheasant Stroganoff (page 144) or with maple syrup for breakfast!

NOTE: You can prepare the waffles ahead of time and reheat on a buttered baking sheet in a 180°C/350°F/Gas 4 oven for about 5 minutes.

# Hashed Brown Potato Cake

Hashed brown potatoes are legendary in the United States and elicit visions of the short order cook behind a grill flipping the crunchy, shredded potatoes before your eyes. I prefer to serve guests an elegant wedge from a large, dramatic cake of such potatoes and have come up with this cake to accompany stews and ragouts.

YIELD: 4-6 SERVINGS
Equipment: a food processor or grater

INGREDIENTS:

675 g/1 ½ lbs boiling potatoes (unpeeled)
1 medium-size onion or 8 spring onions [US scallions],
   finely chopped
2 garlic cloves, finely chopped
Salt and freshly ground pepper to taste
5-6 tablespoons virgin olive oil
75–90 g/2 ½–3 oz [5-6 tablespoons] butter

OPTIONAL ADDITIONS:

Finely chopped smoked ham or bacon
Chopped fresh herbs
Grated cheese

METHOD:

★ Put the potatoes in a large pan, cover with cold water and bring to the boil over high heat. When the water boils, reduce the heat to moderate and simmer the potatoes, uncovered, for about 10 minutes. Drain them in a colander and leave them to cool. Refrigerate them until you are ready to use them – they can be prepared well in advance.

★ When you are ready to make the potato cake, peel the potatoes and grate them coarsely, either in a food processor or with a hand grater. In a large bowl, toss them with the onion, garlic and some salt and pepper, plus any optional ingredients you care to include.

★ Heat 3 tablespoons of the oil with 45 g/1 ½ oz [3 tablespoons] of the butter in a large frying pan (30 cm/12 inches is ideal). When the fat is quite hot, add the potato mixture. Spread it out evenly in the pan and press down with a spatula. Cook for 8-10 minutes or until the base of the cake is brown and crisp. Flip the cake on to a rimless platter or baking sheet, base up. Add more butter and olive oil to the frying pan and heat it, then slide the potato cake back into the pan and brown the other side for 8-10 minutes.

★ Turn the potato cake on to a serving plate. Or you can turn it on to a heatproof platter and keep it warm in a 170°C/325°F/Gas 3 oven until you are ready to serve it. For serving, cut it into wedges.

# Baked Curried Fruit

This is a fruit mixture that is the perfect accompaniment to pork.

YIELD: 6-8 SERVINGS
Oven: 170°C/325°F/Gas 3 and then 180°C/350°F/Gas 4

INGREDIENTS:

3 pears, peeled, halved and cored, or 1 can (400g/14 oz)
   pear halves
3 peaches and 6 apricots, peeled, halved and stoned, or
   1 can (400 g/14 oz) each of peach and apricot halves
½ fresh pineapple, cut into bite-size pieces, or 1 can
   (400 g/14 oz) pineapple chunks

8-10 maraschino cherries, drained, or 1 small bunch fresh
   red grapes, halved and seeded if necessary
55 g/2 oz [4 tablespoons] butter
75 g/2 ½ oz [⅓ cup firmly packed] light soft brown sugar
1 tablespoon garam masala or mild or medium hot curry
   powder

METHOD:

★ The day before serving, drain any canned fruit you are using in a colander and then on paper
towels. Arrange all the fruit attractively, canned or fresh, in a shallow casserole or ceramic or
china flan or quiche dish, putting the cherries or grapes on top for colour.
★ Preheat the oven to the lower temperature.
★ In a small saucepan, melt the butter with the brown sugar and spices. When the mixture is hot
and liquid, pour it over the fruit. Bake the fruit, uncovered, in the preheated oven for 1 hour.
Leave to cool, then refrigerate, well covered, until 30 minutes before you plan to eat the fruit.
★ Preheat the oven to the higher temperature.
★ Bake the fruit again for 30 minutes. Serve it hot from the casserole, with any pork, chicken or
pheasant dish.

# Navajo Fry Bread

A mainstay of the Navajo diet, the origins of this bread can be traced back directly to the Spanish, who introduced wheat to the Southwest. Fry bread is a popular snack at fairs and Indian gatherings, served hot and crispy and slathered with honey or with chili or stew.

YIELD: 4 bread rounds, each 20 cm/8 inches diameter

INGREDIENTS:
240 g/8 ½ oz [2 cups] strong plain flour [US bread flour]
60 g/2 oz [½ cup] non-dairy creamer, such as Coffee-mate
1 teaspoon salt

2 teaspoons baking powder
30 g/1 oz [2 tablespoons] lard or white vegetable fat [US shortening], plus more for deep frying
125 ml/4 fl oz [½ cup] iced water

METHOD:
★ Combine the dry ingredients in a medium-size bowl. Rub in the lard or vegetable fat with your fingers until the mixture resembles a coarse meal. Add the iced water and stir with a wooden spoon until the dough forms a ball. Cover loosely with a towel and leave the dough to rest for a few hours at room temperature.
★ After the resting period and shortly before you plan to serve the bread, divide the dough into four equal portions. Roll out each piece on a lightly floured surface into a 20 cm/8 inch round. In the middle of each round, cut two 2.5 cm/1 inch slits about 2.5 cm/1 inch apart.
★ Melt and heat enough lard or vegetable fat in a large frying pan (23 cm/9 inches or larger) to be at least 2.5 cm/1 inch in depth. When the fat is very hot but not smoking add the bread rounds, one at a time, and fry for about 1 minute on each side or until crisp and brown. Turn with tongs or a large spatula. Drain the bread on paper towels and serve at once.

# Garlic Bread

America is crazy about garlic bread and serves it with everything Italian or barbecued.

YIELD: 6–8 SERVINGS
Oven: 200°C/400°F/Gas 6

INGREDIENTS:
170 g/6 oz [¾ cup] butter, at room temperature
2 tablespoons finely chopped fresh parsley
1 tablespoon finely chopped fresh chives

1 tablespoon freshly squeezed lemon juice
2-3 large garlic cloves, finely chopped
Salt and freshly ground pepper to taste
A large baguette, Italian loaf (ciabatta) or loaf of sourdough bread

METHOD:
★ Combine the butter, herbs, lemon juice, garlic and seasoning and mix well. Leave the mixture to stand, covered, at room temperature for at least 1 hour.
★ Preheat the oven.
★ Cut the bread into 2.5–4 cm/1-1½ inch thick slices, straight down or at an angle. Spread each slice on both sides with the butter mixture. Reassemble the loaf and wrap in foil. Bake in the preheated oven for 10-15 minutes. Open the top of the foil during the last few minutes, so that the top of the bread browns. Serve hot.

# Twice-Baked Potatoes

A very American side-dish with numerous possibilities for variation.

YIELD: 4-8 SERVINGS
Oven: 200°C/400°F/Gas 6

INGREDIENTS:

4 large baking potatoes, weighing about 450 g/1 lb each
80 ml/2 ¾ fl oz [⅓ cup] crème fraîche or sour cream
1 size-1 egg [US jumbo egg]
30 g/1 oz [2 tablespoons] butter, at room temperature
¼ teaspoon salt

Freshly ground pepper
2-3 spring onions [US scallions], finely chopped
120 g/4 oz [1 cup] mature (sharp) Cheddar cheese, grated
Paprika (optional)

METHOD:

★ Preheat the oven.

★ Bake the potatoes in the preheated oven for about 1 hour or until they are tender when pierced with a fork or knife. Depending on how large a serving you will want, either cut the tops off (for 4 servings) or cut the potatoes in half (8 servings) and scoop out most of the flesh, reserving the skins. Mash the potato flesh, or press it through a ricer, and then beat in the cream, egg, butter and seasonings. Fold in the onions and cheese, reserving some cheese to put on top of the potatoes. Spoon the potato mixture back into the skins. Top with reserved cheese and a sprinkling of paprika if you like.

★ Arrange the potatoes on a baking sheet and bake for 20 minutes. Or wrap in foil and bake on the barbecue over medium-hot coals.

# Southwestern Potatoes Au gratin

Au gratin potatoes, a cousin of the French *pommes de terre Dauphinoises*, are very popular in America. This version is spicy and lower in fat, which suits modern preferences perfectly.

YIELD: 4 GENEROUS SERVINGS
Equipment: a mandoline or sharp knife
Oven: 200°C/400°F/Gas 6

INGREDIENTS:
675 g/1 ½ lbs potatoes
1 garlic clove, finely chopped
125 ml/4 fl oz [½ cup] chicken stock, preferably home-made
125 ml/4 fl oz [½ cup] double cream [US heavy cream]
¼ teaspoon ground cumin

Salt and freshly ground pepper to taste
1 can (113 g/4 oz) chopped green chillies, drained
1 teaspoon finely chopped fresh or canned jalapeño peppers, or use any fresh hot green chilli
120 g/4 oz [1 cup] Monterey Jack or Gruyère cheese, grated

METHOD:
★ Preheat the oven. Generously butter a shallow gratin dish.
★ Peel the potatoes and slice them thinly (preferably using a mandoline). Put them immediately into cold water to prevent them from turning brown.
★ In a small saucepan, combine the garlic, stock, cream, cumin and salt and pepper and bring to the boil; reserve. Mix together the chopped green chillies and jalapeño.
★ Drain the potatoes well. Put a layer of potatoes in the bottom of the gratin dish and sprinkle over some of the chillies and cheese. Continue making layers, ending with potatoes and some cheese on top. Pour the cream and stock mixture over the potatoes.
★ Bake in the preheated oven for 30-45 minutes (a lot depends on how thin you are able to cut the potatoes). The potatoes should be tender when you insert a knife and well browned on top.

# Light-As-Air Buttermilk Biscuits

America's favourite bread throughout history and right into fast-food times has been the biscuit. The aroma of their baking make a house a home, their taste completes a breakfast or supper and their quality (or lack of it) have won or lost a cook her reputation. Serve these biscuits as a substitute for bread in any informal meal, or at breakfast or tea with butter, honey and fruit jams.

YIELD: 4-6 SERVINGS
Oven: 200°C/400°F/Gas 6

INGREDIENTS:
120 g/4 oz self-raising flour [US cooks see note below]
60 g/2 oz strong plain flour [see note]
1 ½ teaspoons baking powder
1 ½ teaspoons bicarbonate of soda [US baking soda]

½ teaspoon caster sugar [US granulated sugar]
85 g/3 oz [6 tablespoons] butter
185 ml/6 fl oz [¾ cup] buttermilk

METHOD:
★ Preheat the oven.
★ Sift the dry ingredients into a small bowl and cut or rub in the butter until the mixture resembles coarse meal. Add the buttermilk and stir in, just to blend. Transfer the dough to a lightly floured work surface and pat it into a 20 cm/8 inch round. (Alternatively, you can cut out small rounds, 5–7.5 cm/2-3 inches in diameter.)
★ Transfer the round to a lightly buttered baking sheet and mark into 8 wedges with a knife. Bake in the preheated oven for 15-20 minutes or until golden. Serve warm.

NOTE: US cooks should use 1½ cups all-purpose flour in place of the self-raising flour and strong plain flour.

# CHAPTER FOUR

# EATING ON THE MOVE

*The American Way with
Convenient Fast Food*

"Now here, you see, it takes all the running you can do, to keep in the same place. If you want to get somewhere else, you must run at least twice as fast as that!"
Lewis Carroll *Through the Looking Glass*

VISITORS TO THE UNITED STATES are often struck by the immense size of the country. Unfortunately, this is too often discovered after the whirlwind tour has been scheduled and the weary traveller is forced to jet from New York, to Texas, to the Grand Canyon, to San Francisco and back in one short week. From the beginning, this huge country has forged an adventurous people, always on the move, searching for more land, a better life, or gold, driving cattle, seeking to discover a new frontier. Americans were so prone to travel that the earliest bread, a kind of flat cornmeal bread similar to a pancake, was known as 'the journey cake'.

Since the beginning, Americans have been eating from chuck wagons on cattle drives and wagon trains going west. They had their 'free lunch' in the early saloons and barrooms of the 1800s, where the motto was "Gobble, gulp and go!". Later came the roadside diner where the food was designed to be comforting, accessible and as informal as the surroundings. The fast food industry boom coincided with the car buying boom and 'drive-in' restaurants popped up all over the country in the early 1950s, serving chicken, hot dogs, hamburgers, french fries, root beer, coke and malted milk shakes. Since then, Americans have eaten at the drugstore counter, the deli (or delicatessan), the fast food restaurant, the bistro and the grill. Of course, there are formal restaurants to be found, but to the visitor a lasting impression is sure to be the informality of the country and its eating establishments, where food is eaten with the hands and an open, expansive friendliness prevails.

Americans love their fast food restaurants and convenience foods because time seems to be in diminishing supply. For those of us who want great food in less time – American cooking is full of ideas for sandwiches, salads, breads, dips and grilling. These are the foods that keep pace with America!

# SANDWICHES

Sandwiches are a good example of a portable, easy to prepare, nutritious, well-balanced and versatile food that has kept up with the changes in American society and is still growing in popularity. America has many famous sandwiches, with names like 'The Reuben', 'Club', 'Hero' and 'BLT' (Bacon, Lettuce and Tomato). Of course, we must give credit to the very British Earl of Sandwich for starting it all and demanding that the first sandwich be made so that he could stay at the gambling table. Today, Americans want more than the old-style Peanut Butter and Jelly on white bread – restaurants and delis have popularised more adult sandwiches with interesting new breads, including tortillas, that are filled with a new style of ingredients; everything from grilled vegetables and sun-dried tomatoes to smoked duck and turkey.

PREVIOUS SPREAD: *Cowboys roping cattle by Charles M Russell*
OPPOSITE: *Cowboys eating at their chuckwagon*
BELOW: *Fast food lunch room in New York, 1888*

# A Great Hamburger

Without a doubt, the hamburger is the most famous American sandwich. A gift from our German immigrants, it was first served to the masses at the 1904 Louisiana Purchase Exposition in St. Louis, Missouri. If the hamburgers you have eaten have not impressed you, try making one at home, grilled or pan-fried, from the best quality meat you can find. Once you have eaten a truly great hamburger, you will discover what all the fuss is about and what has made it the most popular sandwich on earth.

YIELD: 4 hamburgers, weighing 170 g/6 oz each

Equipment: a barbecue or frying pan or skillet. You could also use an oven grill [US broiler], but this will not seal in the juices to produce a succulent, well-browned result. You'll need a food processor if mincing the beef yourself.

INGREDIENTS:

675 g/1 ½ lbs boneless beef (chuck or blade steak with 20% fat) or best minced steak [US ground round or sirloin]

3 tablespoons finely chopped spring onions [US scallions]

2 smoked streaky bacon rashers [US thick bacon slices], chopped and fried until almost crisp

3 tablespoons double cream [US heavy cream]

1 tablespoon Worcestershire sauce

12 g/scant ½ oz [¼ cup] fresh basil or parsley, or a combination of both, finely chopped

70 g/scant 2 ½ oz [½ cup] mature (sharp) Cheddar cheese, grated

Vegetable oil and butter if pan-frying

Salt and freshly ground pepper to taste

Hamburger buns, soft rolls, baps or brioche slices

Garnishes: slices of tomato, lettuce leaves, dill-pickled cucumbers, tomato ketchup, mustard, mayonnaise, guacamole (page 198), chutney etc.

METHOD:

★ Buy the best minced steak or purchase boneless beef and mince it roughly in your food processor. If the beef is excellent, simply form it loosely into hamburgers. But if you think it needs more flavour, combine it with the other ingredients, mixing lightly together with your fingertips. (Too much handling will make the hamburgers tough.) Do not season with salt until after the hamburgers have been seared in the cooking process (salt draws out the juices or blood in the meat). Divide into 4 portions and shape each loosely into a burger.

★ If using a barbecue, prepare and light the charcoal fire in good time; for hamburgers, you need a medium hot fire (see page 212 for instructions). Place the hamburgers 7.5–15 cm/3-6 inches above the fire. Cook for 4 minutes on each side for rare, 6 minutes per side for medium and 7–8 minutes for well done. The perfect hamburger has a crust on the outside and is juicy on the inside.

★ If you are pan-frying the hamburgers, heat a heavy frying pan or skillet over a high flame until very hot. Add a thin film of vegetable oil and a bit of butter, then sear the hamburgers on both sides to give them a crisp crust. Reduce the heat to moderate and continue to cook, uncovered, until done to your taste. Rare hamburgers will be very soft to the touch, medium will be springy and well done will be quite rigid with beads of juice on the surface. You will have to turn well-done hamburgers two or three times during the cooking process.

★ Season the hamburgers, put into buns and add garnishes to taste.

# Quesadillas
## THREE WAYS

In Spanish, quesadillas means 'a little something made of cheese', but recently restaurants such as The Coyote Cafe and Santacafe, in the South-western culinary haven of Sante Fe, New Mexico, have been producing spectacular quesadillas filled with much more than cheese. These make a lighter and more unusual sort of sandwich and will offer you some idea of the versatility of the flour tortilla, which has become a staple bread of the western U.S. Here are three different versions of the quesadillas.

YIELD: each filling is enough for 6 large tortillas. These can be cut into wedges for hors d'oeuvres, or eaten like a sandwich, serving perhaps 2 per person.
Equipment: a large frying pan or skillet
Oven (if using): 190°C/375°F/Gas 5

INGREDIENTS:
6 flour tortillas, about 25 cm/10 inches in diameter, for each filling (page 181)

FOR CRAB QUESADILLAS:
¼ onion, finely chopped
1 small garlic clove, finely chopped
1 tablespoon vegetable oil
1 jalapeño pepper, fresh or bottled, seeded and finely chopped
225 g/8 oz crab meat, freshly cooked or canned, drained
65 g/2 ½ oz [¼ cup] cream cheese or other full fat soft cheese, at room temperature
¼ teaspoon salt
1 tablespoon finely chopped fresh coriander [US cilantro]
175 g/6 oz [¾ cup] Monterey Jack or Gruyère cheese, coarsely grated

FOR CHORIZO QUESADILLAS:
350 g/12 oz (about 3) fully cooked chorizo sausages, diced
½ onion, chopped
1 garlic clove, finely chopped
1 tablespoon vegetable oil
1 jalapeño pepper, fresh or bottled, seeded and finely chopped
2–3 tablespoons canned chopped mild green chillies
2 teaspoons mild chilli powder
1 tablespoon finely chopped fresh coriander [US cilantro]
220 g/8 oz [1 cup] mature (sharp) Cheddar cheese, coarsely grated

FOR BRIE AND FRUIT QUESADILLAS:
¼ onion, thinly sliced
15 g/ ½ oz [1 tablespoon] butter
1 jalapeño pepper, fresh or bottled, seeded and finely chopped
1 ripe papaya or mango, peeled, seeded and diced
225 g/8 oz ripe Brie or Camembert cheese, cut into thin slices

METHOD:
★ To make the Crab Quesadillas filling, sauté the onion and garlic in the vegetable oil until soft but not browned. Turn into a small bowl and add the other ingredients. Mix well.
★ To make the Chorizo Quesadillas filling, sauté the chorizo, onion and garlic in the oil until the onion is soft and the chorizo has given up some of its fat. Drain off and discard all but about 1 tablespoon of the fat from the pan. Add the other ingredients, except for the cheese, and mix well. When the mixture has cooled, fold in the cheese.
★ To make the Brie and Fruit Quesadillas filling, sauté the onion in the butter until soft but not browned. Prepare the remaining filling ingredients and reserve.

★ Heat a frying pan or skillet. Lay a tortilla flat on the heated pan and soften for about 15 seconds. Turn the tortilla and add a thin layer of filling to the middle – do not fill to the edges. Fold the tortilla over into a half moon, remove and reserve on a baking sheet. Fill the remaining tortillas in the same way. The Brie and Fruit Quesadillas ingredients should be layered in the tortilla. (The quesadillas can be filled a day in advance and kept refrigerated. Finish them right before serving.)
★ If finishing the quesadillas in the oven, preheat it. Bake the quesadillas for about 5 minutes or until they are hot and golden brown. Alternatively, sauté them in equal parts of butter and oil for about 1 minute on each side or until golden brown. Serve them as they are or cut into wedges as finger food. You may want to offer salsa, sour cream or guacamole (page 198) as accompaniments.

NOTE: If jalapeños are not available, you can substitute any fresh hot green chillies. See appendices for guidelines on handling hot peppers.

# Flour Tortillas

Versatile and quick to prepare, flour tortillas are becoming the predominant bread to many parts of the U.S.. Use these to make Mexican-style Turkey Fajitas (Page 60) or Quesadillas (opposite).

YIELD: eight 23–25 cm/9–10 inch diameter tortillas

INGREDIENTS:
240 g/scant 9 oz [2 cups] strong plain flour [US all-purpose flour]
1 teaspoon salt
¾ teaspoon baking powder
65 g/2 ¼ oz white vegetable fat [US shortening]
125–180 ml/4–6 fl oz [½– ¾ cup] hot water

METHOD:
★ Sift the dry ingredients into a medium-size bowl. Add the vegetable fat and rub in with your fingertips until the mixture resembles a coarse meal. Add the smaller amount of water and stir to form a supple ball; if it is too dry and crumbly, add more water bit by bit. When you have a ball, knead it on a lightly floured surface for a few minutes.
★ Cover the dough with a damp cloth or put it into a plastic bag. Leave it to rest for at least 20 minutes.
★ Heat a large frying pan or skillet over moderately high heat until a drop of water sizzles on it and evaporates quickly.
★ Divide the dough into 8 equal parts. Roll each into a ball about the size of a golf ball.
★ Roll out one ball with a rolling pin into a circle about 23–25 cm/9–10 inches in diameter. Put it immediately on the hot pan and cook for about 30 seconds or until it starts to bubble. If it puffs up too dramatically, push it down with a palette knife [US metal spatula]. Turn and cook for 30 seconds on the other side. Remove and keep warm under a napkin. Roll out the rest of the tortillas, one at a time and cooking each one as soon as it is rolled out.

NOTE: The tortillas can be made in advance and reheated, wrapped in foil, in a 180°C/350°F/Gas 4 oven for 5–10 minutes.

# Grilled Chicken Club Sandwich

The Club Sandwich is a classic American restaurant speciality that has endured. This is a modern version that elevates the sandwich to new heights.

YIELD: 4 SANDWICHES
Equipment: a barbecue or cast iron ridged grill pan

INGREDIENTS:
4 chicken breasts [US chicken breast halves], skinned and boned
125 ml/4 fl oz [½ cup] guacamole (page 198)
4 smoked streaky bacon rashers [US thick bacon slices]
4 tablespoons mayonnaise
1 tablespoon whole-grain mustard
4 ciabatta rolls
4 tomato slices
A large handful rocket [US arugula] or watercress

FOR THE MARINATED PEPPERS:
4 medium-size sweet peppers, 2 red and 2 green
1 tablespoon balsamic vinegar
1 garlic clove, finely chopped
¼ teaspoon salt
80 ml/2 ¾ fl oz [⅓ cup] extra virgin olive oil

FOR THE CHICKEN MARINADE:
4 tablespoons freshly squeezed lemon juice
1 garlic clove, crushed
1 ½ teaspoons grated lemon rind
½ teaspoon each salt and freshly ground pepper
185 ml/6 fl oz [¾ cup] olive oil

METHOD:
★ The day before, prepare the marinated peppers. Roast and peel the peppers (see page 264). Mix together the remaining ingredients, add the peppers and leave to marinate overnight.
★ Split each chicken breast in half lengthways without cutting all the way through. Open up the halves like a book and pound lightly to make an even thickness throughout. Combine the ingredients for the chicken marinade, add the chicken and marinate for at least 4 hours or overnight.
★ On the day you plan to serve the sandwiches, prepare the guacamole; fry the bacon until crisp and mix the mayonnaise and mustard together in a small bowl. Cut the marinated peppers into thin strips. If using a barbecue, prepare and light the charcoal fire in good time; you need a medium hot fire (see page 212 for instructions). A grill pan needs about 10 minutes' preheating.
★ Barbecue grill the chicken breasts, or cook on a grill pan, for about 4 minutes on each side or until the juice runs clear when the meat is pierced with a skewer. Keep warm or cool to room temperature.
★ Cut each ciabatta roll in three horizontally and toast if desired. On the bottom of each roll spread mustard mayonnaise and add a chicken breast and a thin layer of rocket or watercress. Put on the middle bread layer and spread with guacamole. Top with bacon, a tomato slice and some marinated peppers. Put on the top of the roll and use cocktail sticks to hold the sandwich together.

# The Hero Sandwich

This famous American sandwich has numerous variations and almost as many names, such as, 'submarine', 'grinder', 'hoagie', and 'poor boy' to name only a few. There are regional variations, as in the Muffuletta of New Orleans and there are ethnic variations, as in an Italian or French-style Hero. You can be like Dagwood of cartoon fame and create your own Hero from the contents of your refrigerator or use the guidelines that follow.

★ Choose a crusty loaf or roll and slice it in half lengthways. You can make individual Heroes on rolls or a dramatic long sandwich on a loaf to be cut into serving pieces. If you are having a large party you could ask a local bakery to make you an oversize loaf so you can create a table-size Hero that will serve all of your guests!

★ Prepare an oil and vinegar dressing using 1 part vinegar, 1 part freshly grated Parmesan cheese and 3 parts olive or vegetable oil. Pour a thin layer of this on to both cut surfaces of the roll or loaf you have chosen.

★ Layer any of the following combinations *generously* inside the roll or loaf:

**Italian Hero:** tomato, shredded lettuce, mayonnaise, Parma ham or other prosciutto, salami, mortadella, fontina and provolone cheeses, Italian peppers (bottled pickled hot and medium hot peppers) and olives (omit or add as you like).

**French Hero:** use a French baguette and fill with sliced chicken, Bayonne ham or prosciutto cut into julienne (very fine strips), mayonnaise, cornichons, lettuce and tomato.

**All-American Sub:** tomato, shredded lettuce, mayonnaise, ham, turkey, crisp bacon and Cheddar and Gruyère or Swiss cheeses, plus optional guacamole (page 198).

**Modern American Sub:** ham, smoked turkey, goat's cheese, Greek black olives or tapenade and roasted sweet peppers (see page 264); add garlic to the dressing.

★ Do not prepare the Hero too far in advance or it may become a tasteless coward!

# SALADS

Salads are taken quite a bit more seriously in America than in other countries, where the salad may be relegated to a side dish. Salads are everywhere – as main dishes, at salad bars, tossed table-side as part of the entertainment, and, more popular than ever, as take-out food in the glorious presentations of delis (delicatessans) across the country.

# Mary's All-American Potato Salad

My husband's love of potato salad demanded that I go to the source, so I asked my mother-in-law for her recipe. This is Mary Allin's version, loved by the whole family.

## YIELD: 6-8 SERVINGS

### INGREDIENTS:

1.35 kg/3 lbs new potatoes (unpeeled)
   (I like Red Russets.)
6 spring onions [US scallions], chopped
4 tablespoons sweet pickle relish, or use chopped sweet
   pickled cucumbers
2 tablespoons chopped fresh parsley
1 teaspoon celery seed (optional)
125 ml/4 fl oz [½ cup] mayonnaise, bottled or
   home-made

### FOR THE VINAIGRETTE MARINADE:

1 tablespoon Dijon mustard
3 tablespoons white wine vinegar
¼ teaspoon salt
Freshly ground pepper to taste
125 ml/4 fl oz [½ cup] vegetable or olive oil, or a
   combination of both

### METHOD:

★ First prepare the vinaigrette. In a small bowl, whisk together the mustard, vinegar, salt and pepper. In a slow stream, whisk in the oil and continue whisking until it is fully incorporated.

★ Cook the potatoes in boiling salted water to cover until they are just tender. Drain. As soon as they are cool enough to handle, cut into large cubes, removing the peel or not, as you prefer. While they are still warm, toss in the vinaigrette. (Cold potatoes will not absorb the vinaigrette as well.) Add the rest of the ingredients except for the mayonnaise and leave for a good hour at room temperature.

★ Fold in the mayonnaise and refrigerate until serving time. Serve cold. The potato salad can be garnished with sliced hard-boiled eggs.

# Classic Caesar Salad

Originally a 1920s creation of a desperate restaurateur named Caesar, who threw these ingredients together in a crisis, this salad has been a constant on restaurant menus and seems even more popular today. As in all classics, there are many versions. The original was prepared at the table, whisking in each ingredient of the dressing in a dramatic flourish. This version allows you to prepare the dressing in advance. Today, the Caesar Salad is often adapted for a main course by topping it with a grilled chicken breast.

YIELD: 6-8 SALAD-COURSE SERVINGS
Oven: 180°C/350°F/Gas 4

INGREDIENTS:
2 size-1 eggs [US jumbo eggs]
4 canned anchovy fillets, soaked in milk, drained and
    finely chopped
2 teaspoons finely chopped garlic
1 teaspoon Dijon mustard
2 tablespoons freshly squeezed lemon juice
Large pinch of salt
½ teaspoon freshly ground pepper
125 ml/4 fl oz [½ cup] extra-virgin olive oil
2 medium-size Cos or romaine lettuces
100 g/3 ½ oz [½ cup] freshly grated Parmesan cheese

FOR THE CROÛTONS:
80 g/scant 3 oz [2 cups] crusty French or Italian-style
    bread, cut into 2.5 cm/1 inch cubes
55 g/2 oz [¼ cup] butter
4 tablespoons olive oil
1 tablespoon finely chopped garlic

METHOD:
★ Preheat the oven.
★ First prepare the croûtons. Heat the butter and oil in a large frying pan, add the bread cubes and garlic and toss until the cubes are coated all over with fat and have absorbed all of it. Transfer to a baking sheet and bake in the preheated oven, stirring every 5 minutes, for about 20 minutes. If not using immediately, allow to cool and then store in an airtight container.
★ No more than a few hours before serving, prepare the dressing. Bring a small saucepan of water to the boil and lower in the eggs. Simmer for 3 minutes, then drain and cool under cold running water. Break the eggs and add the yolks to a medium-size bowl; discard the whites and shells. Add the anchovies, garlic, mustard, lemon juice, salt and pepper and whisk well. Add the oil in a slow stream, whisking continuously. Refrigerate the dressing until serving.
★ To assemble the salad, tear the lettuce into bite-size pieces in a large salad bowl. Toss with some of the dressing, just enough to coat each piece lightly. Add the croûtons and the grated cheese and toss again. Serve with a pepper mill.

# The Pump Room Spinach Salad

The Pump Room is a famous Chicago restaurant, known for its elegance and the celebrities who have often dined there. A number of years ago, their spinach salad so impressed me that I had to recreate it at home. Each ingredient is finely chopped and lined up for presentation in a gigantic salad bowl and then tossed at the table. Chopped salads are in vogue now in some of America's top restaurants, so if you've got the time and want to impress your guests, do chop. If you don't have the time, simply slice the ingredients.

YIELD: 4 hearty servings or 6-8 side-dish servings
Equipment: for a spectacular presentation, use a large flat salad bowl

INGREDIENTS:
450 g/1 lb fresh spinach, stalks removed
4 size-1 eggs [US jumbo eggs]
24 red radishes, finely chopped
225 g/8 oz smoked streaky bacon [US smoked bacon slices], fried until crisp and chopped or broken into small pieces
2 large bunches (10-12) spring onions [US scallions] including the green tops, finely chopped

FOR THE DRESSING:
2 tablespoons Dijon mustard
4 tablespoons tarragon white wine vinegar
4 teaspoons caster sugar [US granulated sugar] or honey
½ teaspoon salt
Freshly ground pepper
150 ml/ ¼ pint [⅔ cup] vegetable oil, or use a combination of extra virgin olive oil and vegetable oil

METHOD:
★ Immerse the spinach leaves in a sink or basin of cold water and rinse well. Remove to another sink or basin of fresh cold water. Do this a third time to ensure that all sand and dirt is removed from the spinach leaves (the dirt will sink to the bottom). Spin the spinach in a salad spinner and then dry on paper towels or on a clean kitchen towel. Grasp handfuls of spinach leaves into a ball and chop finely with a very sharp chef's knife. (Do not chop the spinach more than a few hours before you plan to serve the salad or it will become too soft.) Prepare bacon, onions and radishes.
★ Put the eggs in a pan of cold water, bring to the boil and simmer for 9 minutes. Remove to a bowl of cold water and leave to cool. When cold, peel the eggs and separate the yolks and whites. Finely chop both the yolks and whites, keeping them separate.
★ Arrange the spinach, egg yolks, egg whites, radishes, bacon and spring onions individually in lines in the salad bowl. Cover and refrigerate until serving time.
★ To make the dressing, in a small bowl whisk together the mustard, vinegar, sugar or honey, salt and pepper. Add the oil in a thin stream, whisking until thick and emulsified.
★ Present the salad to your family or guests and toss it with the dressing at the table for maximum effect!

# Tarragon Chicken Salad Garnished with Melon and Curried Walnuts

There are many interpretations of American chicken salads served for luncheons across the country and most are delicious. What I offer here is my idea of the best combination of tastes and textures – fresh tarragon and chicken, cool melon, crisp, spiced walnuts. If you don't think this is the best chicken salad you have ever eaten, please send me your recipe.

YIELD: 4 LARGE LUNCHEON SERVINGS
Oven: 180°C/350°F/Gas 4

INGREDIENTS:
1.8 kg/4 lbs chicken breasts, or 800 g/1¾ lbs [4 cups] cooked chicken breast meat, cubed
2 tablespoons tarragon white wine vinegar
2 celery stalks (175 g/6 oz), finely chopped
60 g/2 oz [½ cup] finely chopped red onion or spring onions [US scallions]
2 tablespoons chopped fresh tarragon
125 ml/4 fl oz [½ cup] mayonnaise, home-made or bottled
125 ml/4 fl oz [½ cup] sour cream
2 teaspoons creamed horseradish
120 g/4 oz [1 cup] walnuts, toasted and chopped (See page 268)

Salad greens
1 melon, or half each of 2 varieties such as yellow or green-fleshed varieties such as charentais, honeydew, gallia, canteloupe

FOR THE CURRIED WALNUTS:
225 g/8 oz [2 cups] walnut halves
2 tablespoons sugar
1 tablespoon + 1 teaspoon vegetable oil
¼ teaspoon each salt, ground ginger and mild chilli powder
Large pinch each pepper, cayenne pepper, ground coriander and ground allspice
¾ teaspoon ground cumin

METHOD:
★ Preheat the oven
★ To prepare the curried walnuts, first blanch the nuts: drop them into a pan of boiling water, return to the boil and simmer for 1 minute, then drain. While they are still hot, toss the walnuts with the sugar and vegetable oil. Leave them to cool for about 10 minutes. Spread them in a single layer on a baking sheet and bake in the preheated oven for 30-35 minutes, turning and tossing them every 10 minutes. Remove them from the oven. Combine the seasonings and spices and toss the nuts in the mixture while they are still warm. Spread out the nuts on the baking sheet again and leave to cool completely. Store in an airtight container.
★ If using chicken breasts, poach gently for 15 minutes in boiling water in a covered pan. Remove from the heat and leave the chicken in the pan of hot water, still covered, for an additional 15 minutes. Drain and cool, then refrigerate.
★ To prepare the chicken salad, remove the skin and bones from the chicken breasts and cut meat into large chunks. In a medium-size bowl, toss the chicken with the vinegar. Add the chopped celery, onion and tarragon. In a smaller bowl, mix the mayonnaise, sour cream and horseradish together and fold this mixture into the chicken. Shortly before serving fold in the chopped walnuts.
★ To serve, put a mound of the chicken salad on a bed of greens and garnish with slices of melon, or pile the salad in melon halves. Finally, put a few curried walnuts on top of the salad. Serve with popovers (page 211) or muffins (page 200).

# Southern Fried Chicken Salad with Sun-Dried Tomato Vinaigrette

This has become a popular restaurant variation on the classic American chicken salad.

### YIELD: 4 LUNCHEON SERVINGS

INGREDIENTS:

6 chicken breasts [US chicken breast halves], skin and
    bones removed
500 ml/16 fl oz [2 cups] buttermilk
6 smoked streaky bacon rashers [US thick bacon slices]
3 large carrots
3 large oranges
Vegetable oil for frying
120 g/4 oz [1 cup] plain flour [US all-purpose flour]
2 teaspoons garlic salt
2 teaspoons black pepper
¼ teaspoon cayenne pepper
½ teaspoon seasoning salt (page 264)
8 large handfuls mixed greens, including curly endive or
    frisé, oak-leaf or red leaf lettuce and rocket [US arugula]

FOR THE DRESSING:

80 ml/2 ¾ fl oz [⅓ cup] honey
80 ml/2 ¾ fl oz [⅓ cup] tarragon white wine vinegar
4 tablespoons olive oil
4 tablespoons vegetable oil
¼ teaspoon salt
Freshly ground pepper to taste
4 tablespoons finely chopped sun-dried tomatoes
    (preserved in oil)

METHOD:

★ Cut the chicken breasts into goujons or long strips (you should get about 5 strips from each breast). Cover with the buttermilk and refrigerate for at least 4 hours or overnight.

★ On the day you plan to serve the salad, prepare the garnish. Fry the bacon until crisp, then chop or crumble it. Using a vegetable peeler, shave long strips from the carrots. Curl these around your finger and put in bag or other container. Continue making curls until the carrot piece is too thin. Peel the oranges, removing all the white pith. Using a sharp knife cut on both sides of each membrane to remove the orange segments. Reserve the garnishes.

★ To make the dressing, whisk the honey and vinegar together, then add the oils in a thin stream, whisking until the dressing is well combined. Gently whisk in the seasoning and sun-dried tomatoes.

★ Shortly before serving heat 2.5–5 cm/1-2 inches of vegetable oil in a frying pan or wok to 190°C/375°F. In a shallow dish, combine the flour, garlic salt, pepper, cayenne and seasoning salt. Remove the chicken strips from the buttermilk a few at a time and dredge in the seasoned flour. Add a few at a time to the hot oil and cook, turning, until crisp and nicely browned. Remove to a baking sheet lined with paper towels and keep warm in a very low oven until all the chicken has been fried.

★ Toss the greens with some of the dressing and divide among 4 salad plates or bowls. Arrange the strips of chicken like the spokes of a wheel over the greens. Garnish with the orange segments and carrot curls and sprinkle over the bacon pieces. Drizzle with a little more dressing, and serve the remainder separately. Serve with iced tea and popovers (page 211) or muffins (page 200) for a very fine lunch.

# Buckwheat Pasta & Lentil Salad

This earthy salad was inspired by a warm pasta dish in *The Greens Cookbook*: recipes from America's most celebrated vegetarian restaurant. The combination of lentils and buckwheat is hearty and rustic – all you will need is a crusty loaf of bread and a bottle of wine for a picnic.

## YIELD: 4-6 SERVINGS

### INGREDIENTS:
1 red sweet pepper
125 g/4 ½ oz [½ cup] lentils, preferably Puy lentils
1 bay leaf
¼ teaspoon salt
2 carrots, diced
1 red onion, diced
1 celery stalk, diced, or substitute 1 fennel bulb
125 ml/4 fl oz [½ cup] vegetable or chicken stock, preferably home-made
250 g/9 oz soba or other buckwheat noodles (Look for soba in health food shops or specialist shops that sell Japanese ingredients.)
Olive oil
1 tablespoon capers, chopped
12 black oil-cured olives, stoned and chopped

Salad greens
Parmesan cheese (not grated)

### FOR THE VINAIGRETTE:
4 tablespoons vinegar (half balsamic and half red wine is good)
¾ teaspoon salt
¾ teaspoon freshly ground pepper
2 teaspoons finely chopped garlic
1 tablespoon finely chopped fresh basil or 1 teaspoon dried basil
1 tablespoon finely chopped fresh oregano or 1 teaspoon dried oregano
¼ cup chopped fresh parsley
125 ml/4 fl oz [½ cup] olive oil
4 tablespoons vegetable oil

### METHOD:
★ To make the vinaigrette, whisk all the ingredients, except the oils, in a small bowl until combined. Add the combined oils in a stream, whisking continuously. Set aside.
★ Roast and peel the red pepper (see page 264). Cut into julienne (very fine strips).
★ Put the lentils in a small saucepan, cover with water and add the bay leaf and salt. Simmer for about 10 minutes or until just tender. Add more water to the lentils if necessary.
★ When the lentils are tender, drain and return them to the pan. Add the carrots, onion, celery and stock and braise for about 5 minutes, uncovered.
★ Cook the buckwheat noodles in a large pan of boiling salted water until they are tender but still have a little crunch to them (*al dente*). Drain and toss with a little olive oil in a large bowl. Add the warm lentil mixture, red pepper julienne, capers and olives. Toss, while still warm, with the vinaigrette. Spoon on to a bed of interesting salad greens. Shave large curls of Parmesan cheese over the top and serve warm or at room temperature, even cold.

# Summer Salad

This pasta salad, using miniature pasta such as ditalini, evokes all that we love about summer – it's fun, it's refreshing, and you wish it would never end. The dressing is very oriental, the pasta and sun-dried tomatoes are Italian, the addition of carrot and currants are an inspiration – it's all a bit confused but it works, and what could be more American? This is adapted from a popular salad served at the Commissary Restaurant in Philadelphia.

YIELD: 8-12 SERVINGS
Equipment: a mandoline to cut very fine strips of carrot makes this salad more fun to eat

INGREDIENTS:
450 g/1 lb orzo pasta, or substitute another small
    shaped pasta
1 tablespoon sesame oil
180 g/6 oz [1 ½ cups] currants
125 ml/4 fl oz [½ cup] freshly squeezed orange juice
2 tablespoons slivered sun-dried tomatoes (oil-preserved)
375 g/12 oz carrots
140 g/scant 5 oz [1 cup] unsalted sunflower seeds,
    toasted (See page 268)

FOR THE DRESSING:
125 ml/4 fl oz [½ cup] rice wine vinegar
2 tablespoons medium sweet sherry
1 teaspoon soy sauce
1 tablespoon caster sugar [US granulated sugar]
1 teaspoon salt
1 teaspoon freshly ground pepper
¼ teaspoon dried hot red pepper flakes
2 tablespoons thinly sliced spring onions [US scallions]
1 teaspoon finely chopped fresh ginger
½ teaspoon finely chopped garlic
1 tablespoon slivered orange rind, all white pith removed
3 tablespoons finely chopped fresh coriander
    [US cilantro]
125 ml/4 fl oz [½ cup] vegetable oil
4 tablespoons sesame oil

METHOD:
★ Cook the pasta in boiling salted water until it is just tender but still has a bit of a bite (*al dente*), then drain it. Let cold water run through it for a few seconds and thoroughly drain it. Transfer it to a large bowl and toss with the tablespoon of sesame oil to prevent it from sticking together.
★ Put the currants and orange juice in a small saucepan, bring to the boil and simmer for 1 minute. Remove from the heat, cover and leave to plump up for about 15 minutes. Drain the currants and add them to the pasta with the sun-dried tomatoes.
★ Cut the carrots into very fine strips using a mandoline. If you don't have a mandoline, use a food processor or grater to shred the carrots. Reserve.
★ Whisk together all the dressing ingredients except for the oils. Add the oils in a continuous stream, whisking, and continue to whisk until the dressing is well blended. (You can mix the dressing in a food processor, but stir in the orange rind and coriander at the end.)
★ To serve, pour the dressing over the pasta and toss, then fold in the carrots and sunflower seeds. Serve chilled.

NOTE: The salad can be made a day or two in advance and refrigerated. In this case, add the carrots and toasted sunflower seeds no more than 1 hour before serving.

# Winter Salad

A modern version of the classic Waldorf Salad, this gutsy combination is a great accompaniment to stews and soups, and stands in very nicely when lettuce becomes less available in the markets.

## YIELD: 6-8 SERVINGS

### INGREDIENTS:
2 tablespoons currants
3 sweet, crisp apples, such as Golden or Red Delicious, Cox's, sliced (unpeeled)
4 heads of chicory [US Belgian endive], sliced
1 small radicchio, finely shredded
100–200 g/3 ½–7 oz [½-1 cup] Roquefort cheese, crumbled
60 g/2 oz [½ cup] walnuts, toasted

### FOR THE DRESSING:
2 tablespoons finely chopped spring onions [US scallions]
1 tablespoon Dijon mustard
2 teaspoons caster sugar [US granulated sugar]
6 tablespoons walnut oil or fruity olive oil
Salt and freshly ground pepper to taste

### METHOD:
★ Begin by making the dressing in the bottom of the salad bowl. Whisk together the spring onions, mustard and sugar in the bowl. Add the oil in a stream, whisking continuously. The dressing will begin to separate after about 4 tablespoons of oil have been added, but don't worry; it will be fine. Season with salt and pepper. Keep in mind that many Dijon mustards are very salty.
★ To plump the currants, cover them with water in a small pan and bring to the boil. Simmer for 1 minute, then cover and remove from the heat. Leave for about 15 minutes before draining.
★ Add the salad ingredients to the salad bowl, on top of the dressing, in this order: apples, chicory, radicchio and currants. If made in advance, cover the bowl with cling film [US plastic wrap] and refrigerate. Toss at the table, adding the Roquefort and walnuts.

NOTE: Clean the chicory and radicchio with a dampened paper towel, removing any damaged outer leaves. Do not submerge them in water or they will become bitter.

# SNACKS
## *Dips and Spreads*

America is a nation that never seems to stop celebrating something, whether it be a holiday or a winning team, a promotion or a new baby. These frequent, informal gatherings require some quick, healthy things to nibble on and the best solution throughout the years have been dips and spreads. They are easy to prepare and are as good with low fat, vegetable crudités as they are with potato chips!

*A San Francisco pretzel wagon for quick snacks*

# Green Chilli Con Queso Dip

New Mexico is the chilli capitol of the U.S., and produces a variety of chillies that range from mild to fire-hot. Unless you can find dried New Mexican chillies, you will never experience the subtle differences, but will have to try simple recipes like this one using the mild green chillies.

YIELD: about 500 ml/16 fl oz [2 cups], for 6-8 servings
Equipment: a fondue pot with warmer

INGREDIENTS:
½ red sweet pepper
250 g/9 oz [2 cups] mature (sharp) Cheddar cheese,
    coarsely grated
1 tablespoon plain flour [US all-purpose flour]
125 ml/4 fl oz [½ cup] mild taco sauce

1 can (113 g/4 oz) chopped green chillies, such as Old
    El Paso brand
¼ teaspoon salt
4 tablespoons sour cream
Corn or tortilla chips, to serve

METHOD:
★ Roast and peel the red pepper (see page 264). Chop the flesh.
★ Toss the cheese and flour together in a small bowl and reserve.
★ Combine the taco sauce, chillies, chopped red pepper and salt in the fondue pot and heat over moderate heat until it begins to boil. Add the cheese slowly and stir until each batch melts before adding more. Finally, stir in the sour cream. Warm through but do not allow to boil. Serve warm with the chips.

# Potted Roquefort and Chutney Dip/Spread

During the holiday season, I make numerous crocks of this favourite and refrigerate them.

YIELD: about 500 ml/16 fl oz [2 cups]

INGREDIENTS:
175 g/6 oz cream cheese or other full fat soft cheese, at
    room temperature
85 g/3 oz Roquefort cheese
55 g/2 oz [4 tablespoons] butter, at room temperature
30 g/1 oz [¼ cup] finely chopped onion or spring onion
    [US scallion]

1-2 tablespoons milk
½ teaspoon mild curry powder or garam masala
¼ teaspoon salt
3 tablespoons mango chutney [US Major Grey chutney],
    any large pieces finely chopped

METHOD:
★ Beat all the ingredients, except for the chutney, together in a medium-size bowl until creamy. Fold in the chutney.
★ Pack the dip into any non-metal container or crock. Cover tightly and refrigerate for at least 24 hours, but no longer than 2 weeks. Serve with assorted savoury biscuits [US crackers].

# Spinach Dip

This is my favourite dip for health-conscious guests, or anyone, for that matter, who likes something refreshing and light. Dip vegetable crudités into this and watch it disappear.

YIELD: about 500 ml/16 fl oz [2 cups]
Equipment: a food processor

INGREDIENTS:

280 g/10 oz fresh spinach, stalks removed
¼ medium-size onion, finely chopped
15 g/ ½ oz [¼ cup] fresh parsley, finely chopped
4 tablespoons mayonnaise
4 canned anchovy fillets, drained
1 teaspoon prepared horseradish
2 tablespoons freshly squeezed lemon juice

1 tablespoon wine vinegar
1 teaspoon seasoning salt (page 264)
250 ml/8 fl oz [1 cup] sour cream
Salt and freshly ground pepper to taste
1 hard-boiled egg, to garnish
Crudités such as carrots, celery, red and green sweet
     pepper, cucumber, radishes and bulb fennel, to serve

METHOD:

★ Immerse the spinach leaves in a large basin or sink of cold water. Remove the spinach and immerse in a fresh basin of water. Repeat a third time if the spinach is very dirty. Put it in a colander to drain (there will still be water clinging to the leaves). Stir fry the spinach in a wok or large frying pan over high heat until it is just wilted. Transfer it to the colander again and run cold water over it until it has cooled. Drain it well and then squeeze it dry. Cut into small pieces.
★ Combine all the ingredients, except the sour cream and egg, in a food processor. Process until fairly smooth. Remove to a serving bowl and fold in the sour cream. Taste and add salt and freshly ground pepper.
★ Just before serving, separate the white and the yolk of the hard-boiled egg and sieve or chop them finely, keeping them separate. Decorate the dip with lines or rings of egg white and yolk. Serve with crudités.

NOTE: An attractive serving bowl can be made by hollowing out a green or red cabbage. Spoon in the dip just before serving. Arrange the crudités around it.

# Guacamole Dip

Once referred to as 'Indian butter', this Mexican dip has reached celebrity status!

YIELD: about 375 ml/12 fl oz [1 ½ cups]

INGREDIENTS:
2 ripe avocados
1 tomato, diced
30 g/1 oz [¼ cup] finely chopped spring onion
  [US scallion] or red onion

1 small garlic clove, finely chopped
1 teaspoon salt
2 teaspoons finely chopped jalapeño peppers, fresh or bottled, or use any fresh hot green chilli
1 teaspoon finely chopped fresh coriander [US cilantro]

METHOD:
★ Halve the avocados and remove the stones. Scoop out the flesh into a bowl, scraping all of it from the skins. Mash the avocado flesh with a fork, then quickly add the other ingredients and mix with the fork. If you must make the guacamole in advance, cover it with cling film [US plastic wrap], pressing the film against the surface of the guacamole to exclude all air; otherwise it may turn brown. If it does, stir the browned surface into the green guacamole underneath.
★ Serve as a dip with the best quality restaurant-style tortilla chips you can find.

NOTE: Choose ripe avocados without bruises or dark spots. The best variety to use is the Haas avocado, which has a thick black skin, rather than the thin green skinned varieties. A ripe avocado should feel soft but not mushy.

# Hot Crab Dip

This easy dip is ideal for cold weather entertaining – guests will love it and you will be enjoying the party too, not slaving in the kitchen.

YIELD: about 500 ml/16 fl oz [2 cups]
Oven: 190°C/375°F/Gas 5

INGREDIENTS:
225 g/8 oz cream cheese or other full fat soft cheese, at
  room temperature
225 g/8 oz good quality fresh, frozen or canned crab
  meat, all white meat preferably
2 tablespoons finely chopped spring onion [US scallion]
2 tablespoons milk

1 teaspoon creamed horseradish
¼ teaspoon salt
Freshly ground pepper to taste
50 g/scant 2 oz [½ cup] Gruyère cheese, coarsely grated
50 g/scant 2 oz [½ cup] flaked almonds [US sliced
  almonds], toasted

METHOD:
★ Preheat the oven.
★ In a small bowl combine all the ingredients except for the Gruyère and toasted almonds. Mix well. Spread the mixture in an ovenproof serving dish, such as a ceramic flan or quiche dish. Sprinkle with the cheese and then with the nuts.
★ Bake in the preheated oven for 15 minutes. Serve hot with assorted savoury biscuits [US crackers] or crudités.

# BREADS

Americans have never lost their love of the 'journey cake' and love bread, especially the ones that travel well, such as bagels and doughnuts, Danish and coffee cakes, muffins and biscuits. These breads satisfy American 'grazing' tendencies, a term used to describe eating small amounts of food on impulse throughout the day, rather than the three designated times of old. Some of the following breads require more time to prepare than 'quick breads' such as pancakes and muffins, but are included here because they are traditionally offered by America's bakeries and delis, to be taken out and eaten either at home or at work with a steaming cup of coffee. Only occasionally are these made at home, but they should be! If one of your food memories is a cheese Danish from a New York deli or a sticky bun from a café in the South...now you can have them anytime you feel the urge.

# Morning Glory Muffins

This is an adaptation of a recipe from the Morning Glory Café on Nantucket Island. These muffins are very similar to a carrot cake, and could just as well be frosted with cream cheese and taken on a picnic for a dessert.

YIELD: 18 MUFFINS

Equipment: 6 or 12-hole American muffin tins or use deep bun tins that are 7.5 cm/3 inches in diameter and 4 cm/1½ inches deep. You'll also need a food processor or hand grater.

Oven: 190°C/375°F/Gas 5

INGREDIENTS:

150 g/5 oz [1 cup] raisins or sultanas [US golden raisins]
4 tablespoons dark rum
500 g/1 lb 2 oz carrots
2 apples (unpeeled)
220 g/8 oz [1 cup firmly packed] dark soft brown sugar
110 g/4 oz [½ cup] caster sugar [US granulated sugar]
275 g/10 oz [2 cups] self-raising wholemeal flour
  [US whole-wheat flour]
260 g/9 oz [2 cups] self-raising flour [US all-purpose flour]

4 teaspoons ground cinnamon
4 teaspoons bicarbonate of soda [US baking soda]
1 teaspoon salt
85 g/3 oz [1 cup] sweetened dessicated coconut
  [US sweetened flaked coconut]
115 g/4 oz [1 cup] pecans, chopped
6 size-1 eggs [US jumbo eggs]
375 ml/12 fl oz [1 ½ cups] vegetable oil
2 teaspoons pure vanilla essence [US pure vanilla extract]

METHOD:

★ Preheat the oven. Generously butter the muffin cups or line them with paper cases (you will probably have to bake the muffins in batches).

★ Put the raisins and rum in a small saucepan and bring to the boil. Cover, remove from the heat and leave to plump up for 15 minutes. Shred the carrots in a food processor or using a hand grater. Shred the apples.

★ Combine the sugars, flours, cinnamon, bicarbonate of soda and salt in a large bowl. Add the raisins (with any rum that hasn't been absorbed), carrots, apples, coconut and pecans and toss. Combine the eggs, vegetable oil and vanilla in a smaller bowl and whisk together. Add this to the dry ingredients and stir until just combined.

★ Spoon the mixture into the prepared muffin cups and bake in the preheated oven for about 20 minutes. Leave to cool briefly and serve warm. These muffins actually taste better the next day and they freeze well.

*Selling flour in the 1880s*

# Blueberry Sour Cream Muffins

This is America's most famous muffin, but you will seldom taste one as light and delicious as this home-made version.

YIELD: 12 MUFFINS
Equipment: 6 or 12-hole American muffin tins, or use deep bun tins that are 7.5 cm/3 inches in diameter and 4 cm/1 ½ inches deep
Oven: 220°C/425°F/Gas 7

INGREDIENTS:

165 g/5 ½ oz [1 ¼ cups + 2 tablespoons] self-raising flour [US all-purpose flour]
½ teaspoon bicarbonate of soda [US baking soda]
45 g/1 ½ oz [3 tablespoons] unsalted butter, at room temperature
170 g/6 oz [¾ cup] caster sugar [US granulated sugar]
¼ teaspoon salt
2 size-1 eggs [US jumbo eggs]
250 ml/8 fl oz [1 cup] sour cream
Grated rind of 1 lemon
210 g/7 ½ oz [1 ½ cups] fresh or frozen blueberries, dusted generously with flour
Granulated sugar, to garnish

METHOD:

★ Preheat the oven. Generously butter the muffin cups or line them with paper cases.
★ Sift the flour and bicarbonate of soda into a small bowl and reserve.
★ In a medium-size bowl, beat the butter with the sugar and salt until light and fluffy. Add the eggs, one at a time, and continue to beat until well mixed. Add the sour cream and lemon rind and beat to mix. Fold in the dry ingredients quickly followed by the blueberries. (If you are using frozen blueberries, do not thaw, but use them still frozen.)
★ Spoon the mixture into the prepared muffin cups. Sprinkle the top of each muffin generously with sugar (about ½ teaspoon each).
★ Bake the muffins in the preheated oven for 15 minutes. Leave to cool briefly before taking the muffins out of the tins. Serve warm. These freeze well; warm them for serving.

# The Ultimate Bran Muffin

For years I have been testing bran muffin recipes, searching for that healthy but tasty muffin that is just right for everyone in the family. Here is what I have come up with – similar to those found in bakeries across America, but better because they are home-made.

YIELD: 18 LARGE MUFFINS
Equipment: American muffin tins or use deep bun tins that are 7.5 cm/3 inches in diameter and 4 cm/1 ½ inches deep.
Oven: 200°C/400°F/Gas 6

INGREDIENTS:
60 g/2 oz [1 cup] whole bran cereal, such as All-Bran or
    Bran Buds
250 ml/8 fl oz [1 cup] boiling water
125 ml/4 fl oz [½ cup] vegetable oil
4 tablespoons honey
55 g/2 oz [¼ cup firmly packed] dark soft brown sugar
2 size-1 eggs [US jumbo eggs]
500 ml/16 fl oz [2 cups] buttermilk
325 g/11 oz [2 ½ cups] self-raising wholemeal flour
    [US whole-wheat flour]
2 ½ teaspoons bicarbonate of soda [US baking soda]
½ teaspoon salt

25 g/¾ oz [¼ cup] porridge oats or rolled oats
35 g/1 ¼ oz [½ cup] wheat germ
40 g/scant 1 ½ oz [¾ cup] natural bran
95 g/3 ¼ oz [¾ cup] sunflower seed kernels
120 g/4 oz [1 cup] dried dates, stoned and chopped
150 g/5 oz [1 cup] raisins or sultanas [US golden raisins]

FOR THE GLAZE:
55 g/2 oz [¼ cup] caster sugar [US granulated sugar]
55 g/2 oz [¼ cup firmly packed] dark soft brown sugar
3 tablespoons honey
55 g/2 oz [¼ cup] butter, at room temperature

METHOD:
★ Preheat the oven.
★ Put the cereal in a medium-size bowl, pour the boiling water over and leave it to soak until the water is totally absorbed. Add to this the vegetable oil, honey, brown sugar, eggs and buttermilk and whisk to combine.
★ In a large bowl, mix together all the dry ingredients with the sunflower seeds, dates and raisins. Stir the wet ingredients into the dry ingredients and mix just until combined.
★ Prepare the glaze by beating the sugars and honey into the soft butter. With a pastry brush, coat the bottom and sides of the muffin cups with the glaze. Fill to the top with the muffin mixture.
★ Bake in the preheated oven for 20-25 minutes. Cool, in the tins, on racks for a few minutes, then turn upside-down over foil, leaving the tins over the muffins for a few minutes so that all the glaze comes out. After a few minutes lift off the tins and leave the muffins to cool. Eat the muffins while they are still warm or reheat for serving. These freeze very well.

# Sticky Buns

Almost every bakery in America will have their own version of 'Sticky Buns' or Caramel Rolls, but nothing is quite as good as the home-made variety. Although this is a yeast bread and not a quick bread, these buns are a good example of the kind of food Americans pick up at their local bakeries and eat 'on the run'.

YIELD: 24 BUNS
Equipment: an electric mixer with dough hook and a baking pan measuring about
31 x 21 x 4 cm/12 ½ x 8 ½ x 1 ½ inches, or two 25 cm/10 inch round cake pans
Oven: 200°C/400°F/Gas 6

INGREDIENTS:
110 g/ 4 oz [½ cup] caster sugar [US granulated sugar]
4 tablespoons warm water (80°C/175°F)
2 ½ teaspoons dried yeast
4 tablespoons milk
225 g/8 oz [1 cup] butter, cut into pieces
½ teaspoon salt
6 size-1 eggs [US jumbo eggs]
700 g/1 lb 9 oz [6 cups] strong plain flour
    [US bread flour]

FOR THE FILLING:
140 g/scant 5 oz [¾ cup] raisins or currants
4 tablespoons boiling water
170 g/6 oz [1 ½ cups] pecans
110 g/4 oz [½ cup] granulated sugar
1 tablespoon ground cinnamon
55 g/2 oz [¼ cup] butter

FOR THE GLAZE:
330 g/12 oz [1 ½ cups firmly packed] soft brown sugar
125 ml/4 fl oz [½ cup] water
55 g/2 oz [¼ cup] butter

METHOD:
★ Stir 1 teaspoon of sugar into the warm water in a small bowl. Sprinkle over the yeast and leave for about 5 minutes. The mixture should bubble and become frothy. (If using easy blend yeast [US rapid-rise yeast], follow the instructions on the packet.)
★ Warm the milk and butter together in a small saucepan until the butter melts completely. Remove from the heat.
★ Put the remaining sugar and the salt in the bowl of the electric mixer (fitted with the ordinary beater) and add the warm milk and butter mixture. Beat until the sugar has dissolved and the mixture feels just warm. Add the yeast mixture and the eggs, one by one, and continue beating at medium speed until well mixed. Add about 450 g/1 lb [3 ½ cups] of the flour and mix until smooth.
★ At this point, switch the beater to a paddle or dough hook. Add the rest of the flour and continue to beat and knead with the machine until the dough begins to pull away from the sides of the bowl or until you can touch it with your fingers and it will not stick to them. This will take about 5-10 minutes with a machine, 15 minutes if you are doing this by hand.
★ Transfer the dough to a greased or buttered bowl and cover tightly with cling film [US plastic wrap] or a damp towel. Leave the dough to rise in a warm place for 1–1 ½ hours or until it has doubled.
★ Punch the dough to knock out the air and turn it on to a lightly floured board. Knead for a few minutes, then cover and leave to rise again until doubled. This will take about an hour this time. (If you want to make the dough in advance, punch it down and refrigerate after the first ris-

ing; let it make its second rising when you intend to bake it. If you want to freeze the dough, punch it down and refrigerate it until it is cold, then wrap well and freeze.)

★ To prepare the filling, put the raisins or currants in a bowl and pour the boiling water over them. Leave to plump up for about an hour before draining.

★ Preheat the oven. Toast the pecans in the oven for 5–10 minutes, stirring once or twice. Chop one-third of the nuts very finely and mix with the sugar and the cinnamon. Chop the remaining pecans into rough quarters. Melt the butter. Reserve.

★ For the glaze, combine the brown sugar, water and butter in a saucepan and bring to the boil. Reduce the heat to moderate and simmer for about 10 minutes or until slightly thickened. Reserve.

★ Butter the pan(s) and sprinkle the quartered pecans over the bottom. Pour half of the syrup over the nuts.

★ Cut the dough in half and put one half on a lightly floured board. Roll it out into a 30 x 25 cm/12 x 10 inch rectangle. Brush the dough with the melted butter and sprinkle evenly with half of the sugar/cinnamon/nut mixture. Sprinkle half of the raisins or currants over and drizzle over half of the remaining syrup. Starting from a long edge, roll up the dough into a tight cylinder. Cut across into twelve 2.5 cm/1 inch rounds with a sharp knife. Arrange the rounds, cut side up, evenly in the prepared pan so they are almost touching. Roll out the second half of the dough and repeat the process. Leave the buns to rise again until doubled and covering the pans completely.

★ Preheat the oven again, with a heavy baking sheet on the middle shelf.

★ Set the pan of buns on the hot baking sheet in the preheated oven and bake for 10 minutes (the baking sheet boosts the heat under the buns and helps them to rise a little bit more). Reduce the oven temperature to 180°C/350°F/Gas 4 and continue baking for 20-25 minutes or until firm throughout. Cool for 5-10 minutes in the pan, then turn over upside-down on a piece of foil, leaving the pan over the buns until all the glaze has fallen out. Serve warm.

*Illustrated on pages 204–205*

# Chocolate Chip and Almond Coffee Cake

If you visit the United States, you will most likely be offered 'coffee cake' at one time or another. This is our version of 'tea bread' and we eat it for breakfast or with coffee, which is our hot beverage of preference. The combination of chocolate and almond in this recipe is wonderful.

YIELD: 2 coffeecakes, 12 servings each
Equipment: a food processor
Oven: 180°C/350°F/Gas 4

## INGREDIENTS:

One recipe of sweet bread dough from Sticky Buns (page 206)
Toasted flaked almonds [US sliced almonds], to garnish

### FOR THE CHOCOLATE CHIP AND ALMOND FILLING:

565 g/1 ¼ lbs blanched almonds
220 g/8 oz [1 cup] sugar
2 teaspoons pure almond essence [US pure almond extract]
150 g/5 oz [⅔ cup] unsalted butter, at room temperature
½ teaspoon salt
2 tablespoons plain flour [US all-purpose flour]

2 size-1 eggs [US jumbo eggs]
2 teaspoons freshly squeezed lemon juice
115 g/4 oz bittersweet or plain dark chocolate chips [US semi-sweet chocolate chips] or chopped lightly sweetened dark continental chocolate

### FOR THE GLAZE:

85 g/3 oz [6 tablespoons] unsalted butter
180 g/6 oz [1 ½ cups] icing sugar [US confectioners' sugar]
4 tablespoons boiling water
1 teaspoon pure vanilla essence [US pure vanilla extract]

## METHOD:

★ Make the sweet bread dough, taking it through the second rising.

★ Meanwhile, prepare the filling. Process the almonds with the sugar in a food processor until very fine. Transfer the mixture to a bowl and add the rest of the filling ingredients, stirring with a wooden spoon. Reserve.

★ Divide the sweet dough in half and roll out each piece into a rectangle about 25 x 35 cm/ 10 x 14 inches. Spread half of the filling over each rectangle, leaving a border clear of about 2.5 cm/ 1 inch all around.

★ Lightly score the filling on one of the dough rectangles, marking it into three equal portions lengthways. Using a sharp knife or kitchen scissors, make diagonal cuts in the outside portions at 2.5 cm/1 inch intervals (the middle third of the rectangle will remain uncut and will be the base of the coffee cake). Alternately fold the cut strips from the outside portions over each other, crossing on the middle third. Seal the ends and tuck them under the coffee cake. Repeat with the second dough rectangle.

★ Set the coffee cakes on foil-lined and buttered baking pans. Leave to rise again in a warm spot until doubled in size.

★ Preheat the oven. Bake the coffee cakes in the preheated oven for 25-30 minutes or until lightly browned. Cool on a rack and glaze while still warm but not hot.

★ To prepare the glaze, melt the butter in a small pan and cook until it turns light brown (noisette, as the French call it). Mix in the sifted icing sugar and then the boiling water, 1 teaspoon at a time, to make a spreading consistency. Add the vanilla. Drizzle the glaze over the coffee cake. Sprinkle toasted almonds over the top if you like.

NOTE: When browning the butter for the glaze, if you listen to the sound of the butter cooking, you will notice that it stops "singing" when it becomes browned to the right degree. This browning technique lends a good deal of flavour to the glaze and indeed to many other things you may want to try it on!

# Macadamia Nut Pancakes

We all have special food memories that come back to us from time to time and one of mine is Macadamia Nut Pancakes. While on holiday in Maui, one of the Hawaiian islands, my husband and I discovered a small beachfront restaurant whose speciality was these heavenly pancakes. We ate them, protected by the hut from a tropical shower, and decided they were the best pancakes we had ever eaten, in the most beautiful setting. I developed this recipe just to recreate that wonderful experience over and over again. Maybe you don't have the beach, but close your eyes and pretend you are in Hawaii while eating these. Macadamia nuts are native to Australia but a speciality of Hawaii. The difficulty of shelling them makes them expensive but their unique taste and crunch makes them well worth the price.

YIELD: 12 medium-size pancakes, to serve 2–3

INGREDIENTS:
100 g/3 ½ oz [1 cup] sponge or plain flour
   [US cake flour]
1 teaspoon caster sugar [US granulated sugar]
½ teaspoon salt
½ teaspoon bicarbonate of soda [US baking soda]
¾ teaspoon baking powder
1 size-1 egg [US jumbo egg]
250 ml/8 fl oz [1 cup] buttermilk
30 g/1 oz [2 tablespoons] butter, melted
60 g/2 oz [½ cup] macadamia nuts, finely chopped

FOR THE SYRUP:
125 ml/4 fl oz [½ cup] honey
125 ml/4 fl oz [½ cup] water
4 tablespoons pure maple syrup
30 g/1 oz [2 tablespoons] butter
60 g/2 oz [½ cup] macadamia nuts, finely chopped

METHOD:
★ First make the syrup: in a small saucepan combine the honey, water, syrup and butter and bring to the boil. Simmer for 10-15 minutes. Add the finely chopped nuts and continue to simmer until slightly thickened. Reserve.
★ Sift the flour, sugar, salt, bicarbonate of soda and baking powder into a medium-size bowl. In a smaller bowl, whisk together the egg, buttermilk and melted butter. Whisk this mixture into the dry ingredients, mixing only until combined.
★ Heat a frying pan or griddle that has been lightly buttered. Drop the pancake batter in spoonfuls on to the hot pan, frying 4–6 pancakes at a time, and fry until golden brown on the base. Sprinkle each pancake with a good pinch of chopped macadamia nuts, then turn and fry to a golden brown on the other side. Serve immediately, stacking up the pancakes and pouring the syrup over.

# $\mathcal{P}opovers$

A close relative to Yorkshire Pudding, these are a quick and dramatic alternative to rolls or biscuits and a welcome accompaniment to any meal. Serve with butter and honey or jam. They can also be filled with soft scrambled eggs and chopped chives for breakfast.

YIELD: 8 POPOVERS
Equipment: 8 individual soufflé dishes or ramekins, 9 cm/3 ½ inches in diameter and 4 cm/1 ½ inches deep
Oven: 220°C/425°F/Gas 7. If you have a convection oven, which produces the best results, set it to 200°C/400°F/Gas 6

INGREDIENTS:
3 size-1 eggs [US jumbo eggs]
250 ml/8 fl oz [1 cup] milk
120 g/4 oz [1 cup] strong plain flour [US all-purpose flour]

½ teaspoon baking powder
½ teaspoon salt
15 g/ ½ oz [1 tablespoon] butter, melted

METHOD:
★ Preheat the oven.
★ Whisk the eggs until frothy and lightened, then add the milk. Sift the dry ingredients over this mixture and whisk together. Finally add the melted butter.
★ Generously butter the soufflé dishes or ramekins. Arrange them on a baking sheet and heat in the preheated oven for 10 minutes.
★ Pour the batter into the dishes, filling them about three-quarters full. Bake for 15 minutes, then lower the oven temperature to 170°C/325°F/Gas 3 (or 150°C/300°F/Gas 2 if using a convection oven) and continue to bake for 20 minutes. Try not to open the oven door during the baking process. The popovers should puff dramatically. Serve hot. *(See picture on page 142)*

# AMERICAN-STYLE GRILLING

A discussion of America's ways of preparing food fast and conveniently would not be complete without including the art of grilling. From the beginning Americans have cooked out of doors over an open fire. Early settlers learned many tricks from their friends the Indians. Indians used stones and wood planks placed over the fire and it's not hard to see the connections between their methods of cooking and our modern barbecue or grill. Although backyard grilling has always been popular, the chefs and restaurants of California have in recent years taken it to new heights, using interesting fruit woods and mesquite to add smoke, grilling fruits and vegetables, and serving up the best, freshest local meats, poultry, fish and game from our old friend the grill. 'California Cuisine' has swept the United States and made grilling a part of many new restaurant menus as far away as London or Tokyo.

The origins of the word 'barbecue' are still being debated. The Louisiana Acadians claim it comes from the French *barbe à queue* or "from whiskers to tail", as spit-roasted whole animals were often cooked. The Acadians, of French descent, are the originators of Cajun cooking, which brings us many charcoal smoked foods. But Texans, always prone to argument, claim the Spaniards were the first to learn of barbecue cooking from the Carib Indians who created a green wood lattice over the fire. The Spaniards called this lattice *barbacoa*.

Grilling is defined as fast cooking over live coals or any source of strong heat from 200 degrees C. to 500 degrees C. (400-1,000 degrees F.). Grilling sears food quickly to retain its juices and is most appropriate for tender cuts of meat and poultry, such as steaks, chops and breasts.

Grilling should not be confused with the slow, soulful and time-consuming art of barbecuing, even though the words are sometimes used interchangeably. Grilling is not always barbecuing, but barbecuing is always grilling. Barbecuing is done in an enclosed unit with long, smoky cooking over a hardwood fire or a charcoal fire with hardwood added. Barbecued meat is cooked very slowly and sometimes with a thick, sweet tomato-based sauce characteristic of the American South. Barbecue remains a regional speciality, but grilling has become an American export, now becoming popular around the world.

## GUIDELINES TO GOOD GRILLING:

- Use tender cuts for grilling, otherwise marinate less tender cuts for 8 hours or overnight.
- Have food at room temperature before grilling.
- Start charcoal 40-60 minutes before grilling. The coals should be covered in grey ash and be glowing red inside.
- Always use charcoal grills outdoors – toxic carbon monoxide is generated by charcoal fires.
- Use only approved starter fluids, not kerosene or gasoline. And never add starters after the fire has been lit.

• Use enough charcoal to cover the area under the food you are grilling. Pile high when starting the fire and spread just before grilling.

• Use a medium to medium-hot fire. To test the fire, hold a hand at cooking level. If you can hold your hand there for 5 seconds, it is a low temperature under 150 degrees C.; 3 seconds is a medium temperature of 150-180 degrees C.; 2 seconds is medium-hot,180-200 degrees C. and 1 second is hot or 200-250 degrees C.

• To lower the grilling temperature: close the grill vent, spread the coals further apart, raise the cooking rack. To raise the grilling temperature: open the grill vent, push coals together, and/or lower the cooking rack.

• On windy, cool days grilling may take longer than usual, increase the amount of charcoal used and plan for a longer cooking time.

• Avoid fire flare-ups by trimming off excess fat on meat and spray flare-ups cautiously with water in a spray bottle.

• Especially when entertaining, grill to sear meat and other foods on both sides and then finish cooking them indoors in your oven. This way you get the best of both worlds—the wonderful taste and colour of the grill and the control of cooking time in your oven.

• Don't turn food too often, turn once half-way through cooking time. Use tongs to turn the food, not a fork that pierces the food and allows juice to escape.

You will find recipes that use grilling throughout this book, as well as the more time-consuming barbecue recipes, but the following are a few basic recipes, to start you thinking about grilling vegetables and fish, if you have not already tried cooking them on a grill.

*Indians in Virginia cook fish over a fire in 1590*

# Grilled Swordfish in a Lime and Coriander Marinade

Swordfish is an ideal fish for grilling and tastes deliciously earthy with this marinade.

### YIELD: 4 SERVINGS
Equipment: a barbecue or cast iron ridged grill pan

### INGREDIENTS:

Juice of 3 limes, or 2 limes and 1 lemon
125 ml/4 fl oz [½ cup] extra-virgin olive oil
1 large bunch (about 50 g/1 ¾ oz) fresh coriander
   [US cilantro], finely chopped

4 swordfish steaks, or any other firm-fleshed fish suitable
   for grilling, such as halibut and shark
Salt and freshly ground pepper to taste

### METHOD:

★ Whisk together the lime juice, olive oil and most of the coriander in a shallow glass container. Add the fish and leave to marinate for several hours in the refrigerator.

★ If using a barbecue, prepare and light the charcoal fire well in advance; bring the coals to a medium heat (see page 212 for instructions). A grill pan will need about 10 minutes' preheating.

★ About half an hour before cooking, remove the fish from the refrigerator and allow it to come to room temperature. When you are ready to cook, remove the fish from the marinade, reserving it. Barbecue grill the fish or cook it on the grill pan, turning it once and basting with the marinade from time to time, just until the flesh begins to flake. A 2.5 cm/1 inch steak will need about 10 minutes total cooking time. To test for doneness, insert a fork into the middle: the flesh should be opaque and beginning to flake; alternatively, insert a wooden skewer, which should not meet with resistance.

★ Serve the fish at once, seasoned with salt and pepper and drizzled with a bit of the marinade and the remaining coriander. This would be wonderful with a pasta salad, especially Summer Salad (page 193).

# Grilled New Potato Salad with Rosemary

Grilling brings out the best in potatoes and combines with robust rosemary in a true symphony of tastes.

YIELD: 4 SERVINGS

Equipment: a barbecue and wire hinged basket or a cast iron ridged grill pan

INGREDIENTS:

900 g/2 lbs new potatoes (unpeeled)
6 tablespoons extra-virgin olive oil
2 tablespoons finely chopped fresh rosemary

FOR THE DRESSING:

3 tablespoons mayonnaise, bottled or home-made
2 tablespoons white wine
1 tablespoon white wine vinegar
1 ½ teaspoons Dijon mustard
3 spring onions [US scallions], thinly sliced
3 tablespoons finely chopped fresh parsley
Salt and freshly ground pepper to taste

METHOD:

★ Put the potatoes in a medium-size saucepan, cover with salted water and bring to the boil. Simmer for 10–12 minutes or until they are just tender, then drain. Mix together the olive oil and rosemary in a bowl. Add the potatoes while they are still warm, slicing them in half as you add them. Toss with the oil. (The potatoes can be prepared up to a day in advance.)

★ Mix the dressing ingredients together and refrigerate until needed, up to a day in advance.

★ Up to 1–2 hours in advance of serving the salad, grill the potatoes. If you are using a barbecue, prepare and light the charcoal fire well in advance; you want a medium-hot fire (see page 212 for instructions). A grill pan will need about 10 minutes' preheating.

★ If you are barbecue grilling, put the potatoes in a flat wire hinged basket. Place them over the charcoal fire and cook for 8–10 minutes on each side or until they are quite brown. For indoor grilling, place them directly on the hot grill pan and cook for 5–8 minutes on each side or until brown.

★ Transfer the potatoes to a serving bowl and toss with the dressing. Serve immediately or at room temperature.

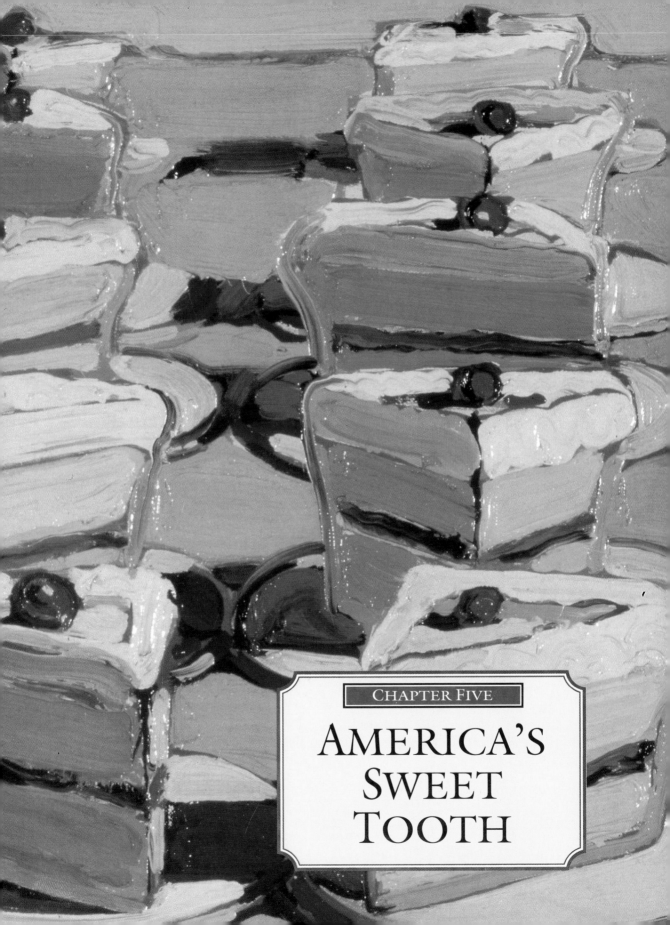

CHAPTER FIVE

# AMERICA'S
# SWEET
# TOOTH

NATIVE AMERICAN INDIANS already had a sweet tooth when the early colonists arrived. The Indians added maple sugar to water as a beverage and they mixed it with bear's fat as a sauce for their roasted meats. Colonists observed that sugar was to the Indians what salt was to Europeans. From the Indians, the early settlers learned to collect the maple tree's sugar during the "maple moon" in late February, when the sap begins to rise during the day. This augmented their diminishing supply of refined sugar brought with them from Europe. For these settlers, sugar made the unknown foods they found growing wild in their new country more palatable, it was a reward at the end of a long day and it brought them pleasure in a sometimes hostile new place.

Columbus had brought sugar cane shoots to the New World on his second voyage and had planted them in the Caribbean, where they flourished. Out of this sugar cane production came numerous sweet products, including refined white sugar, cane syrup, brown sugar, molasses and black strap molasses. Molasses and maple sugar were the cheapest and therefore the most popular sweeteners in America before the middle of the 19th century. These sweeteners precluded anything too fancy in cooking methods and resulted in more rustic, simpler desserts, often made with the bountiful fruits of the country. By the 1880s, white sugar had become cheaper than maple sugar and became the sweetener of choice. The consumption of white sugar doubled between 1880 and 1915. This was a boom time for home baking, as homemakers competed with each other to make the best 'fancy' desserts, such as cakes, cookies and candy.

But American desserts were never as fancy or as refined as their European counterparts. The spirit and character of the land made way for desserts characterised by their simplicity and generosity. Many Early American desserts incorporated the local fruits, sweetened and stewed in a kettle over the fire, with a simple crown of cake that baked or steamed along with it. These had names like slump, grunt, pandowdy, and cobbler, names that were a kind of self-parody of the crudeness of the offering and perhaps the cook as well. This simplicity and homeliness of style continues today and demands that the ingredients be fresh and high quality, since they must stand on their own with little adornment. Generosity is evident in the filled-to-the-brim pies, tall multi-layer cakes, and over-sized cookies filled with nuts, chocolate and other goodies. They may lack the elegance of a Gateau Saint-Honoré, but their flavour and simplicity gives an advantage to the home baker, who can offer these wonderful desserts to the family.

In the following chapter, you will find a sampling of what I believe to be the best version of the most popular American desserts. They have been adapted so that they will appeal to today's taste and to the non-American palate, while maintaining as close as possible the authenticity of the dish. You will find recipes for traditional desserts, unique interpretations of these classics, as well as some modern desserts that have become popular in recent years. Pies, although not originating in America, are a more popular dessert in the United States than anywhere else in the world. Cakes have become symbols of celebration and hospitality, as demonstrated by a popular American song of the 1940s , "If I knew you were coming, I'd have baked a cake". Cookies are our favourite dessert to take along on picnics or with a packed lunch, the fast food of desserts. Ice-cream is a virtual dessert phenomenon in America, where it has been embraced like no other food. In 1917 ice-cream was classified by the government as an "essential foodstuff", and considered indispensable to the morale of the U.S. Army by the Secretary of War. Immigrants to the U.S. from 1921 onwards were served ice-cream when they arrived on Ellis Island. Americans may not have invented it, but we invented more uses for it – the ice-cream cone, the ice-cream sundae (including banana splits), the ice-cream soda and malt, and more recently, deluxe versions called 'gourmet ice-creams', including a brand sold under the sophisticated-sounding name of Haagen-Dazs.

Today, diet consciousness has hit an all-time high, and "low-fat, low-cholesterol, and low-calorie" is on everyone's lips. But in reality Americans are still passionate about their delicious ice-creams, chocolate, cakes, pies and cookies!  Sociologists describe today's American lifestyle as 'save and splurge' and this behaviour carries over into the way we eat as well. We may try to eliminate fat, red meat, cholesterol from our diets, but we still want a rich, sinful dessert at the end of it and we will fight for our right to have it. With American affluence has come a different attitude to eating than that of our forefathers. It is now more than just a necessity – it's got to be fun too. Eating is after all a social event, a celebration; sometimes ceremonial in the part food plays at weddings, birthdays and anniversaries. Dessert is the climax of the unfolding menu. Dinner, like a play, cannot end logically without a dramatic ending, something sweet and memorable. Most Americans agree with the sentiment of Pierette Brillat-Savarin's last words, "Bring on the dessert. I think I am about to die."

PREVIOUS SPREAD: *"Boston Cremes" by Wayne Thiebaud*
BELOW: *Malted milk shakes and ice-cream sodas in a 1950s diner*

# Basic American Pie Crust

Americans are crazy about pie – fruit, chiffon, pecan and lemon meringue to name only a few. But while almost any kind of pie will do, Americans are rather particular about their crust – it must be light, flaky and savoury to contrast with the sweetness of the filling. Originally, pie crust was made from lard, which provided the ultimate in taste and flakiness. This recipe is adjusted for modern tastes, using only a small quantity of lard. It is the best of both worlds.

YIELD: 20 cm/8 inch top and bottom crusts or a 25 cm/10 inch pie shell

INGREDIENTS:

240 g/8 ½ oz [2 cups] strong plain flour [US all-purpose flour]

½ teaspoon salt

115 g/4 oz [½ cup] unsalted butter, chilled

45 g/1 ½ oz [3 tablespoons] lard or white vegetable fat [US shortening], chilled

4–5 tablespoons iced water

METHOD:

★ Sift the flour and salt into a medium-size bowl. Cut or rub in the chilled fats until the mixture is the consistency of sand (this can be done with a fork, a pastry cutter or your fingertips).

★ Sprinkle 1 tablespoon of iced water on one area at a time, mixing it in to moisten the mixture. Add only enough water to make a dough that will hold together in a ball that is moist and supple, but not sticky.

★ Turn the dough out on to a work surface. With the heel of your hand push the dough away from you, smearing it on the surface. This will make sure that all the butter has been evenly distributed in the dough.

★ Flour the dough lightly, wrap in paper and refrigerate for 30 minutes to an hour before rolling it out. Dough can be successfully frozen.


FOR A PIE SHELL:

★ On a lightly floured surface, roll the dough out, working from the centre to the outer edges with each roll. Gently move the dough from time to time to be sure it is not sticking underneath, but refrain from turning it over and working in too much additional flour, because that will produce tough pastry. Roll it out to a 32.5 or 35 cm/13 or 14 inch circle (or about 5 cm/2 inches greater in diameter than the pan you intend to use). The dough should be about 3 mm/ ⅛ inch thick.

★ To transfer the dough to the 25 cm/10 inch pie tin or plate, simply roll it around the rolling pin and unroll over the tin, centring it. Trim about 2.5 cm/1 inch beyond the edge of the pie tin or plate, fold the excess dough under and flute or crimp the edge. (Fluting is a zig-zag pattern made by holding the edge of the dough between thumb and bent-under forefinger of both hands and pushing it in opposite directions, forming a 'zig' and a 'zag'. Do this all around the edge in a uniform pattern. It takes practise, but looks lovely.) Or simply trim the dough even with the tin or plate and use a fork to make a design on the edge.

★ If the pie shell is to be baked blind (without a filling), prick the bottom and sides well with a fork. Refrigerate or freeze for 10–20 minutes to firm the dough and reduce shrinking.

★ To bake blind, preheat the oven to 200°C/400°F/Gas 6. Line the pie shell with greaseproof or parchment paper and fill with dried beans or other weights. Bake for 10 minutes, then remove the beans and paper. Continue baking for a further 10–15 minutes or until the pastry is golden brown. If you require a partially baked shell, stop baking after the first 10 minutes.

FOR A LATTICE-TOP CRUST:

★ Roll out half of the dough as for a pie shell and use to line a 20 cm/8 inch pie tin or plate. Trim to leave a 2.5 cm/1 inch overhang all around. Put the filling in the pie shell.

★ Roll out the remaining dough and cut it into strips 1.5–2 cm/ ½-¾ inch thick, using a knife or pastry wheel. Lay half of the strips over the filling at 2.5 cm/1 inch intervals. Fold back alternate strips as you weave the remaining strips through in the opposite direction.

★ Fold the overhanging lower crust over the irregular lattice top and flute the edge decoratively.

FOR A DOUBLE CRUST:

★ Roll out half of the dough as for a pie shell and use to line a 20 cm/8 inch pie tin or plate. Trim even with the edge of the pie tin or plate. Put the filling in the pie shell.

★ Roll out the remaining dough and lay over the filled pie. Tuck the top crust under the edge of the lower crust and seal. Flute the edge decoratively. Be sure to cut slits in the top crust to allow steam to escape during baking.

*The children enjoy cooking at the turn of the century*

# All-American Apple Pie with Cheddar Cheese Crust

It seems almost sacrilegious to alter the recipe for an American symbol like apple pie, but with this recipe you will have a sweet and a savoury dessert rolled into one. If you are a purist, simply omit the cheese in the crust and you have a classic apple pie the way Americans love it – lots of apples, flaky crust and a hint of cinnamon and nutmeg. In early America and well into the 19th century, pie was a typical breakfast dish and with this one you will be tempted.

YIELD: 6-8 SERVINGS
Equipment: a 23–25 cm/9-10 inch pie tin or plate or flan/quiche dish
Oven: 230°C/450°F/Gas 8 and then 180°C/350°F/Gas 4

INGREDIENTS:

1 ½ recipes of Basic American Pie Crust dough (page 220) (The large amount of apples in this recipe require more crust to enclose them!)
60 g/2 oz [½ cup] plain flour [US all-purpose flour]
220 g/8 oz [1 cup] sugar (or use half soft brown sugar and half caster)
1 ½ teaspoons ground cinnamon
¼ teaspoon freshly ground nutmeg
½ teaspoon salt

1.8 kg/4 lbs (about 8–10 large) apples (The pie will be as interesting as the apples you choose. This recipe was tested with half Granny Smiths and half Golden Delicious apples, which makes a nice combination of sour and sweet, with apples that are always readily available. I also like Cox's apples, but they produce a lot of juice and the flour may need to be increased.)
2 tablespoons freshly squeezed lemon juice
15–30 g/ ½–1 oz [1–2 tablespoons] butter, at room temperature
120 g/4 oz [1 cup] mature (sharp) Cheddar cheese, grated

METHOD:

★ Prepare the pie crust dough and divide it into thirds. Wrap one-third separately for the bottom crust and the remaining two-thirds for the top crust. Refrigerate for at least 20 minutes, or for a few days if you are making the dough in advance.

★ Combine the flour, sugar, cinnamon, nutmeg and salt in a large bowl. Peel and core the apples and slice them thinly. Add them to the bowl as they are sliced, sprinkling with the lemon juice and stirring to coat them with the other ingredients. If you work quickly the apples will not turn brown. Allow the apples to blend with the other ingredients for about 15 minutes, stirring from time to time.

★ Roll out the dough for the bottom crust into a circle 5 cm/2 inches greater than the diameter of your pie tin. Put the dough into the tin and allow the edges to drape over the sides. Add the apple filling and dot the top with the butter.

★ Preheat the oven to the higher temperature.

★ On an unfloured surface, roll out the dough for the top crust to a circle about 20 cm/8 inches in diameter. Sprinkle the grated cheese over the dough, fold it over in half and roll out again until the cheese is well distributed throughout the dough.

★ Flour the work surface and roll out the dough to a 37.5–40 cm/15-16 inch circle. Lay this top crust over the pie. Moisten the bottom crust where it touches the top crust and squeeze them together. Fold the crusts under, on to the edge of the pie tin, and then crimp or flute attractively. Cut a few slits in the top crust to allow the steam to escape during baking (a star pattern radiating out from the centre of the pie is traditional).

★  Bake the pie for 10 minutes, then reduce the oven temperature. Continue baking for 1 hour. If you like, put a foil-lined pan under the pie to catch any juice that may escape from it, although if the crusts have been sealed properly, this will be minimal.

★  Serve the pie warm if possible, and *à la mode* (with vanilla ice-cream) if you like.

NOTE:  If you want a classic apple pie, omit the cheese from the top crust. Just brush the top crust with egg white and sprinkle with a bit of sugar. Bake as above, but be careful the top doesn't burn. Foil can be placed over the pie to prevent it from browning too much.

*Picking apples in a family orchard, a familiar fall scene*

# Mississippi Mud Pie

Mississippi Mud Pie is often sold in an ice-cream version. There is really no classic version, only a basic guideline that it be dark, rich and chocolate – the colour of Mississippi mud. Here is one version in all its sinful glory: a dramatic finish to a meal when only chocolate will do.

YIELD: 8-10 SERVINGS
Equipment:  a 23–25 cm/9-10 inch pie tin or plate, an electric mixer and a food processor
Oven: 200°C/400°F/Gas 6

INGREDIENTS:

FOR THE CRUST:
120 g/4 oz [1 cup] digestive biscuits [US graham crackers] or other plain sweet biscuit or cookie, pulverised in a food processor until fine
60 g/2 oz [½ cup] pecans or walnuts, toasted and finely chopped (or pulverise with the biscuits in the food processor)
75 g/2 ½ oz [⅓ cup firmly packed] light soft brown sugar
75 g/2 1/2 oz [⅓ cup] unsalted butter, at room temperature

FOR THE FILLING:
115 g/4 oz unsweetened bitter dark chocolate or lightly sweetened dark continental chocolate, chopped into small pieces

170 g/6 oz [¾ cup] unsalted butter, at room temperature
220 g/8 oz [1 cup firmly packed] light soft brown sugar
1 teaspoon pure vanilla essence [US pure vanilla extract]
4 size-1 eggs [US jumbo eggs] (See note)

FOR THE TOPPING:
1 teaspoon powdered gelatine [US unflavoured gelatin]
2 tablespoons cold water
500 ml/16 fl oz [2 cups] whipping cream
55 g/2 oz [½ cup] icing sugar [US confectioners' sugar], sifted
2 teaspoons pure vanilla essence [US pure vanilla extract]
½ teaspoon coffee essence [US coffee extract] (Trablit is an excellent brand), or use 1 teaspoon instant coffee granules dissolved in ½ teaspoon boiling water
Dark chocolate, to garnish

METHOD:
★  First make the crust and preheat the oven. In a medium-size bowl, mix the pulverised biscuits with the nuts and brown sugar and stir in the softened butter until well incorporated. Press evenly over the bottom and sides of the pie tin. Bake in the preheated oven for about 8 minutes or until lightly browned. Cool.
★  For the filling, melt the chocolate in the top of a double boiler over simmering water. Remove and set aside to cool. In a medium-size bowl, beat the butter until it is light and fluffy. Add the sugar and vanilla and beat for several minutes or until this mixture is also fluffy. Add the cooled chocolate. Beat in the eggs one at a time, beating for several minutes after each addition. The mixture should be smooth, silky and thick. Pour the filling into the cooled crust and refrigerate.
★  Sprinkle the gelatine over the cold water in a small metal or heat-proof cup and leave to soften for a few minutes. Put the cup into a shallow pan of simmering water and heat just until the gelatine dissolves (gelatine needs this gentle approach!).
★  Set aside about 4 tablespoons of the whipping cream in a small bowl and put the rest in a medium-size bowl. Whip with an electric mixer until beginning to thicken, then add the icing

sugar and vanilla and continue whipping until the cream forms soft peaks. Quickly add the gelatine to the reserved cream in the small bowl and beat briefly. Add this to the whipped cream and continue to whip until the cream forms soft but firm peaks.

★ Remove about 250 ml/8 fl oz [1 cup] of the whipped cream and fold the coffee essence or instant coffee mixture into it.

★ Spread the remaining vanilla whipped cream over the filling in the pie shell. Spoon the coffee whipped cream evenly over the top and swirl it through the vanilla cream with a knife to create an attractive, marbled pattern.

★ Hold a large piece of dark chocolate firmly and shave off curls, using a very sharp knife and pushing it flat against the chocolate. Decorate the top of the pie with these curls. Refrigerate until serving time. This pie can be made a day in advance.

NOTE: Since the eggs in the filling are not cooked in any way you might want to take the precaution of using pasteurised eggs in this recipe. Pasteurising removes the risk of salmonella. These eggs taste and behave just as regular fresh eggs do and have the added advantage of being lower in cholesterol. Substitute 240 g/scant 9 oz liquid pasteurised eggs for the 4 fresh eggs called for in the ingredients.

# Black Bottom Pie

This pie is a southern speciality evocative of summer afternoon tea on the porch. It is light, not too sweet, and a little sinful on the bottom.

YIELD: 8-12 SERVINGS
Equipment: a 23–25 cm/9–10 inch pie tin or plate or flan/quiche dish

INGREDIENTS:

1 tablespoon powdered gelatine [US unflavoured gelatin]
4 tablespoons cold water
85 g/3 oz unsweetened bitter dark chocolate or lightly sweetened dark continental chocolate
400 ml/14 fl oz [1 ¾ cups] milk
170 g/6 oz [¾ cup] caster sugar [US granulated sugar]
1 tablespoon cornflour [US cornstarch]
3 size-1 eggs [US jumbo eggs], separated

¼ teaspoon coffee essence [US coffee extract], or use
    ½ teaspoon instant espresso granules dissolved in
    ½ teaspoon hot water
One pie shell made with Basic American Pie Crust dough, baked blind (page 220)
2 tablespoons dark rum
¼ teaspoon each salt and cream of tartar
125 ml/4 fl oz [½ cup] whipping cream, whipped
Chocolate curls (page 265), to garnish

METHOD:

★ Sprinkle the gelatine over the cold water and set aside to soften. Melt the chocolate in the top of a double boiler over simmering water and remove to cool.

★ To make the custard, heat the milk in a saucepan until bubbles appear around the edge. Mix 110 g/4 oz [½ cup] of the sugar with the cornflour in a small bowl and add the egg yolks, whisking until light. Add a little of the hot milk to the egg and sugar mixture, whisking, and then pour it into the remaining milk in the saucepan. Cook over moderate heat, stirring, until thickened. Remove from the heat.

★ Add 250 ml/8 fl oz [1 cup] of the custard to the melted chocolate together with the coffee essence or instant coffee mixture. Mix well. Cool slightly, then pour into the pie shell. Chill.

★ Stir the softened gelatine into the remaining custard and transfer to a bowl. Put this bowl inside a larger bowl filled with ice and cold water and whisk the custard until it is well chilled but not set. Add the rum.

★ Whisk the 3 egg whites with the salt and cream of tartar until soft peaks form. Gradually add the remaining sugar and continue whisking until the whites are stiff and glossy.

★ Whip the cream until firm.

★ With the bowl still in the bath of iced water, fold the whisked egg whites and whipped cream into the rum custard. Pour this over the chocolate layer in the pie shell and refrigerate until firm. Garnish with chocolate curls before serving.

# Strawberry Rhubarb Tart

There is no more heavenly combination than strawberry and rhubarb. Rhubarb was considered to be a spring tonic to Early Americans, since it was the first fresh produce to come out of their gardens in cold climates. It was such a favourite pie ingredient that it became known as the 'pie plant'.

YIELD: 6-8 SERVINGS
Equipment: a 25 cm/10 inch loose-bottomed tart tin or use a flan/quiche dish
Oven: 190°C/375°F/Gas 5

INGREDIENTS:

FOR THE SWEET PASTRY:
180 g/6 ½ oz [1 ¼ cups + 2 tablespoons] plain flour [US all-purpose flour]
55 g/2 oz [¼ cup] caster sugar [US granulated sugar]
115 g/4 oz [½ cup] unsalted butter
1 size-1 egg [US jumbo egg], separated
1–2 tablespoons double cream [US heavy cream]

FOR THE FILLING:
525 g/1 ¼ lb [4 cups] rhubarb, cut into 1.5 cm/ ½ inch pieces
220 g/8 oz [1 cup] sugar
50 g/1 ¾ oz [5 tablespoons] cornflour [US cornstarch]
¼ teaspoon salt
1 tablespoon grated orange rind
1 tablespoon Grand Marnier or other orange liqueur

FOR THE GARNISH:
75 g/2 ½ oz [¼ cup] seedless strawberry jam or jelly, or substitute another red jam or jelly
1 tablespoon Grand Marnier
225 g/8 oz fresh strawberries, halved

METHOD:
★ First make the pastry. Sift the flour and sugar into a medium-size bowl. Cut the butter into the flour using a pastry cutter or simply use your fingertips to break the butter up into the flour. It should be the consistency of a thick grain. In a small cup, whisk together the egg yolk with 1 tablespoon of cream and add to the flour mixture. Mix to moisten. If the dough does not hold together in a supple ball, add more cream. Wrap the dough well and refrigerate for at least 20 minutes.
★ Mix the rhubarb filling ingredients together in a medium-size bowl. Set aside for a good 15 minutes, stirring from time to time, so that the juices of the rhubarb can mix with the cornflour and sugar. (Note: If baked immediately, the filling will be very dry with a crusty, hard top.)
★ Preheat the oven.
★ Roll out the dough to a circle about 30–32.5 cm/12–13 inches in diameter. Place in the tart tin or dish. (I prefer to use a ceramic or china flan or quiche dish because its rounded edges don't cut the dough when it is being pressed in, and because of the ease and attractiveness of presentation at the table.) Trim and crimp the edges attractively. Paint the tart shell with the egg white (this will seal it from the juice of the rhubarb).
★ Add the rhubarb filling to the tart shell. Bake in the preheated oven for about 30 minutes or until the rhubarb is tender but not mushy. Push the top rhubarb down into the juices about half way through the baking time to insure even cooking. Allow the tart to cool to room temperature.
★ Just before serving (or 1–2 hours before if necessary), melt the strawberry jam with the liqueur, stirring. Heat just until melted; do not boil. Chill briefly or cool at room temperature until this glaze thickens sufficiently to coat the back of a spoon. Decorate the top of the tart attractively with the strawberry halves. With a pastry brush, paint each strawberry with the glaze. Serve the tart with sweetened whipped cream (see Strawberry Shortcake, page 232).

# Key Lime Pie

A famous American pie named after the small "key" limes available in Florida. It works perfectly well with any lime and provides a refreshing, light end to a meal. This version is so light it may float away and, like any meringue based dessert, it is best made on a dry day.

YIELD: 6-8 SERVINGS
Equipment: a 23–25 cm/9–10 inch pie tin or plate and an electric mixer
Oven: 180°C/350°F/Gas 4

INGREDIENTS:

6 size-1 eggs [US jumbo eggs], separated
220 g/8 oz [1 cup] caster sugar [US granulated sugar]
125 ml/4 fl oz [½ cup] freshly squeezed lime juice (from about 3 large limes)
1 tablespoon grated lime rind (from about 2 large limes)

2 drops of green food colouring
¼ teaspoon salt
One pie shell made with Basic American Pie Crust dough, baked blind (page 220) and cooled

METHOD:

★ In the top section of a double boiler, off the heat, or in a heatproof bowl, beat the egg yolks with an electric mixer until they are light and lemon-coloured. Add half of the sugar and continue beating until the sugar is no longer grainy. Add the lime juice and rind and set over the bottom pan of boiling water. Cook for about 15 minutes, beating often. The mixture should be very thick and lines drawn across it with the beaters will remain. Remove from the heat and beat in the green food colouring.

★ Preheat the oven.

★ Whisk the egg whites with the salt in a medium-size bowl, until soft peaks form. Add the remaining sugar, a little at a time, and continue to whisk until a glossy and stiff meringue has formed. Whisk about 125 ml/4 fl oz [½ cup] of the meringue into the lime mixture and then fold this into the rest of the meringue. Fold gently but thoroughly until no white meringue is visible in the mixture.

★ Fill the prebaked pie shell with the mixture and smooth the top attractively. Bake in the preheated oven for 15–20 minutes or until the meringue is nicely browned. Serve warm or chilled.

NOTE: Lemons can be substituted for the limes, but the result will be a sweeter, less refreshing pie.

# Blueberry-Raspberry Buckle

Early American desserts were often make-shift adaptations of desserts made in Europe, re-created in a kettle over the fire. They were called by such amusing names as slumps, grunts, cobblers and buckles, silly names that were descriptive of the strange things these sweets did in the baking process. Buckle means 'to crumple up', which the top will do and recipes for this dessert can be found in many old Southern cookbooks. This is a homely dessert, meant to be served warm with cream or ice-cream.

YIELD: 8-10 LARGE SERVINGS
Equipment: a 30 cm/12 inch flan/quiche dish or a 35 x 25 cm/14 x 10 inch gratin dish
Oven: 180°C/350°F/Gas 4

INGREDIENTS:
225 g/8 oz [1 cup] unsalted butter, at room temperature
75 g/2 ½ oz [⅓ cup] caster sugar [US granulated sugar]
1 size-1 egg [US jumbo egg], beaten
120 g/4 oz self-raising flour [US cooks see note below]
120 g/4 oz strong plain flour [see note]
2 teaspoons bicarbonate of soda [US baking soda]
250 ml/8 fl oz [1 cup] buttermilk
Grated rind of 1 lemon
260 g/9 ½ oz [2 cups] blueberries
260 g/9 ½ oz [2 cups] raspberries

FOR THE TOPPING:
110 g/4 oz [½ cup] granulated sugar
115 g/4 oz [½ cup firmly packed] dark soft brown sugar
120 g/4 oz [1 cup] self-raising or plain flour [US all-purpose flour]
115 g/4 oz [½ cup] unsalted butter, at room temperature
50 g/1 ¾ oz [⅓ cup] pecans, toasted and chopped
½ teaspoon freshly grated nutmeg

METHOD:
★ Preheat the oven. Butter and flour the baking dish.
★ In a large bowl, beat the butter and sugar together until they are light and fluffy. Add the egg and continue to beat. Add the flours and bicarbonate of soda alternately with the buttermilk, ending with a final addition of flour. Fold in the lemon rind. Spread this batter in the bottom of the baking dish and sprinkle the berries over it.
★ Combine the topping ingredients in a small bowl, using your fingertips to distribute the butter throughout the other ingredients. Sprinkle the topping evenly over the batter and berries.
★ Bake the buckle in the preheated oven for 1 hour. Leave to cool for 15-30 minutes before serving, with cream or ice-cream.

NOTE: US cooks should use 2 cups all-purpose flour to replace both the self-raising flour and the strong plain flour in the batter.

# Angel Food Cake

This is a cake rarely found outside the United States, but Americans have been having a love affair with it since its invention in the 1870s. It is still chic and popular today, a classic cake with the added benefits of no fat or cholesterol. Delicious served with whipped cream and fresh berries or drizzled with chocolate, the lightness of this cake will amaze you.

### YIELD: 10-12 SERVINGS
Equipment: an angel food tube pan (which comes in two pieces), measuring 25 x 11 cm/10 x 4 ½ inches and with a capacity of 3 litres/4 ⅔ pints [3 quarts]. Or you can use a 23 x 12.5 x 7.5 cm/9 x 5 x 3 inch loaf pan with a greaseproof or parchment paper collar tied around it to create another 5 cm/2 inches in height. (If using the loaf pan, cut the recipe in half.) You'll also need an electric mixer or whisk.
Oven: 170°C/325°F/Gas 3

### GUIDELINES:
- Choose a day of low humidity for baking this cake.
- Egg whites must be free of any trace of yolk and equipment must be cleaned of all traces of grease or fat.
- Use a copper bowl and large whisk for best results or an electric mixer and a stainless steel mixing bowl.
- Work quickly once the egg whites are whisked and bake immediately after mixing.

### INGREDIENTS:
Whites from about 12 size-1 eggs [US jumbo eggs] to yield 520 g/1 lb 2 ¼ oz or 420 ml/14 fl oz [1 ¾ cups]
1 teaspoon cream of tartar
¼ teaspoon salt
385 g/scant 14 oz [1 ¾ cups] caster sugar [US superfine sugar]

125 g/4 ¼ oz [1 ¼ cups] sifted sponge or plain flour [US cake flour]
1 ½ teaspoons pure vanilla essence [US pure vanilla extract]
¾ teaspoon almond essence [US almond extract]
¾ teaspoon freshly squeezed lemon juice

### METHOD:
★ Preheat the oven.
★ Whisk the egg whites until frothy. Add the cream of tartar and salt and continue to whisk until soft peaks form.
★ Sprinkle the sugar by the tablespoon over the whites, whisking after each addition. Whisk until the whites are stiff and glossy. Do not overbeat and let the whites become dry.
★ Sift the flour over the whites little by little, folding it in gently but thoroughly. Try not to lose the volume you have whisked into the whites.
★ Finally, sprinkle the essences and the juice over the mixture and fold them in.
★ Pour the cake mixture into the ungreased tube pan and smooth the top. Bake for about 1 hour and 10 minutes or until the top is golden brown and the cake springs back when pressed lightly with a finger.
★ Turn the tube pan over and insert the central funnel into the top of a bottle, so that the pan is suspended well over the work surface. Leave the cake to cool upside down for about 1 hour. Run a knife around the edges and remove the cake. Store it in an airtight container. Angel food cake will keep for a few days, but is best eaten the day it is baked.

# CHOCOLATE FROSTING FOR ANGEL FOOD CAKE

6 tablespoons icing sugar [US confectioners' sugar]
⅛ teaspoon salt

6 tablespoons unsweetened cocoa powder
750 ml/1 ¼ pints [3 cups] whipping cream

Mix together the dry ingredients and reserve. Whip the cream in a chilled bowl until soft peaks begin to form. Sift the dry ingredients over the cream and whip until stiff. Use to ice the cake. Garnish with toasted almonds or chocolate curls (page 265), if desired.

## ...dUE

This variation (                          )itchens of the Switzerland
Association in Nev                        chocolate. This is a fun finish
to any meal that i                        dunk fresh fruit sparingly into
the chocol                                ound cake a bath in it.

e forks

INGREDIENTS:
A 250 g Toblerone chocolate bar or equivalent (The Toblerone bar is Swiss milk chocolate with honey and almond nougat.)
60–125 ml/2–4 fl oz [¼ –½ cup] whipping cream
1–2 tablespoons Kirsch or Grand Marnier or other liqueur of choice (optional)

pineapple, strawberries, bananas, cherries, oranges, mango etc., all cut into bite-size pieces
Angel Food Cake (opposite) or other plain cake, cut into 2.5 cm/1 inch cubes
Marshmallows

METHOD:
★ Melt the chocolate and cream together slowly in the fondue pot. Start with the smaller amount of cream and add more if you need to. Whisk to combine into a smooth dip, then add liqueur if desired.
★ Transfer the pot to the table and set it over a small burner to keep the fondue warm. Pass the fruit, cake and marshmallows so guests can dip them into the chocolate as they like.

# Old-Fashioned Strawberry Shortcake

Many restaurants in the U.S. now serve a sponge cake version of Strawberry Shortcake, but it is nothing like the original. Shortcake by definition is a cake made short and crisp with butter, like a biscuit. Many remember their mothers' Strawberry Shortcake and the special additions she made to make it the best they've ever eaten. This adaptation of the classic recipe comes with a sauce that soaks into the cake, inspiration from just such a childhood memory. Shortcake is best served warm.

YIELD: 4-6 SERVINGS
Oven: 200°C/400°F/Gas 6

INGREDIENTS:
85 g/3 oz [6 tablespoons] unsalted butter
120 g/4 oz strong plain flour [US cooks see note]
120 g/4 oz self-raising flour [see note]
1 tablespoon baking powder [see note]
1 teaspoon salt
2 tablespoons caster sugar [US granulated sugar]
Grated rind of 1 lemon
15 g/ ½ oz [1 tablespoon] lard or white vegetable fat
   [US shortening]
125–185 ml/4–6 fl oz[1 ¾ cup] single cream
   [US light cream]

FOR THE SAUCE:
225 g/8 oz fresh strawberries, sliced
110 g/4 oz [½ cup] sugar
4 tablespoons freshly squeezed lemon juice

FOR THE GARNISH:
225 g/8 oz fresh strawberries, halved
300 ml/ ½ pint [1 ¼ cups] whipping cream
2 tablespoons icing sugar [US confectioners' sugar]
½ teaspoon pure vanilla essence [US pure vanilla extract]
A few beautiful whole strawberries

METHOD:
★ Well in advance, make the sauce. Combine all the sauce ingredients in a medium-size saucepan and bring to the boil over moderate heat. Cook until thickened and reduced to about 250 ml/8 fl oz [1 cup] (there will be some strawberry pieces in the syrup, and that's okay!). Cool and then chill until needed.
★ For the garnish, sprinkle the strawberries with a little granulated sugar. Whip the cream with the icing sugar and vanilla. Keep refrigerated until needed.
★ Preheat the oven.
★ For the shortcake, set 30 g/1 oz [2 tablespoons] of the butter aside to soften at warm room temperature. Sift the flours, baking powder, salt and sugar into a bowl and stir in the grated lemon rind. Cut or rub in the remaining butter and the lard or vegetable fat using your fingertips or a pastry blender. Mix to an even, grainy consistency. Slowly add the cream to make a supple dough that is not too wet; you probably won't need all of the cream.
★ Turn the dough on to a floured board and cut in half. Roll out half of the dough to a circle about 20 cm/8 inches in diameter and place it in a buttered baking pan that is 20 cm/8 inches or larger in diameter. With a pastry brush or your fingers, smooth the softened butter over the top of the dough.
★ Roll out the remaining dough in the same manner and place it on top of the dough in the pan. Bake in the preheated oven for 20-25 minutes or until golden brown. (If you must bake the shortcake in advance, warm it briefly in the oven before adding the garnish.)

★ Let the shortcake cool slightly, then split the two halves (the butter layer will facilitate this). Moisten both layers with the sauce. Cover the bottom layer with most of the whipped cream and the halved strawberries. Set the second layer on top and garnish with the rest of the whipped cream and a few beautiful whole strawberries. Cut at the table after displaying this creation and receiving applause.

NOTE: US cooks should use 2 cups all-purpose flour to replace both the self-raising flour and the strong plain flour in the shortcake dough, and add an additional 1 ½ teaspoons baking powder.

# Brownie Cheesecake

Tradition has it that cheesecake was introduced to Britain and Western Europe during the Roman conquests. In each country, cheesecake developed differently using different cheeses and additions to it. In 1872, the American dairy industry gave cheesecake in the United States the boost it needed while attempting to recreate the French cheese, neufchatel. They created an unripened cheese that was even richer and decided to call it 'cream cheese'. Brownie cheesecake is very different from the classic or New York Cheesecake – it's a lighter, custard cheesecake with a crunchy, naughty brownie top.

YIELD: 12-24 servings, depending on serving size
Equipment: a 25 cm/10 inch springform cake pan
Oven: 170°C/325°F/Gas 3

INGREDIENTS:

FOR THE SHORTBREAD SHELL:
120 g/4 oz strong plain flour [US cooks see note below]
60 g/2 oz plain flour [see note]
55 g/2 oz [¼ cup] caster sugar [US granulated sugar]
115 g/4 oz [½ cup] unsalted butter, at room temperature
¼ teaspoon salt
1 size-1 egg [US jumbo egg], separated
1 teaspoon Tia Maria or other coffee liqueur (optional)

FOR THE FILLING:
450 g/1 lb cream cheese or other full fat soft cheese, at room temperature
220 g/8 oz [1 cup] caster sugar [US granulated sugar]
2 tablespoons plain flour [US all-purpose flour]
8 size-1 eggs [US jumbo eggs]
750 ml/1 ¼ pints [3 cups] milk
1 teaspoon pure vanilla essence [US pure vanilla extract]
350 g/12 oz [3 cups] brownies (use Fudge Brownie recipe, page 241, with or without nuts), cut into 1.5 cm/ ½ inch cubes and frozen

METHOD:
★  To make the shortbread dough, sift the flours and sugar into a medium-size bowl. Add the softened butter, salt, egg yolk and Tia Maria, if using. Mix with a fork to combine and then use your fingers to mix to a smooth pliable dough. Shape into a ball and refrigerate for 20 minutes (or freeze for 10).
★  Preheat the oven.
★  Roll the dough out between two sheets of greaseproof or parchment paper or cling film [US plastic wrap] until it is 35–37.5 cm/14–15 inches in diameter. Using the bottom of the springform pan as a guide, cut out a circle of dough. Reserve the dough trimmings for making the sides later.
★  Put the dough circle on the bottom of the springform pan and prick all over with a fork. Bake in the preheated oven for about 15 minutes or until golden brown. Remove from the oven and leave to cool.
★  Using your hands, press the dough trimmings on to the sides of the pan, extending almost all the way up to the rim. Don't worry about the patchwork sides – it won't show after the cheesecake has been baked. Be careful to join the prebaked bottom with the unbaked sides very well, so that the cheesecake filling will not ooze out of a small hole. Finally, brush the bottom and sides with the egg white, to seal them from the moisture of the filling.
★  Beat the cream cheese with the sugar and flour until smooth and fluffy. Add the eggs, two at a time, beating well after each addition. Add the milk and vanilla and beat to combine.

★ Carefully pour the filling into the prepared shell and bake in the middle of the preheated oven for 30 minutes. Remove the cheesecake and scatter the frozen brownie pieces over the whole cake, sinking some but allowing others to float on the surface. Bake the cheesecake for a further 1 hour or until the filling is no longer liquid in the centre. Allow to cool to room temperature and then chill well before serving.

NOTE: US cooks should use 1 ½ cups all-purpose flour to replace both the plain flour and the strong plain flour in the shortbread dough.

# New York Style Cheesecake

This is the classic cheesecake for which New York is famous. It is a simple list of ingredients, but the result is a very tall and impressive cheesecake with a texture that is fine and light.

YIELD: 20 or more servings depending on how you cut it
Equipment: a 23 cm/9 inch springform cake pan
Oven: 200°C/400°F/Gas 6

INGREDIENTS:
900 g/2 lbs cream cheese (You can substitute the "light" version if you must, but the cheesecake just won't be as good.), at room temperature
170 g/6 oz [¾ cup] caster sugar [US granulated sugar]
2 size-1 eggs [US jumbo eggs], beaten lightly

1 teaspoon pure vanilla essence [US pure vanilla extract]
2 tablespoons cornflour [US cornstarch]
250 ml/8 fl oz [1 cup] sour cream
One pre-baked biscuit crust (see Mississippi Mud Pie recipe, page 224), made with or without nuts

METHOD:
★ Preheat the oven.
★ In a large bowl, beat together the cream cheese and sugar until smooth and light. Beat in the eggs, vanilla and cornflour just until well combined. With a whisk, beat in the sour cream.
★ Pour the filling into the prepared crust. Bake in the preheated oven for 45 minutes. Leave the cheesecake to cool in the turned-off oven, with the oven door only slightly opened, for 3-4 hours. Then chill in the refrigerator until firm.

# Chocolate Fudge Turtle Cake

Chocolate layer cake is reputed to be America's favourite dessert and you will often see a 'death by chocolate' dessert listed on menus across the country. This is such a dessert – rich fudgy cake, filled with an irresistible caramel custard filling and frosted in soft and creamy chocolate inspired by a confection called a "turtle". European flours make it difficult to bake American layer cake. In this cake height and moistness is achieved by juggling flours and adding a secret ingredient, date purée.

### YIELD: 12-24 SERVINGS
Equipment: 2 round 23 cm/9 inch cake pans, a food processor and a hand-held electric mixer
Oven: 190°C/350°F/Gas 4

### INGREDIENTS:
120 g/4 oz [½ cup packed] pitted dates, chopped
125 ml/4 fl oz [½ cup] boiling water
¾ teaspoon bicarbonate of soda [US baking soda]
170 g/6 oz lightly sweetened dark continental chocolate [US semi-sweet chocolate]
110 g/4 oz [½ cup] caster sugar [US granulated sugar]
4 size-1 eggs [US jumbo eggs], separated
115 g/4 oz [½ cup] unsalted butter, at room temperature
220 g/8 oz [1 cup firmly packed] soft brown sugar
60 g/2 oz strong plain flour [US cooks see note below]
180 g/6 oz self-raising flour [see note]
1 teaspoon baking powder [see note]
½ teaspoon salt
4 tablespoons cold water
125 ml/4 fl oz [½ cup] sour cream
1 teaspoon pure vanilla essence [US pure vanilla extract]
Toasted pecan halves, to garnish

### FOR THE CARAMEL PECAN FILLING:
330 g/12 oz [1 ½ cups] granulated sugar
30 g/1 oz [¼ cup] plain flour [US all-purpose flour]
¾ teaspoon salt
375 ml/12 fl oz [1 ½ cups] whipping cream
170 g/6 oz [¾ cup] unsalted butter, cut into small pieces
115 g/4 oz [1 cup] pecans, toasted and chopped
2 teaspoons pure vanilla essence [US pure vanilla extract]

### FOR THE CHOCOLATE FROSTING:
220 g/8 oz [1 cup] sugar
250 ml/8 fl oz [1 cup] whipping cream
170 g/6 oz unsweetened bitter dark chocolate or lightly sweetened dark continental chocolate
Pinch of salt
115 g/4 oz [½ cup] unsalted butter
½ teaspoon coffee essence [US coffee extract], or use instant espresso or coffee granules
1 teaspoon pure vanilla essence [US pure vanilla extract]

### METHOD:
★ Butter and flour the cake pans. Set aside. Preheat the oven.
★ To make the date purée, put the dates in a small bowl and pour the boiling water over them. Add ¼ teaspoon of the bicarbonate of soda and stir to mix. Purée the mixture in a food processor fitted with a metal blade.
★ In a small saucepan, combine this purée with the chocolate, caster sugar and 1 egg yolk. Cook over moderate heat, stirring constantly with a wooden spoon, until it becomes almost too hot to touch and is slightly thickened (there will still be some lumps of date visible). Never allow it to boil. Remove from the heat and leave to cool.
★ In a large bowl, beat the butter with the brown sugar using an electric mixer until light and fluffy. Add the remaining 3 egg yolks, one at a time, beating well after each addition.
★ Sift the flours, baking powder, remaining bicarbonate of soda and the salt together. Mix the cold water, sour cream and vanilla together. Add the dry and liquid ingredients to the butter mixture alternately, in 3 parts, ending with the dry ingredients. Beat well after each addition. Beat in the cooled chocolate custard until it is evenly combined.

★ Whisk the 4 egg whites until stiff but not dry and fold into the cake mixture gently but thoroughly. Pour into the prepared pans and bake in the preheated oven for 25–30 minutes or until a skewer inserted into the centre comes out dry. Cool, in the pans, on a rack. (The cake layers can be baked as much as 2–3 weeks in advance and frozen.)

★ In the meantime, prepare the filling. Combine the sugar, flour and salt in a heavy saucepan and gradually whisk in the cream and butter. Cook over low heat, stirring, until the butter has melted, then leave to simmer for 25–30 minutes or more until golden brown in colour. During this time, whisk occasionally to combine the browned bits at the bottom with the whole. Be sure to cook the filling long enough to caramelise it – the colour change will be subtle, not dramatic. Leave to cool to room temperature and then stir in the nuts and vanilla. Refrigerate the filling until it is thick enough to spread and retain its shape. (The filling can be prepared a day in advance and refrigerated. Bring it back to room temperature before using.)

★ When the cakes have cooled completely, remove one layer to a serving plate. Reserve 250 ml/8 fl oz [1 cup] of the filling and spread the remainder over the cake layer. Put the second layer on top.

★ To make the frosting, put the sugar and cream in a heavy saucepan and bring to the boil over moderate heat. Reduce the heat and simmer for 6 minutes, stirring occasionally. Remove from the heat and add the chocolate, stirring until it has melted. Add the rest of the ingredients and stir until the butter melts completely. Put the frosting into a medium-size bowl and put this bowl into a larger bowl that is filled with ice and water. Beat the frosting with a hand-held electric mixer until its colour changes slightly and it has a spreading consistency.

★ Spread the frosting generously over the top and sides of the cake, reserving enough frosting to make about 6–8 mounds on top (about 2 tablespoons of frosting for each mound). Refrigerate for about 30 minutes.

★ Warm the reserved caramel filling slightly until it is of pouring consistency (don't let it get too hot or it will melt the frosting). Drizzle the filling over the top of the cake, especially over and around the mounds of frosting. Push 2 pecan halves into each mound, leaving the nuts sticking out on each side so they resemble the feet of a turtle. Refrigerate briefly to set this topping, but serve the cake at room temperature.

NOTE: US cooks should use 2 cups all-purpose flour to replace both the self-raising flour and the strong plain flour in the cake mixture and increase the baking powder to 1 ½ teaspoons.

# Celebration Cake

Of course any event can be a celebration, but this cake is well-suited for birthdays or anniversaries. It is lemon meringue heaven – elegant, light and refreshing. You can change this cake to suit anyone's preference, filling it with different mousses, plain whipped cream and a variety of fruits, or even drizzle it with chocolate.

YIELD: 8-12 SERVINGS
Equipment: two 23 cm/9 inch springform cake pans and an electric mixer (countertop or hand-held)
Oven: 180°C/350°F/Gas 4

INGREDIENTS:

30 g/1 oz [¼ cup] blanched almonds, very finely chopped
  (chop in a food processor if you like)
115 g/4 oz [½ cup] unsalted butter, at room temperature
440 g/1 lb [2 cups] caster sugar [US granulated sugar]
Yolks from 4 size-1 eggs [US jumbo eggs]
4 tablespoons milk, or use half cream and half milk
½ teaspoon almond essence [US almond extract]
100 g [1 cup] sifted sponge or plain flour [US cake flour]
1 ½ teaspoons baking powder
Salt
Whites from 6 size-1 eggs [US jumbo eggs]
1 teaspoon pure vanilla essence [US pure vanilla extract],
  or use half almond essence and half vanilla essence
Strawberries or raspberries, to garnish

FOR THE FILLING AND TOPPING:

65 g/2 ¼ oz [¼ cup + 1 tablespoon] granulated sugar
2 tablespoons cornflour [US cornstarch]
⅛ teaspoon salt
4 tablespoons water
4 tablespoons freshly squeezed lemon juice
Yolk of a size-1 egg [US jumbo egg]
1 teaspoon grated lemon rind
15 g/ ½ oz [1 tablespoon] unsalted butter
250 ml/8 fl oz [1 cup] whipping cream
1 tablespoon icing sugar [US confectioners' sugar]
Garnish with strawberries or raspberries

METHOD:

★ Generously butter the springform pans and sprinkle the finely chopped almonds over the bottoms. Preheat the oven.

★ In a large bowl, beat the butter with 110 g/4 oz [½ cup] of the sugar, using an electric mixer, until light and fluffy. Add the 4 egg yolks, one at a time, beating well after each addition. Combine the milk and almond essence, and sift together the flour, baking powder and ¼ teaspoon salt. Add the milk and the dry ingredients alternately to the butter mixture, ending with the dry ingredients. Continue beating at high speed for about 2 minutes.

★ Divide the cake mixture evenly between the two prepared pans and spread it out with a rubber spatula.

★ In a clean, greaseless bowl and with very clean beaters, whisk the egg whites with a pinch of salt until they are firm. Add the remaining sugar, little by little, continuing to beat until the meringue is very firm and glossy and will hold peaks indefinitely. Finally, whisk in the vanilla. Divide the meringue in half and spread over the cake mixture in the pans, peaking and swirling the top attractively.

★ Bake the cakes in the preheated oven for 35 minutes. The meringue will be well cooked and golden brown. Cool in the pans set on racks.

★ Prepare the lemon filling while the cakes are baking (or prepare it in advance). Combine the granulated sugar, cornflour and salt in a medium-size saucepan and whisk in the water and lemon juice. Bring the mixture to the boil and cook until thick and glossy, whisking continuously. Off the heat, add a small amount of the hot mixture to the beaten egg yolk and then return it to the remaining hot mixture, whisking. Put the pan back on the heat and cook, whisking, for an additional minute or two until thick. Remove from the heat and whisk in the lemon rind and butter. Cool to room temperature and then refrigerate, covered.

★ When you want to assemble the cake, whip the cream until it starts to become firm. Remove the lemon custard from the refrigerator and whisk it briskly until softened. Fold half of the whipped cream into the lemon custard. Continue whipping the rest of the cream with the icing sugar until it is firm and peaks well.

★ Loosen the cakes by cutting around them, then remove from the pans. Set one cake on a serving plate with the meringue side down. Mound the lemon custard filling over this cake layer and place the second cake layer on top, with the meringue side up. Decorate the top of the cake with mounds of the plain whipped cream and garnish with strawberries or raspberries. Refrigerate until serving.

# Lemon Bars

Bars are a treat that are just as good as cookies, but easier to make. This recipe is a very popular one, great served with tea or for dessert with ice-cream or fresh fruit.

YIELD: 16 bars, each 5 cm/2 inches square
Equipment: a 20 cm/8 inch square cake pan
Oven: 180°C/350°F/Gas 4 and then 160°C/315°F/Gas 2 ½

INGREDIENTS:

115 g/4 oz [½ cup] unsalted butter, at room temperature
120 g/4 oz [1 cup] self-raising flour [US all-purpose flour]
30 g/1 oz [¼ cup] icing sugar [US confectioners' sugar], plus more for the top

Salt
2 size-1 eggs [US jumbo eggs]
220 g/8 oz [1 cup] caster sugar [US granulated sugar]
Grated rind and juice of 1 large lemon
30 g/1 oz [¼ cup] plain flour [US all-purpose flour]
½ teaspoon baking powder

METHOD:

★ Lightly butter the cake pan and set aside. Preheat the oven to the higher temperature.

★ In a medium-size bowl, beat the softened butter with the self-raising flour, icing sugar and a pinch of salt until well combined. Use your fingers to press this shortbread dough evenly on to the bottom of the prepared pan. Bake in the preheated oven for 20 minutes. Meanwhile, prepare the topping.

★ In a medium-size bowl, beat the eggs well and gradually whisk in the caster sugar. Slowly add the lemon rind and juice, plain flour, baking powder and ¼ teaspoon salt, whisking well.

★ When the shortbread base has finished baking, remove it from the oven. Pour the lemon topping over the hot base and return to the oven at once. Reduce the oven temperature and bake for a further 30–35 minutes or until the top is a light golden colour.

★ Remove the pan and run a knife around the edge of the cake. Leave to cool in the pan for about 20 minutes and then cut into 5 cm/2 inch squares. Sprinkle the tops with sifted icing sugar and arrange on a lace doily on a plate for serving. The bars can be kept in an airtight container, but only for a day or two.

# The Best Fudge Brownies

Brownies became popular in the United States sometime after World War I and all the major chocolate companies came out with versions of their own. They were voted most popular snack by the time World War II arrived and then rationing made them almost impossible to make. Today we don't have to abstain and they are still popular for their rich goodness and ease of preparation.

YIELD: 12-16 BROWNIES
Equipment:  a 25 x 20 x 5 cm/10 x 8 x 2 inch baking pan, or a 23 cm/9 inch square pan, and an electric mixer
Oven: 180°C/350°F/Gas 4

INGREDIENTS:

120 g/4 oz [1 cup] strong white flour [US all-purpose flour]
⅛ teaspoon salt
170 g/6 oz unsweetened bitter dark chocolate (Chocolat Amer by Valhrona is a good brand) or lightly sweetened dark continental chocolate
1 teaspoon instant espresso coffee granules

115 g/4 oz [½ cup] unsalted butter, at room temperature
170 g/6 oz [¾ cup] caster sugar [US granulated sugar]
110 g/4 oz [½ cup firmly packed] soft brown sugar
1 teaspoon pure vanilla essence [US pure vanilla extract]
130 g/4 ½ oz [⅓ cup] golden syrup [US light corn syrup]
3 size–1 eggs [US jumbo eggs]
170 g/6 oz [1 ½ cups] pecan halves or large pieces, toasted

METHOD:

★  Butter the cake pan, line it with greaseproof or parchment paper and butter again. Finally, flour it lightly. Preheat the oven.

★  Mix the flour and salt together and reserve. Chop the chocolate finely and melt it in the top of a double boiler, or in a heatproof bowl over a pan of hot water. Add the instant coffee and stir until smooth. Remove from the heat and reserve.

★  Beat the butter with the sugars and vanilla until light and fluffy. Add the syrup and mix well. Add the eggs one at a time, beating well after each addition. Finally, beat in the cooled, melted chocolate. Add the flour and beat on low speed until a smooth mixture is achieved. Stir in two-thirds of the nuts.

★  Pour the mixture into the prepared pan and spread to level. Place the rest of the nuts decoratively on the top, so that each brownie will have a nut in the centre when cut.

★  Bake in the preheated oven for 45–50 minutes or until a wooden cocktail stick inserted in the centre comes out clean but not dry. Cool in the pan for 30 minutes and then invert on to a rack. Peel off the paper and leave to cool completely. Refrigerating or freezing the brownies briefly will ease the cutting process. Store in an airtight container or wrap individually in cling film [US plastic wrap]. These freeze well.

# Old-Fashioned Sugar Cookies

There was a time when this cookie filled the cookie jars of America and this recipe found its way into all the church and community cookbooks of the land. This is the cookie of ice-cream socials and make-'em-for-your-beau fame.

YIELD: 4-5 DOZEN LARGE COOKIES
Oven: 190°C/375°F/Gas 5

INGREDIENTS:

225 g/8 oz [1 cup] butter, at room temperature
250 ml/8 fl oz [1 cup] vegetable oil
120 g/4 oz [1 cup] icing sugar [US confectioners' sugar]
220 g/8 oz [1 cup] caster sugar [US granulated sugar]
2 size-1 eggs [US jumbo eggs]

1 teaspoon each of salt, bicarbonate of soda [US baking soda], cream of tartar and pure vanilla essence [US pure vanilla extract]
240-360 g/8 ½–12 ¾ oz self-raising flour [US cooks see note below]
240 g/8 ½ oz strong plain flour [see note]

METHOD:

★ Whisk or beat the butter and oil together until smooth. Add the sugars and beat until the mixture is fluffy and light. Add the eggs, salt, bicarbonate of soda, cream of tartar and vanilla.

★ Reserve 120 g/4 oz of the self-raising flour and add the remainder with the strong plain flour to the bowl. Mix well. Add just enough of the reserved self-raising flour to make a dough that is firm enough to shape into balls. Refrigerate the dough for about ½ hour.

★ Preheat the oven.

★ Scoop up the dough by large tablespoons and roll into balls with your hands, placing the balls on ungreased baking sheets. Leave at least 5 cm/2 inches space between the balls. Using a heavy, flat-bottomed glass and dipping it in sugar each time, flatten the balls quite thinly.

★ Bake in the preheated oven for 10-12 minutes. The cookies should be lightly browned (if they are too white they will not be crisp, too dark and they will taste burnt). Remove the cookies to a rack or paper to cool. Keep in a cookie jar in plain view of kids of all ages. Delicious with ice-cream or tea (or both).

NOTE: US cooks should use 4–5 cups all-purpose flour to replace both the self-raising flour and the strong plain flour. Reserve 1 cup flour adding just enough to make the cookie dough.

# Chocolate Chunk Cookies

These were invented out of desperation when I was living in Europe and my children clamoured for chocolate chip cookies but no chocolate chips were available. Happily, these cookies are actually better because the cook can control the size and the quality of the chocolate chunks according to taste. The word 'cookie' came to the United States with the Dutch, who called little cakes *koekje*. Chocolate chip cookies have achieved an unparalleled success and are found in every country to which I have travelled. But none have been as good as these.

YIELD:  3-6 dozen cookies, according to size
Oven: 190°C/375°F/Gas 5

INGREDIENTS:
270 g/9 ½ oz [2 ¼ cups] self-raising flour [US all-purpose flour]
1 teaspoon baking powder
1 teaspoon salt
100 g/3 ½ oz [½ cup] white vegetable fat [US shortening], at room temperature
115 g/4 oz [½ cup] unsalted butter, at room temperature

170 g/6 oz [¾ cup] caster sugar [US granulated sugar]
170 g/6 oz [¾ cup firmly packed] soft brown sugar
2 size-1 eggs [US jumbo eggs]
1 teaspoon pure vanilla essence [US pure vanilla extract]
280–365 g/10–13 oz best quality bittersweet dark or milk chocolate, or a combination of both, chopped into bite-sized pieces
60–115 g/2–4 oz [½–1 cup] pecans, chopped (optional)

METHOD:
★ Preheat the oven.
★ Sift the flour, baking powder and salt into a medium-size bowl. In a larger bowl, beat the vegetable fat and butter together with the sugars until the mixture is light and fluffy. Add the eggs one at a time, beating well. Add the vanilla and then the dry ingredients. Fold in the chocolate and nuts, blending evenly.
★ Drop the dough by tablespoons on to ungreased baking sheets, leaving 2.5–5 cm/1–2 inches between the cookies. Bake in the preheated oven for about 8 minutes or until lightly browned. Remove the cookies to a rack or paper to cool.

# White Chocolate and Macadamia Nut Cookies

There is a growing fascination with white chocolate in the United States, and this combination vyes for popularity with the chocolate chip cookie. Macadamia nuts are a speciality of Hawaii and are wonderful combined with white chocolate.

YIELD: 4 DOZEN LARGE COOKIES
Equipment: a food processor
Oven: 170°C/325°F/Gas 3

INGREDIENTS:

100 g/3 ½ oz [½ cup] white vegetable fat [US shortening], at room temperature
115 g/4 oz [½ cup] butter, at room temperature
220 g/8 oz [1 cup firmly packed] soft brown sugar
110 g/4 oz [½ cup] caster sugar [US granulated sugar]
2 size-1 eggs [US jumbo eggs]
1 teaspoon pure vanilla essence [US pure vanilla extract]
180 g/6 oz [1 ½ cups] self-raising flour [US all-purpose flour]
½ teaspoon salt

1 teaspoon baking powder
1 teaspoon bicarbonate of soda [US baking soda]
160 g/5 ½ oz [2 cups] porridge or rolled oats, processed in a food processor until medium fine, or use medium oatmeal
115 g/4 oz white chocolate, finely chopped
340 g/12 oz white chocolate chips, or use white chocolate cut into chunks
225 g/8 oz [1½ cups] macadamia nuts, chopped, or you can substitute almonds

METHOD:

★ Preheat the oven.
★ Beat the vegetable fat and butter with the sugars until the mixture is light and fluffy. Add the eggs and vanilla and continue beating to combine well.
★ Sift the flour, salt, baking powder and bicarbonate of soda into a medium-size bowl and stir in the oats. Add these dry ingredients to the butter mixture and combine with a wooden spoon. Finally, fold in the chocolate and nuts.
★ Put the mixture on baking sheets by the ample tablespoon, leaving at least 5 cm/2 inches between each cookie. Bake in the preheated oven for 8–10 minutes or until nicely browned (the more you let them brown the crisper they will be). Leave to cool on the baking sheet for half a minute before removing the cookies to a paper-lined rack for cooling.

NOTE: For a crispy chocolate chip cookie, substitute milk chocolate for the 115 g/4 oz of finely chopped white chocolate, dark chocolate chips or chunks of bitter dark chocolate for the 340 g/12 oz white chocolate chips, and pecans for the macadamia nuts.

# Easy Marshmallow Fudge

Candy-making has all but left the home front in America – except for fudge. This is an easier version than the old-fashioned recipe that required lots of beating, but it is just as good. I once made this for a neighborhood craft sale in France and it was so popular I couldn't keep up with the orders for pounds and pounds of it.

YIELD: ABOUT 1.1 KG/2½ LBS
Equipment: a 20 cm/8 inch square pan

INGREDIENTS:

115–225 g/4–8 oz [1–2 cups] pecan or walnut halves, toasted
295 g/10 ½ oz [1 ⅛ cups] sugar
150 ml/ ¼ pint [⅔ cup] evaporated milk
55 g/2 oz [4 tablespoons] unsalted butter
16 large marshmallows, quartered, or 1 jar (200 g/7 oz) marshmallow cream

¼ teaspoon salt
350 g/12 oz [2 cups] best-quality plain or dark continental chocolate [US semi-sweet chocolate], chopped, or use chocolate chips
1 teaspoon pure vanilla essence [US pure vanilla extract], or use ½ teaspoon coffee essence [US coffee extract]

METHOD:

★ Reserve a large handful of the toasted nuts to decorate the top of the fudge; chop the remaining nuts. Butter the pan and set aside.

★ In a heavy saucepan, combine the sugar, evaporated milk, butter, marshmallows and salt. Bring to the boil over moderate heat, stirring frequently. As soon as the mixture reaches the boil, start timing it: boil for just 5 minutes, stirring frequently.

★ Remove the pan from the heat and add the chocolate. Beat it in until completely melted. Then stir in the chopped nuts and vanilla. Working quickly, spread in the buttered pan. Smooth the top and press on the reserved nuts in an even spacing so that when cut, each square of fudge will have a nut centred in the middle.

★ Leave the fudge to cool, then refrigerate until it is firm. Cut the fudge into squares. Wrap the pieces individually in cling film [US plastic wrap] or store in an airtight container. If the fudge is not to be eaten within a few days, it should be frozen.

# Fudge Peanut Butter Ripple Ice-Cream

Ice-cream knows no season in America – it's eaten all year long. It is served on pie, in pies and cakes, in sundaes, sodas, floats or just on its own. This creation is like so many popular today because it is inspired by a popular candy bar that combines chocolate and peanut butter.

YIELD: about 1 litre/1⅔ pints [1 quart]
Equipment: an ice-cream machine

INGREDIENTS:
500 ml/16 fl oz [2 cups] milk
500 ml/16 fl oz [2 cups] whipping or double cream
  [US heavy cream]
1 vanilla pod [US vanilla bean], preferably split open down
  the length
Yolks from 6-12 size-1 eggs [US jumbo eggs], according to
  richness desired
220 g/8 oz [1 cup] sugar

FOR THE FUDGE PEANUT BUTTER RIPPLE:
160 g/5 ½ oz [½ cup] Mom's Chocolate Fudge
  Sauce (page 248)
65 g/2 ¼ oz [¼ cup] chunky-style peanut butter
35 g/1 ¼ oz [2 tablespoons] golden syrup [US light
  corn syrup]
50–100 g/1¾–3½ oz [½–1 cup] dry-roasted peanuts

METHOD:
★ In a medium-size heavy saucepan, bring the milk and cream almost to the boil, then remove from the heat. Add the vanilla pod. Cover and set aside to infuse for about 15 minutes.
★ Meanwhile, whisk together the egg yolks and sugar until fluffy and light in colour.
★ After the cream and milk and bean have infused for 15 minutes, bring almost to the boil again. Remove from the heat. Whisk half the liquid into the yolks and sugar, then pour this mixture into the saucepan. Return to the heat and cook very gently, stirring constantly with a wooden spoon, until the custard has thickened enough to coat the spoon. (To test the consistency, dip the spoon into the custard and run your finger over the back of the spoon. If your finger leaves a clean trail, the custard is ready.) Do not let the custard boil or it will curdle. If it does get a little too hot and starts to curdle on the bottom, strain the mixture. Leave the custard to cool at room temperature.
★ Strain the custard to remove the vanilla pod. Scrape the interior with a knife to release the little vanilla seeds and add these to the custard if you like. Refrigerate the custard until cold.
★ Pour the custard into the ice-cream machine and freeze, following the manufacturer's instructions.
★ To make the fudge peanut butter, warm the fudge sauce, peanut butter and golden syrup in a small saucepan until well combined. Leave to cool to room temperature.
★ When the ice-cream has almost finished freezing but is not completely firm, add the fudge peanut butter sauce and the peanuts. Allow them to be swirled into the ice-cream briefly, but don't mix them in completely – a ripple effect is the desired result. Transfer the ice-cream to a freezer container. The fudge peanut butter mixture freezes very hard, so you may want to remove the ice-cream from the freezer a few minutes before serving.

# Peppermint Stick Ice-Cream

Peppermint sticks were one of the earliest candies invented, and certainly one of the first to be added to ice-cream (now it's a trend). But this old-fashioned treat is one you will have to make yourself to enjoy today. Nothing compares to its palate-cleansing refreshment, and it is divine served with a warm brownie and hot fudge sauce.

YIELD: about 1 litre/1 ⅔ pints [1 quart]
Equipment: an ice-cream machine

INGREDIENTS:
350 g/12 oz best-quality peppermint sticks or candies
   (Find ones that use real flavourings if possible. The red and white ones are the prettiest.)

500 ml/16 fl oz [2 cups] milk
Yolks from 8 size-1 eggs [US jumbo eggs]
500 ml/16 fl oz [2 cups] cream (use either double cream [US heavy cream] or whipping cream)

METHOD:
★ Reserve 100 g/3 ½ oz of the peppermint. Put the remainder in a heavy plastic bag and break the candies into small pieces with a hammer. Do not pulverise them however. Add them to the milk and refrigerate for 8 hours or overnight.
★ Whisk the egg yolks and cream together in a heavy saucepan. Stir with a wooden spoon over very low heat until this custard has thickened enough to coat the back of the spoon. (To test the consistency, dip the spoon into the custard and run your finger over the back of the spoon. If your finger leaves a clean trail, the custard is ready.) Do not let the custard boil or it will curdle. If it does get a little too hot and starts to curdle on the bottom, strain the mixture immediately. Once the desired consistency is reached, strain the custard and leave to cool at room temperature.
★ Add the custard to the peppermint-flavoured milk. Pour into the ice-cream machine and freeze, following the manufacturer's instructions.
★ In the meantime, crush the reserved peppermint candies into very small pieces. Add to the ice-cream when it has begun to thicken.

# Mom's Chocolate Fudge Sauce

The Hot Fudge Sundae is the most popular offering of America's ice-cream parlours and shops, and you will find more of these in the United States than in any country in the world. Perhaps we can trace this sundae back to Aztec times, when legend has it that Montezuma enjoyed hot chocolate poured over snow that had been rushed to him from the mountain tops. Today, it is much easier to serve this sauce warmed over a rich vanilla ice-cream or use it to make Fudge Peanut Butter Ripple Ice-Cream.

YIELD: about 750 ml/1 ¼ pints [3 cups]

INGREDIENTS:
85 g/3 oz unsweetened bitter dark chocolate (such as Chocolat Amer from Valhrona) or lightly sweetened dark continental chocolate
435 ml/14 fl oz [1 ¾ cups] single cream [US light cream]
170 g/6 oz [¾ cup] sugar

30 g/1 oz [¼ cup] plain flour [US all-purpose flour]
¼ teaspoon salt
15 g/ ½ oz [1 tablespoon] butter
1 teaspoon pure vanilla or coffee essence [US pure vanilla or coffee extract]

METHOD:
★ Gently melt the chocolate in the cream until smooth, stirring occasionally.
★ Combine the sugar, flour and salt in a small bowl. Add enough of the chocolate mixture to make a smooth paste, then add this to the remaining chocolate mixture in the pan. Cook, stirring, until smooth and thick.
★ Remove from the heat and stir in the butter and vanilla or coffee essence. Serve warm.

NOTE: The fudge sauce can be kept refrigerated for 1–2 weeks. Warm it before serving.

# Banana Sorbet with Hawaiian Fruits and Pineapple Sauce

Often a light and refreshing dessert is called for, and this one celebrates America's 50th State – Hawaii. It is a delicious combination of flavours, perfect after an oriental-influenced meal or a summer barbecue.

YIELD: about 1 litre/1 ⅔ pints [1 quart]
Equipment: an ice-cream machine (useful but not absolutely essential) and a food processor

INGREDIENTS:
450 g/1 lb (4–6) ripe bananas
Juice of ½ lemon
185 ml/6 fl oz [¾ cup] still mineral water
2 teaspoons rum (preferably white)
Fresh fruits of your choice: pineapple, papaya, mango, carambola (star fruit) etc.

FOR THE SUGAR SYRUP:
275 g/10 oz [1 ¼ cups] sugar
250 ml/8 fl oz [1 cup] water

FOR THE PINEAPPLE SAUCE:
Flesh of ¼ fresh pineapple, puréed in a food processor
55 g/2 oz [¼ cup] sugar
2 tablespoons dark rum
1 tablespoon freshly squeezed lime or lemon juice

METHOD:
★ For the sugar syrup, put the sugar and water in a saucepan over high heat and stir until the sugar dissolves. Bring to a complete boil, then remove from heat and leave to cool.
★ Peel the bananas and purée the flesh in a food processor until smooth. (Do not use an electric blender because it will add too much air to the purée.) Measure the purée – you will need a generous 415 ml/13½ fl oz [1⅔ cups]. In a bowl, mix the banana purée with 330 ml/10½ fl oz [1⅓ cups] of the sugar syrup, the lemon juice, mineral water and rum.
★ Pour into the ice-cream machine and freeze, following the manufacturer's instructions. If you do not have an ice-cream machine you can use the still-freezing method: pour the mixture into a metal bowl, cover and freeze for about 2 hours or until the outside 5 cm/2 inches of the mixture is firm. Remove from the freezer, scrape the frozen parts into the centre and beat with an electric mixer (or in small amounts in a food processor) until smooth. Cover and return to the freezer. Repeat this procedure 3 times, leaving the mixture to freeze solid after the final beating. For an extra-smooth texture, chill the food processor container and blade in the freezer.
★ Transfer the sorbet to a freezer container, leaving 1.5 cm/½ inch headspace for expansion, and cover tightly. Place in the freezer compartment of the refrigerator to "ripen" 1–2 hours before serving.
★ To make the pineapple sauce, stir the ingredients together in a small bowl until the sugar dissolves.
★ Create a work of art on each serving plate or a large platter with balls of sorbet and attractively cut fruit. Serve the sauce on the side or lay a thin layer on the plate before arranging the fruit and sorbet.

# Frozen Cappuccino with Chocolate Leaves

Sometimes time is lacking, but not the desire to serve a special dessert. This dramatic, adult dessert is quick and easy to prepare, but will receive raves. Your guests won't believe you made the chocolate leaves yourself – but even they are easy.

### YIELD: 4-6 SERVINGS
Equipment: a food processor and fresh non-toxic leaves from the garden

## INGREDIENTS:
1 litre/2 pints [1 quart] good-quality coffee ice-cream
4 tablespoons light rum
4 tablespoons dark rum

4 tablespoons coffee liqueur such as Kahlua or Tia Maria
About 100 g/3 ½ oz good-quality plain or dark
    continental chocolate [US semi-sweet chocolate],
    finely chopped

## METHOD:
★ Chill a food processor bowl and metal cutting blade. Combine the ice-cream, rums and liqueur in the food processor and process just until blended. (Do not process too much or the ice-cream will start to melt.)
★ Pour into small freezerproof wine glasses or serving dishes and freeze.
★ To make chocolate leaves, melt the chocolate gently in a double boiler or in a heatproof bowl set over a pan of hot water (or in a microwave).
★ Choose large fresh leaves that are firm and have prominent veins (rose leaves are very pretty). Simply paint the chocolate on to each leaf in a thin, even layer. Refrigerate until needed.
★ Just before serving, peel the leaf off the chocolate and lay two or three chocolate leaves on each dessert, prettiest side up.

ABOVE: *Thanksgiving Day Turkey, painted by Norman Rockwell, 1943*
OPPOSITE: *A Fourth of July Invitation from Uncle Sam*

"Fourth of July" Greetings

# CHAPTER SIX

# MENUS FOR AMERICAN-STYLE CELEBRATIONS

A MERICANS LOVE TO CELEBRATE! We celebrate Thanksgiving, our Forefathers' first harvest feast and day of thanks and on the Fourth of July, commemorate our independence. We celebrate love on Valentine's Day, Father's Day, Mother's Day and even Grandparent's Day. Christmas is a festival of lights, with every household trying to outdo the next in their decorating, both inside and out. It is a holiday resplendent with rejoicing and entertainment. Some of our favourite celebrations are outdoors when "the weather is hot and the living is easy" and we picnic, barbecue and enjoy a friendly game of softball. But no matter what the celebration, it is usually associated with special food.

These menus will enhance any celebration. Let them transport you into another style and world of eating. That's what cookbooks should be about – being transported – away from everyday cares and into the fun of another country's cuisine and people.

### AN AMERICAN THANKSGIVING
Sugar & Spice Roasted Nuts (recipe follows)
Sparkling apple juice (add Calvados for the adults)
Thanksgiving Roast Turkey with Sausage-Chestnut Stuffing
Thanksgiving Potatoes (recipe follows)
Corn Crêpes with Sweet Potato Soufflé or Corn Pudding
Cranberry & Orange Relish
Ginger Pumpkin Pie with a Brown Sugar-Cinnamon Crust (recipe follows) or Pecan Pie

### FOURTH OF JULY BARBECUE
Guacamole and corn chips
Time-Stealing Barbecued Ribs and Grilled Teriyaki Chicken Breasts
Corn on the Cob and Boston Baked Beans
Mary's All-American Potato Salad
Layered Picnic Salad (recipe follows)
Fourth of July Tipsy Watermelon (recipe follows) and Old-Fashioned Sugar Cookies

### SUPER BOWL ALL-AMERICAN BRUNCH
A Pitcher of Bloody Marys
Fruit Kebabs (recipe follows)
Salmon Hash
Blueberry & Sour Cream Muffins and Apple Pizza
Coffee

### CHRISTMAS TREE TRIMMING PARTY OR OPEN HOUSE
Eggnog and Holiday Punch for Kids (recipe follows)
Fruited tea bread sandwiches:
Cranberry Orange Bread with ham
Banana Bread with Goat's Cheese Spread (recipe follows)
Truffle Cookies (recipe follows) and Old-Fashioned Sugar Cookies

A MEXICAN-STYLE COCKTAIL PARTY
Killer Margaritas, Sangria, Mexican beers
Quesadillas – 3 Ways
Guacamole and corn chips
Green Chile Con Queso Dip
Fresh Fruit and Tequila Dip


A SUMMER DINNER PARTY OUT-OF-DOORS
Killer Margaritas or A Pitcher of Bloody Marys
Spicy Roasted Pecans (recipe follows)
Grilled Baby Chicken & Salsa Verde
Pump Room Spinach Salad
Fresh Fruit and Tequila Dip
Old-Fashioned Sugar Cookies and Truffle Cookies (recipe follows)


A VALENTINE DINNER FOR TWO
Champagne
Benne Biscuits
Classic Caesar Salad
San Francisco Cioppino
Crusty Italian bread (ciabatta)
Frozen Cappuccino with Chocolate Leaves


SOUTHERN DINNER BUFFET
Mint Juleps
Benne Biscuits
Time-Stealing Barbecue Ribs
Southern Fried Chicken
Okra Fritters
Skillet Cornbread
Louisiana Bread Pudding Soufflé with Whiskey Sauce


TEENS' LOW-FAT LUNCHEON
Turkey Burgers on wholemeal buns
Summer Salad
Angel Food Cake and fresh fruit


NEW YEAR BEAT-THE-BLUES-AND-EXTRA-POUNDS DINNER PARTY
Double Rich Mushroom Soup with Wild Rice
Grilled Swordfish in a Lime & Coriander Marinade
Classic Caesar Salad
Banana Sorbet with Hawaiian Fruits & Pineapple Sauce

# Sugar and Spice Roasted Nuts

Roasted and spiced nuts make a wonderful holiday treat, both to give to friends and to have in bowls around your house. It's hard to decide which is best – the spicy hot ones or the aromatic sweet ones, but you should try both and decide for yourself.

YIELD: 450 g/1 lb nuts from each recipe
Oven: 180°C/350°F/Gas 4 for the spicy pecans and 140°C/275°F/Gas 1 for the sweet mixed nuts

FOR SPICY PECANS:
Whites from 2 size–1 eggs [US jumbo eggs]
1 teaspoon salt
1 teaspoon freshly ground black pepper
½ teaspoon ground white pepper
½ teaspoon cayenne pepper
½ teaspoon dried thyme
½ teaspoon dried basil
1 tablespoon Worcestershire sauce
1 teaspoon Tabasco sauce
450 g/1 lb pecan halves

FOR SWEET SPICED NUTS:
165 g/5 ½ oz [¾ cup] sugar
1 teaspoon ground cinnamon
½ teaspoon ground cloves
¼ teaspoon each freshly grated nutmeg and ground ginger
½ teaspoon salt
1 egg white, beaten until frothy
2 tablespoons water
450 g/1 lb whole blanched almonds, walnut halves and whole hazelnuts (a mixture according to your preference)

METHOD:
★ For the spicy pecans, preheat the oven and brush a baking sheet with oil. Whisk the egg whites in a small bowl until foamy and add all the seasonings. Add the nuts and toss them in the mixture. Spread the nuts on the baking sheet. Bake in the preheated oven for 12-14 minutes, stirring once or twice to loosen the nuts from the pan and turn them over so that they brown evenly. Remove from the oven and serve warm or store in an airtight container until you plan to use them. They will keep for a few days.
★ For the sweet spiced nuts, preheat the oven and lightly brush a baking sheet with softened butter. Combine the sugar, spices and salt and stir in the egg white and water to make a paste. Add the nuts and toss in the mixture to coat them well. Remove the nuts from the mixture with a fork to the prepared baking sheet. Bake in the preheated oven for 45 minutes or until the nuts are crisp and coloured. Stir them once or twice during baking. Leave to cool to room temperature before serving or storing in an airtight container.

# Thanksgiving Potatoes

I always make these potatoes for a big celebration, because with all the other last-minute things I have to prepare, I don't want to whip potatoes! They are rich, fattening and delicious, but this celebration happens only once a year!

YIELD: 6–12 SERVINGS
Equipment: an electric mixer and a large soufflé dish
Oven: 170°C/325°F/Gas 3

INGREDIENTS:

1.5 kg/3 ⅓ lbs (about 6) large baking potatoes, peeled and quartered
55 g/2 oz [4 tablespoons] butter
165 g/5 ½ oz [½ cup + 2 tablespoons] cream cheese or other full fat soft cheese
125 ml/4 fl oz [½ cup] sour cream

1 size-1 egg [US jumbo egg], beaten
½ teaspoon salt
¼ teaspoon white pepper
¼ teaspoon freshly grated nutmeg
35 g/1 ¼ oz [½ cup] freshly grated Parmesan cheese
2 tablespoons chopped fresh chives (optional)

METHOD:

★ Cook the potatoes in a large pan of boiling salted water until tender. Drain the potatoes, put into a large bowl and beat them until smooth with an electric mixer. Add the butter, Neufchatel or other cream cheese, sour cream and beaten egg and beat well. Add the salt, pepper, nutmeg and most of the Parmesan cheese (save some for the top). Fold in the chives.

★ Pour the mixture into a buttered large soufflé dish. Sprinkle the top with the remaining Parmesan cheese and refrigerate until about 40 minutes before you want to serve them.

★ Preheat the oven.

★ Bake the potatoes in the preheated oven for 25-35 minutes or until firm and slightly browned on top. This dish is not too finicky and will tolerate being left in the oven until the gravy is made and the turkey carved.

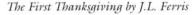

*The First Thanksgiving by J.L. Ferris*

# Ginger Pumpkin Pie

Warm pumpkin pie with a dollop of whipped cream is the traditional sweet ending to the Thanksgiving feast. Fresh pumpkin purée and freshly grated ginger elevate this pie to new heights. Choose a small pumpkin with dark-coloured flesh or substitute a hubbard or butternut squash.

YIELD: a 25 cm/10 inch pie that serves 6-8
Equipment: a 25 cm/10 inch ceramic or china flan/quiche dish
Oven: 200°C/400°F/Gas 6 and then 180°C/350°F/Gas 4

INGREDIENTS:

FOR THE PIE SHELL:
120 g/4 oz strong plain flour [US cooks see note below]
60 g/2 oz plain flour [see note]
¼ teaspoon salt
75 g/2 ½ oz [⅓ cup firmly packed] dark soft brown sugar
1 tablespoon wheat germ (optional)
½ teaspoon ground cinnamon
75 g/2 ½ oz [⅓ cup] unsalted butter
Yolks from 3 size-1 eggs [US jumbo eggs]
1 tablespoon iced water
½ teaspoon pure vanilla essence [US pure vanilla extract]
2–3 tablespoons apricot jam

FOR THE FILLING:
450 g/1 lb [2 cups] fresh pumpkin purée (follow instructions in Halloween Pumpkin Cake, page 41, for making fresh pumpkin purée), or use canned pumpkin purée
110 g/4 oz [½ cup] caster sugar [US granulated sugar]
¼ teaspoon salt
¼ teaspoon freshly grated nutmeg
¼ teaspoon ground cinnamon
1 teaspoon finely grated fresh ginger or ½ teaspoon ground ginger
2 size-1 eggs [US jumbo eggs]
150 ml/ ¼ pint [⅔ cup] whipping or double cream [US heavy cream]
1 teaspoon pure vanilla essence [US pure vanilla extract]
Whipped cream, to garnish

METHOD:
★ First prepare the pie shell dough. In a medium-size bowl, combine the flours with the salt, brown sugar, wheat germ and cinnamon. Rub in the butter with your fingertips until the mixture resembles coarse meal. Add the egg yolks and mix with a fork or your fingers, then sprinkle over the water and vanilla and mix until the dough forms a ball. Wrap the dough in paper or cling film [US plastic wrap] and refrigerate for at least an hour.
★ Roll this fragile dough out between two lightly floured pieces of greaseproof or parchment paper into a circle about 30 cm/12 inches in diameter. Carefully remove the top paper. Invert the dough into the flan dish, pressing it in gently to line evenly, and carefully peel off the remaining paper. Trim the dough, letting it extend about 1.5 cm/½ inch above the rim of the dish, and crimp the edges decoratively. Refrigerate for 20-30 minutes, crimping again when the dough is easier to handle.
★ Preheat the oven to the higher temperature.
★ Melt the apricot jam in a small saucepan with a little water until it is completely liquid. Brush this glaze over the entire crust, bottom and sides. This will seal it from the liquid filling so that it does not get soggy in the baking process.
★ Whisk together the ingredients for the filling. Pour the filling into the prepared pie shell and bake in the preheated oven for 15 minutes. Lower the oven temperature and continue to bake the pie for 30-40 minutes longer or until the filling is set.
★ Serve the pie warm with whipped cream (slightly sweetened with icing sugar [US confectioners' sugar] if you like and flavoured with a little rum or vanilla).

NOTE: US cooks should use 1½ cups all-purpose flour to replace both the strong plain flour and the plain flour in the dough.

# Layered Picnic Salad

This salad looks beautiful in a glass bowl because of all the colourful layers, and the ingredients are assembled the night before so they get crisp and cold. A wonderful invention for everyone with limited time to cook and a delicious contribution to a picnic or any summer gathering. Protein can be added too – sliced ham, chicken, turkey and hard-boiled eggs would all be good in this salad.

### YIELD: 12 OR MORE SERVINGS

INGREDIENTS:

1 head of lettuce such as iceberg, Cos or romaine, torn into small pieces
1 red sweet pepper, cut into thin slices
4 celery stalks, thinly sliced
1 large red onion, diced
340 g/12 oz [2–3 cups] frozen petit pois [US tiny peas]
200 g/7 oz [2 cups] cherry tomatoes, halved
1 large cucumber [US seedless cucumber], halved, seeded and sliced
16 red radishes, sliced

200 g/7 oz [2 cups] French beans [US thin green beans], cooked until tender but crisp, refreshed and chilled
250 ml/8 fl oz [1 cup] mayonnaise
250 ml/8 fl oz [1 cup] sour cream
1 teaspoon mild or medium-hot curry powder
125 ml/4 fl oz [½ cup] mango chutney
225 g/8 oz [2 cups] mature (sharp) Cheddar cheese, grated
8 smoked streaky bacon rashers [US thick bacon slices], cooked until crisp and then chopped or crumbled

METHOD:

★ Layer the vegetables in a large clear glass or plastic bowl, in the order given above. The peas should be added frozen.

★ Mix together the mayonnaise, sour cream, curry powder and chutney in a small bowl. If there are large chunks of fruit in the chutney, remove them and chop them finely before adding. Pour this dressing over the vegetables, then sprinkle with the cheese and bacon. Cover well and refrigerate for about 8 hours or overnight.

★ Toss the salad just before serving.

# Fourth of July Tipsy Watermelon

Watermelon season begins in July and is always a part of the festivities on the Fourth of July. Adding alcohol to this all-American fruit has been in practice before and after the days of Prohibition, and always makes for a fun adult treat at any picnic or outdoor gathering.

INGREDIENTS:
1 sweet watermelon (it should sound hollow when "plunked" with your knuckles)

An alcohol of your choice, such as rum, Cognac, bourbon whiskey, Champagne or calvados

METHOD:
★ Cut a deep plug about 2.5–5 cm/1–2 inches diameter in the watermelon and remove it. Make a few deep cuts into the flesh revealed, using a long knife. Slowly pour in as much alcohol as the watermelon will absorb. (A small melon should absorb at least 125 ml/4 fl oz [½ cup].)
★ Put the plug back into the watermelon and tape over it. Chill for about 24 hours, turning the melon a number of times to allow the alcohol to permeate the flesh evenly.
★ Slice and enjoy! Serve with Old-Fashioned Sugar Cookies (page 242).

# Fruit Kebabs

These are ideal for serving at buffet dinners or brunches. They are attractive and refreshing, and the ginger sugar syrup keeps the fruits moist and aromatic.

An attractive presentation can be made by using the scooped out pineapple halves as a base for a "hedgehog" display of the fruit kebabs. Lay the halves prickly side up on a platter and stick in the kebabs at intervals all over.

INGREDIENTS:
330 g/12 oz [1 ½ cups] sugar
250 ml/8 fl oz [1 cup] water
Juice of ½ lemon
Six 1.5 cm/½ inch slices (about 55 g/2 oz) peeled fresh ginger

Assorted fresh fruits, such as pineapple, mango, papaya, orange segments, kiwi fruit, lychees, melon, strawberries etc.
Stem ginger in syrup, sliced (optional)
Wooden skewers

METHOD:
★ Combine the sugar, water, lemon juice and fresh ginger in a small saucepan. Bring to the boil over moderate heat and simmer for a few minutes. Leave to cool.
★ Cut the fruit into bite-size pieces and thread on to wooden skewers. Add slices of stem ginger if you like.
★ Lay the kebabs in a pan or dish large enough to hold them in a single layer and pour the cooled syrup over the fruit. Refrigerate overnight or for a few hours.

# Holiday Punch For the Kids

Kids sometimes feel left out of holiday festivities – this frothy, fruity punch gives them a special treat too.

YIELD: 16-20 SERVINGS
Equipment:  a punch bowl

INGREDIENTS:
1 litre/1 ⅔ pints [4 cups] each of orange juice, apricot
    nectar and pear nectar

1 small carton (500 ml or 1 pint) raspberry sorbet
1 litre/1 ⅔ pints [4 cups] ginger ale or fizzy lemon-lime
    drink, chilled

METHOD:
★  Mix the fruit juices together in a large pitcher and refrigerate.
★  When ready to serve, scoop the sorbet into a punch bowl, pour over the juices and the ginger ale and stir gently. Ladle into cups, adding a portion of the sorbet to each serving.

# Goat Cheese Spread

This savoury spread complements fruited tea bread, such as Banana Bread (page 262).

YIELD:  280 g/10 oz [1 cup]
Equipment: a food processor or electric mixer

INGREDIENTS:
115 g/4 oz cream cheese or other full fat soft cheese, at
    room temperature

115 g/4 oz soft goat's cheese, at room temperature
55 g/2 oz [4 tablespoons] unsalted butter, at room
    temperature

METHOD:
★  Put the ingredients in a food processor and work until smoothly blended, or beat in a bowl with an electric mixer.
★  This can be kept in the refrigerator for 3–4 days.

# Banana Bread

Banana bread has a definite place in American culture and cuisine. It is the favourite fruit bread, offered at brunches and breakfast buffets across the country and baked and given away more often than any other bread. A recent film scene had the heroine, going through one of life's crises, being visited by a friend with a loaf of banana bread, which she added to her freezer full of other such loaves, given by other concerned friends.

YIELD: 2 medium-size loaves or 4 small loaves
Equipment:  2 loaf pans, each 25 x 11 cm/10 x 4½ inches, or 4 loaf pans, each
15 x 11 cm/6 x 4½ inches, and an electric mixer
Oven: 180°C/350°F/Gas 4

INGREDIENTS:
Sesame seeds for the loaf pans
220 g/8 oz [1 cup] caster sugar [US granulated sugar]
110 g/4 oz [½ cup firmly packed] light soft brown sugar
225 g/8 oz [1 cup] unsalted butter, at room temperature
6-8 over-ripe bananas (675 g/1½ lbs peeled weight)
4 size-1 eggs [US jumbo eggs]
1 teaspoon pure vanilla essence [US pure vanilla extract]
½ teaspoon pure almond essence [US pure almond extract]

170 g/6 oz [1 ½ cups] sponge or plain flour [US cake flour]
135 g/4½ oz [1 cup] wholemeal flour [US whole-wheat flour]
2 teaspoons bicarbonate of soda [US baking soda]
1 teaspoon salt
½ teaspoon freshly grated nutmeg

METHOD:
★  Butter the loaf pans and sprinkle with sesame seeds to coat the bottom and the sides. Preheat the oven.
★  In a medium-size bowl, beat the sugars and butter together with an electric mixer until light and fluffy. Mash the bananas with a fork [US cooks should measure 3 cups purée]. Add the bananas to the butter mixture with the eggs and essences and beat to combine.
★  Sift together the dry ingredients and sift again over the banana mixture. Add the bran sifted out if necessary. Fold together gently, mixing just until combined.
★  Pour the mixture into the pans, filling them about three-quarters full. Bake in the preheated oven for 45 minutes to 1 hour or until the loaves are firm in the centre and are beginning to come away from the sides of the pan.
★  Cool on a rack for about 15 minutes before removing the loaves from the pans. Banana bread keeps for 3-4 days well-wrapped, and also freezes well.

# Truffle Cookies

These are adult cookies for serious chocolate lovers, reminiscent of the dense rich truffles I love in France and hence the name. These are the one chocolate cookie I make during the holidays and love to give as gifts.

YIELD: 3-4 DOZEN COOKIES
Equipment: a food processor
Oven: 150°C/300°F/Gas 2

INGREDIENTS:

115 g/4 oz [½ cup] unsalted butter, at room temperature

100 g/3 ½ oz [½ cup] lard or white vegetable fat [US shortening]

150 g/5 oz [1 ¼ cups] icing sugar [US confectioners' sugar]

130 g/4 ½ oz [1 cup] walnuts, toasted

255 g/9 oz [1 ¾ cups] lightly sweetened dark continental chocolate [US semi-sweet chocolate]

205 g/7 oz [2 ¼ cups] sifted sponge or plain flour [US all-purpose flour]

1 teaspoon pure vanilla essence [US pure vanilla extract]

¼ teaspoon coffee essence [US coffee extract]

110 g/4 oz [½ cup] caster sugar [US granulated sugar]

METHOD:

★ Preheat the oven.

★ Using an electric mixer or wooden spoon, beat the butter and lard or vegetable fat until soft and light. Add the icing sugar and beat until well combined.

★ Chop the walnuts finely in a food processor fitted with the steel blade. Chop the chocolate in the food processor until it is in very small pieces, but not into powder. Add these to the butter mixture together with the flour and essences. Stir together well with a wooden spoon.

★ Take about 2 teaspoons of dough and roll into a small ball. Put on an ungreased baking sheet. Continue rolling balls of dough, leaving about 2.5 cm/1 inch space between them on the baking sheets (they will flatten in the baking process, but not too much).

★ Bake in the preheated oven for 15 minutes. Remove from the oven and allow the cookies to cool on the sheets for about 5 minutes. Then remove and roll in the caster sugar while still warm. Allow to cool completely on a rack or on greaseproof or parchment paper. Store in airtight containers.

# Appendices

## American-Style Seasoning Salt

Always looking for a quick flavouring boost, Americans have used commercially produced seasoning salts for years. Now you can make this version yourself or modify it with your own favourite spices. If you like it, why not bottle it to give to your friends.

INGREDIENTS:

220 g/8 oz [1 cup] salt
¼ teaspoon each dried basil, tarragon, thyme, cayenne pepper, ground nutmeg and mild chilli powder
1 tablespoon sweet paprika
1 ½ teaspoons garlic salt
1 teaspoon black pepper, dry mustard, mild or medium hot curry powder and caster sugar [US granulated sugar]

METHOD:

Combine all the ingredients in a food processor and process until large pieces have been pulverised to a powder. Store in a tightly closed container.

## Home-made Tomato Essence

This is what the French call *tomates concassées*, and I like to substitute this sweet essence in place of tomato sauce or paste in many of my recipes – the result is worth the trouble. This is also a wonderful topping for omelettes. In winter, add 3–4 oil-preserved sun-dried tomatoes, finely chopped, to boost the taste.

YIELD: about 500 ml/16 fl oz [2 cups]

INGREDIENTS:

30 g/1 lb [2 tablespoons] butter
2 shallots, finely chopped
1.35 kg/3 lbs ripe red tomatoes, preferably plum or beef-steak, skin and seeds removed, coarsely chopped
A large bouquet garni including 10–12 parsley sprigs, a bay leaf and 4-6 fresh thyme sprigs
Salt and pepper to taste

METHOD:

★ Melt the butter in a large frying pan and add the shallots. Sauté them until soft, then add the tomatoes and bouquet garni, with sun-dried tomatoes if using. Season with salt and pepper. Cook over moderate heat, stirring frequently, until almost all of the moisture has evaporated.
★ Taste for seasoning. Keep refrigerated or freeze until putting it to use.

## Roasted Peppers

Many of the world's cuisines, especially those of Spain and Portugal, roast peppers, both sweet and chillies, to enhance their flavour and to enable their tough skin to be removed. The amazing flavour that roasted peppers impart is sought after in modern American cooking and is integral to many of the recipes contained in this book.

Roasted peppers can be used in many recipes or marinated in a vinaigrette to be served cold or at room temperature as an accompaniment to grilled fish and meat. A platter of marinated red and green sweet peppers is especially festive for the Christmas holidays.

Some cookbooks suggest you can roast peppers, under the oven grill [US broiler] or over an electric burner, but you will not achieve the success you'll have over a gas fire or a flame-licking charcoal fire in a barbecue. The goal is to blacken all the skin so that it can be removed easily, but not to cook the pepper flesh to a pulp.

If roasting fresh chilli peppers, first make a small slit near the stalk, or they may explode. Place the sweet or chilli pepper directly on the metal pan support of the gas burner, flame turned to high, or on the grill over flaming charcoal. Turn the pepper frequently with tongs until all the surface is blackened. Place the pepper in a plastic bag and leave to cool for a few minutes, then immerse in a bowl of iced water or hold under cold running water. Gently remove the blackened skin with your fingers.

## Using Fresh Hot Chillies

Some precautions should be taken when using fresh chillies, to avoid contact with the oils contained in them. Wear rubber gloves or coat your hands with vegetable oil. Don't hold the chilli under running water, since the water spray can carry the chilli oils to the face and eyes. Most of the 'heat' of the chillies is contained in the inner veins and seeds. To remove them, cut off the stalk, slice the chilli in half and cut around the inside core, removing the ribs and seeds. Wash your hands, utensils and cutting boards well after preparing chillies.

The level of 'heat' in chillies varies from variety to variety and even within the same variety, so always use caution when adding an unknown chilli to a recipe. Start small and add more after tasting the completed dish. Remember that you can always add that extra 'heat' at the table with Tabasco sauce, or add cayenne pepper as you adjust the seasonings in the completed dish.

## Notes on Working with Chocolate

Chocolate has been called "the devil of the kitchen", because of the difficulty almost every chef or cook has with it at one time or another. If chocolate is over-heated or if water gets into it when it is being melted, it will tighten or 'seize'. When this happens it becomes very firm, grainy and impossible to work with or to melt again. To rescue seized chocolate, try adding a teaspoon of vegetable oil to every 55 g/2 oz of chocolate. But to prevent chocolate from seizing in the first place, melt it gently, over indirect heat – in a double boiler or heatproof bowl set over a pan of hot but not simmering water – or use a microwave.

If using indirect heat, finely chop the chocolate and stir it occasionally until it is just melted and smooth. Milk chocolate and white chocolate (not really chocolate since it contains no cocoa solids) have high proportions of milk proteins,

butterfat and sugar and therefore burn and seize even more easily than other chocolates. So extra caution should be taken with them.

To melt chocolate in a microwave oven, place finely chopped chocolate in a microwave-safe bowl and melt at 50% power for between 90 seconds and 3 minutes (according to the quantity of chocolate and the power of your microwave), interrupting the process to stir every 30 seconds.

If chocolate is to be melted with butter or a liquid such as water or milk, this can be done in a heavy pan directly over very low heat. Stir and watch the process carefully. Adding alcohol to chocolate, in liquors or even in flavouring essences [US extracts], can sometimes cause chocolate to seize. Smooth it by adding the oil suggested earlier.

### SUBSTITUTES

The amount of sugar added to dark chocolate varies and such variation does not usually alter the recipe result dramatically. You can substitute lightly sweetened dark or bitter chocolate for unsweetened chocolate, but always use the best quality chocolate available to you – those with the higher percentages of cocoa solids or chocolate liquor in them.

With unsweetened chocolate, 30 g/1 oz can also be replaced by 3 tablespoons unsweetened cocoa powder + 15 g/ ½ oz [1 tablespoon] fat. Unsweetened chocolate can be made into semisweet chocolate by adding 1 tablespoon sugar to each 30 g/1 oz of melted chocolate.

To intensify the chocolate taste in any recipe, try adding a pinch or few drops of ground cinnamon, instant coffee powder or coffee essence [US coffee extract] or pure vanilla essence [US pure vanilla extract]. These flavours enhance that of chocolate and cut the sweetness, and will not generally be detectable in the dish.

To make chocolate curls, to decorate desserts: Hold a large piece of dark chocolate firmly and shave off curls, using a very sharp knife and pushing it flat against the chocolate. Refrigerate the curls until serving time.

Chocolate is a volatile substance and should be stored carefully. All types should be wrapped first in foil and then in plastic before being stored in an airtight container. (The foil protects the chocolate from light and the plastic from moisture and foreign aromas.) Don't wrap directly in plastic, because the fats in the chocolate may absorb the taste of plastic. Store in a cool, dark, dry place with an even temperature. Properly stored, dark chocolate can last up to 5 years with no change in quality, milk chocolate up to one year and white chocolate for 6-8 months. Quality chocolate brands include: Valrhona, Callebaut, Lindt and Suchard/Tobler.

## Notes on Working with Yeast Dough

Yeast is a living plant which responds to temperature in the following ways:
• At the right temperature (30°C/80°F for fresh yeast and 40-45°C/105–115°F for dried yeast), it grows and produces bubbles of carbon dioxide which raise the dough.
• At lower temperatures, yeast acts more slowly. It becomes dormant at freezing, though it does not die.
• High temperatures (above 54°C/130°F) kill yeast.
Both fresh and ordinary dried yeast are normally sprinkled over lukewarm water (or better yet, water at the right temperatures above) and left for 5–10 minutes before using in a recipe. This procedure checks that the yeast is alive and ready to do its work. Adding a little sugar will encourage the yeast to start growing. (Salt retards the growing process, so should never be added directly to the yeast at the beginning.) Easy-blend dried yeast [US rapid-rise yeast] does not require this initial stage.

Kneading helps to distribute the yeast evenly throughout the dough, which helps it to rise well. Kneading also develops the gluten in the flour. The higher the gluten content of the flour, the more even-textured the finished bread will be. Gluten becomes elastic through the addition of moisture and by kneading it and this elasticity adds strength to a dough, making it capable of retaining the gases the growing, fermenting yeast creates.

There are about 30,000 different varieties of wheat, which are used in various combinations to produce white flour. They are classified according to their growing season and to the 'strength' of the flour they produce. Winter or hard wheat is sown in the autumn and harvested the following summer; it is high in gluten and low in starch. This wheat flourishes in North America (Canada and the US). Soft, spring grown wheat is lower in gluten and higher in starches and grows best in the temperate climates of Europe and the southern regions of the US.

In converting American recipes for use in the UK, I have often used a mixture of strong bread flour and self-raising, sponge or plain flour, to approximate the make-up of American all-purpose flour, which combines hard and soft wheat. All of the recipes in this book have been tested using both American and British flours.

## An Alternative to Buttermilk

Buttermilk is widely used in American cooking. If you cannot find it in your local shop or supermarket, you can substitute milk soured with lemon juice or vinegar. To each 375 ml/12 fl oz [1½ cups] of milk, add 2 tablespoons lemon juice or vinegar. Leave this soured milk to stand for about 5 minutes before using it.

## Preparing Fresh Chestnuts

Use a sharp knife to cut a cross on the flat side of each chestnut. Put the chestnuts into a pan of boiling water, return to the boil and cook for 5 minutes. Drain the chestnuts and keep them warm in a towel, or return to the pan and cover, while you work quickly to peel them. If they cool, they will be impossible to peel.

## Preparing Fresh Clams

Scrub the clams well, discarding any that are open. Place them in a large pot with 1.5 cm/½ inch of water on the bottom. Cover and cook over moderately high heat until the shells open. Remove the clams. Strain the liquid and reserve to include in the dish. Take the clams out of their shells or just remove the top shells.

## Fresh Pork Sausagemeat

YIELD: about 900 g/2 lbs
Equipment: a food processor or mincer
[US grinder]

INGREDIENTS:
565 g/1 ¼ lbs lean pork fillet [US pork tenderloin]
300 g/10 oz fresh pork fat
1 ¼ teaspoons each salt, dried thyme and dried sage, or
    use 1 tablespoon fresh thyme and sage if available
1 teaspoon dried hot red pepper flakes
¾ teaspoon each freshly ground nutmeg and pepper
¼ teaspoon ground allspice
4 tablespoons Cognac

METHOD:
★ Cut the pork into medium-size cubes and the pork fat into small cubes and put in a bowl. Add the spices and herbs.
★ Process the mixture (or put through a mincer) in three batches: the first batch should be roughly minced [US roughly ground], the second medium, and the third medium-fine. Do not over-process – some coarseness is desired. Add the Cognac and pulse to combine.
★ Put the sausagemeat into a bowl and cover it tightly. Refrigerate overnight.

## Preparing Whole Live Lobster at Home

Perhaps the most sensual dining experience in America is eating whole fresh lobster, preferably out-of-doors. And, of course, the best place to do that is somewhere on the East Coast, from Maine to Cape Cod. It's not a neat affair, but it epitomises the plain simplicity of New England cuisine and a celebration of seafood in its unadulterated splendour. Once abundant and inexpensive, the American lobster is now in diminishing supply, but connoisseurs declare it the best for its salty-sweet flesh. If you have an opportunity to buy a fresh American or Canadian lobster – jump at it. A 675g / 1 ½ lb lobster will serve each guest royally!

### STEAMING

Most experts advise that steaming is the best way to cook a lobster, avoiding the tendency to water-log the beast. You will need a very large pot with a cover and a rack that fits inside. Put in 5–7.5 cm/2–3 inches of salted water (1 tablespoon of salt for every 1 litre/1⅔ pints [1 quart] of water) and bring to a rapid boil. Put lobsters in head first. I find wearing rubber gloves gives me more courage to grasp the lobsters. Cover the pot and when the boiling resumes begin timing. Steam a 450–565 g/1–1¼ lb lobster for 10-12 minutes, a 565–900 g/1½–2 lb lobster for 15-18 minutes and should you have a larger one in the 1.12–2.25 kg/ 2½–5 lb range, steam for 20–25 minutes. Before serving, hold the lobster upside down and cut the tip off each claw with kitchen scissors, allowing any water inside to drain out. Then turn the lobster, soft belly up, on a working surface and cut down the middle of the body and tail, either with a sharp chef's knife or with kitchen scissors. Remove the dark intestinal vein running down the tail and discard the stomach sac in the head. The soft green tomalley and red coral (in the female) is considered a delicacy. The majority of the meat is in the tail and claws, but small morsels can be found throughout the lobster. Serve with lots of melted butter and lemon wedges and the utensils to dig out the meat – a nutcracker and small pointed forks, such as those used for hors d'oeuvres.

### BOILING

Boiling, another satisfactory method of cooking lobster, is especially appropriate when preparing the lobster for use in another recipe, where it will receive a second cooking. Bring enough salted water (same quantities of salt as above) to the boil so that the lobster can be totally submerged. When the water is boiling rapidly, submerge the lobster, head first. Cover, return to the boil and reduce the heat so that the water simmers. Cook the lobster for 5 minutes for the first 450 g/1 lb and 3 minutes more for each additional 450 g/1 lb.

### BARBECUE GRILLING

Kill the lobster by plunging it headfirst into salted boiling water and cook for 1 minute. Remove and drain. Grill the lobster over medium-hot coals (see page 212 for instructions) for about 8-10 minutes, turning occasionally to avoid burning a particular area. Crack a claw to see if the lobster is done – the meat should be opaque.

## Removing Skin and Seeds from Tomatoes

First remove the stalk, then cut an 'x' in the base. Plunge the tomato into boiling water for a few seconds, then lift out and refresh under cold running water. Remove the skin – it should slip off easily. Cut the tomato in half and squeeze gently to remove the seeds.

## Toasting Nuts

Most nuts and seeds benefit from toasting, to enhance their flavour and aroma. Preheat the oven to 180°C/350°F/Gas 4. Spread the nuts or seeds in a small cake pan or on a baking sheet (depending on how many nuts you are toasting). Bake for 5–10 minutes or until the nuts or seeds are lightly browned (should you be able to distinguish a colour change) and are smelling wonderfully nutty. Watch carefully as they can burn, and stir once or twice so they toast evenly.

# BIBLIOGRAPHY

*American Cooking*, Dale Brown and the Editors of Time-Life Books, Time-Life Books, New York, 1968.

*Food*, Waverly Root, Simon and Schuster, New York, 1980.

*I Hear America Cooking*, Betty Fussell, Elizabeth Sifton Books, Viking Penguin Inc., New York, 1986.

*On Food and Cooking*, Harold McGee, Charles Scribner's Sons, New York, 1984.

*A Nation of Nations*, Louis Adamic, Harper & Brothers Publishers, N.Y. & London, 1945.

*American Food, The Gastronomic Story*, Evan Jones, E.P. Dutton & Co. Inc., N.Y., 1975.

*Americans, The View From Abroad*, James C. Simmons, Harmony Books, N.Y., 1990.

*First Generation: In the Words of 20th Century American Immigrants*, James Namias, Beacon Press, Boston, 1978.

*The Uprooted*, Oscar Handlin, Little, Brown & Co., Boston, 1951.

*They All Chose America*, Albert Q. Maisel, Thomas Nelson & Sons, N.Y., 1957.

*Time Magazine*, Special Issue 'The New Face of America', Fall 1993, Vol. 142, No. 21, Time Inc., N.Y.

*American Heritage Cookbook*, Editors of American Heritage, Simon & Schuster, Inc., 1964.

*Gourmet Magazine*, April 1993, Volume LIII, Condé Nast Publications, Inc., N.Y.

*Road Food & Good Food*, Jane & Michael Stern, Alfred A. Knopf, N.Y., 1986.

# INDEX

# PICTURE ACKNOWLEDGEMENTS

**Anthony Blake Photo Library, London**: p54, p79.

**Bridgeman Art Library, London**: p29 *Maple Sugaring* 1856 coloured lithograph by Currier and Ives, p51 *Thanksgiving Turkey Shoot* C19th Anon, p151 *The Stampede* 1932 by Robert O Lindneux (b1871), p253, p257 *The First Thanksgiving* by J L Ferris (1863-1930).

**Crocker Art Museum, Sacramento CA**: p216-7 *Boston Cremes* 1962 by Wayne Thiebaud (b1920) oil on canvas 35.6x45.7cm. Gift of the Crocker Art Gallery Association.

**George Eastman House**, Reproduced by courtesy: p65 *Italian family on a ferry boat leaving Ellis Island* (detail) 1905 photograph by Lewis Hine.

**Image Bank, London**: p11 Paul Trummer, p16 John Kane, p17 Lisl Dennis, p33 Walter Bibikow, p40 Peter Miller, p45 Michael Salas, p59 Marc Romanelli, p67 Place, p75 Peter Miller, p91 Alvis Upitis, p116-7 Place, p123 Peter Miller, p155 Murray Alcosser, p161 Grant V Faint, p163 Guido Alberto Rossi, p185 Infocus International, p199 Julius Ciss, pp211, 223, 231 Liberty Collection, p214 Michael Schwab, p221 Mercury Archive.

**John Lee, London**: pages 2, 4, 14-15, 19, 26, 31, 36, 43, 53, 56, 69, 82, 93, 102, 105, 109, 115, 120, 135, 137, 142, 148, 164-5, 179, 182, 189, 202, 204-5, 209, 233, 237, 240, 250.

**National Trust (Yorkshire Region)**/photo Jim Kershaw: p89 *Dutch Kitchen Scene* by Joachim de Beuckelaer (c1530-1573).

**Peter Newark's American Pictures, Bath**; p1: p8-9 *Indian Encampment on Lake Huron* by Paul Kane (1810-71), p13, p23, p35, p50 *Wild Turkey* by John James Audubon (1780-1851), p77 *Quaker Farm in Pennsylvania* c1800 Anon, p86, p88 *New Amsterdam* c1650 Anon, p94 *Duck Hunters on the Hoboken Marshes* 1849 by William Ranney (1813-1857), p96 *Country Breakfast* 1884 by Edward L Henry (1841-1919), p107, p113, p119, p128, p130, p169 *Autumn Fruits* 1861 coloured lithograph by Currier and Ives, p174-5 *Cowboys Roping Cattle* by Charles M Russell (1865-1926), p176 Nebraska State Historical Society, p177, p195, p201, p213 *Virginian Indians Cooking Fish* 1590 engraving by Theodore de Bry after a painting by John White, p225 *On the Mississippi* 1869 coloured lithograph by Currier and Ives, p252.

**The New York Historical Society Collection**: p62-3 *Hester Street New York* 1898 photographer unknown.

**Norman Rockwell Family Trust © 1943**: p252 *"Freedom From Want" – Thanksgiving Day Turkey* by Norman Rockwell (1894-1978). One of "The Four Freedoms" paintings which appeared first in the *Saturday Evening Post* in 1943 reproduced by permission of the Norman Rockwell Family Trust.

**ZEFA Picture Library (UK)**: p219, p247.

Endpapers: **Museum Quilts Publications, London**: *Album Quilt* (detail) made in 1862 by the Ketcham Family of New Jersey.

With thanks to:
Page 115: Japanese plate courtesy of Saga Japanese Restaurant, London
Page 137: Silver mint julep cup courtesy of Garrard, London
Page 188: J. R. Bonner olive ash bowl courtesy of Divertimenti, London